ETHNOPOLITICAL ENTREPRENEURS

ETHNOPOLITICAL ENTREPRENEURS

Outsiders inside Armenian Los Angeles

Daniel Fittante

CORNELL UNIVERSITY PRESS   ITHACA AND LONDON

First published 2023 by Cornell University Press

Library of Congress Cataloging-in-Publication Data

Names: Fittante, Daniel, 1982- author.
Title: Ethnopolitical entrepreneurs : outsiders inside Armenian Los Angeles / Daniel Fittante.
Description: Ithaca [New York] : Cornell University Press, 2023. | Includes bibliographical references and index.
Identifiers: LCCN 2023002720 (print) | LCCN 2023002721 (ebook) | ISBN 9781501770326 (hardcover) | ISBN 9781501771477 (paperback) | ISBN 9781501770333 (pdf) | ISBN 9781501770340 (epub)
Subjects: LCSH: Immigrants—Political activity—United States. | Armenians—Political activity—California—Glendale. | Ethnicity—Political aspects—United States. | Political culture—United States.
Classification: LCC JV6477 .F58 2023 (print) | LCC JV6477 (ebook) | DDC 305.891/992079493—dc23/eng/20230130
LC record available at https://lccn.loc.gov/2023002720
LC ebook record available at https://lccn.loc.gov/2023002721

To Lilia

Contents

Preface

I think it fair to assume that most non-Armenian scholars who study Armenians have memorized an answer for the often-asked question, why do you study Armenians? I imagine many people who are reading this book might have come to it with a similar question in mind. In truth, my answer to such a question is a bit lackluster and bookish: studies of Armenians have a great deal to offer social scientific scholarship. I am, in fact, perplexed that so few scholars, particularly non-Armenian scholars, study Armenians. While my answer to the previously mentioned question may not satisfy many who would ask, another question—about how I came to study Armenians—is, I believe, more interesting. In this book, I share the stories and journeys of the many Armenians with whom I have had the privilege to interact. Therefore, it seems only fair that I share my own story, at least as it relates to how I ended up writing this book.

My first conscious encounter with Armenians occurred in 2007, when I traveled to Armenia as a volunteer. For a brief stint, I co-taught an English language class at Goris State University in Armenia's southernmost province (or *marz*), Syunik. I lived with an exceedingly hospitable family, whose home was located directly across the street from the state university. I did not remain in Goris or Armenia long enough to acquire any proficiency in the Armenian language, nor did I leave with any profound understanding of the people around whom I had volunteered for several months. Nonetheless, these initial months in Armenia left a rather indelible impression on my mind.

After doing a bit of independent traveling, I eventually began my graduate training at the University of Chicago in 2009. At Chicago, I had the good fortunate of meeting an Armenian language lecturer, Hripsime Haroutunian, from the Department of Near Eastern Languages and Cultures (NELC). With Hripsime, I learned basic (Eastern) Armenian and developed a research topic that dealt with Armenian cultural identity in the United States and Armenia. While doing research for this project, I was struck by how few scholarly studies existed on topics related to Armenians in the United States. In terms of academic books, I could find only a handful, such as Robert Mirak's *Torn between Two Lands: Armenians in America, 1890 to World War I* (1983) and Anny Bakalian's *Armenian-Americans: From Being to Feeling American* (1993). While this exiguity imposed certain constraints on the amount of information I could acquire through secondary sources, it also inspired me to contribute something on this conspicuously understudied topic.

At that early stage, my interest in Armenians related most centrally to the multilocal nature of the global Armenian diaspora. In particular, I was interested in the implications of the convergence of this multilocal population in what had become the world's most internally diverse Armenian diasporic node—that is, the Armenians of Greater Los Angeles. While still in Chicago, I was introduced to one of Hripsime's colleagues, S. Peter Cowe, who is a scholar of Armenian studies in the Department of NELC at the University of California, Los Angeles (UCLA). After leaving Chicago, I continued my study of the Armenian diaspora at UCLA. However, as I began my doctoral studies, it became evident that I had only a vague understanding of the Armenian diaspora. Indeed, the entirety of my experiences at that point was limited to the time I had spent in Armenia and my interactions with Hripsime, an Armenian from Armenia. As a result, the Armenian diaspora was largely theoretical for me.

I therefore decided to learn as much about this complex population as possible. In Los Angeles, I was able to meet Armenians from vastly different backgrounds. However, learning by proxy did not quite satisfy my desire to understand the people I had chosen to study. Therefore, I undertook fieldwork in as many sites of concentrated Armenian settlement as I could manage. I consciously opted to include not only the most sizable and visible but several smaller communities as well. To date, these fieldwork stints have included Argentina, Australia, Bulgaria, the Czech Republic, Italy, France, Latvia, Romania, Russia, Sweden, and, of course, the United States. While still at UCLA, I also spent one academic year in Yerevan, Armenia, where I taught at the American University of Armenia and undertook fieldwork on the topic of diasporic return migration. From these experiences, I have acquired deep insights about the global Armenian diaspora and formed close relationships with Armenians around the world. In fact, Lilia, the woman I ultimately married, is a diasporic Armenian from Tehran, Iran. All these experiences, insights, and relationships inform this book. To be sure, it is a book about the Armenians of Los Angeles and, more specifically, Glendale, where Armenians from every corner of the world have converged on one site. But I have also made a concerted effort to visit many of those corners of the world to try to make sense of the internally diverse Armenians of Greater Los Angeles.

And that is how I came to study Armenians and write this book.

Acknowledgments

I would like to begin by thanking my mentors, Khachig Tölölyan, Roger Waldinger, and S. Peter Cowe, for guiding me throughout this entire process. In addition, I would like to acknowledge the others who read my manuscript and offered valuable feedback; in particular, I am very grateful to James Barry, Rik Adriaans, Eli Watson, and Min Zhou. Thanks are also due to several other people with whom I worked at various stages of the book's development: Talia Fittante, who wrote the alternative text for the figures; Hasmik Sargisyan, who provided a translation of the Armenian Angeleno Survey (AAS) into (Eastern) Armenian; Bryan Wilcox-Archuleta, who helped me distribute and analyze data from the AAS; and Diana Ter-Ghazaryan, who created the two maps of Glendale. I would also like to acknowledge and thank Jim Lance as well as the editorial and faculty boards at Cornell University Press. In addition, this book would not have been possible without the support and assistance from several elected officials and administrative staff from the City of Glendale. I am especially indebted to Ardy Kassakhian, who permitted me to observe his 2016 election and helped me with my research. In addition, I would like to extend my thanks to Eric Hacopian, Berdj Karapetian, Tom Lorenz, Nayiri Nahabedian, Adrin Nazarian, Paul Krekorian, and Zareh Sinanyan.

I also want to acknowledge the support I received from the administrative staff and academic faculty in the Department of NELC at UCLA, including Aaron Burke, Kara Kooney, Rubina Peroomian, and Isamara Ramirez.

In terms of financial support, I would like to acknowledge the generous funding I received from the Calouste Gulbenkian Foundation, the National Association for Armenian Studies and Research, the Narekatsi Chair in Armenian Studies, NELC (at UCLA), and the Publications Committee at Södertörn University. In addition, I am very grateful to the Foundation for Baltic and East European Studies (Östersjöstiftelsen) at Södertörn University.

Many personal contacts also have helped me complete this book. I am especially grateful to my very close friend Hakop Azatyan, who supported and assisted me from the beginning of fieldwork to the final stages of production. Several others from my personal network also played important roles in the book's development: the Azatyan family, Lee Beaudoen, Senem Cevik, Neyla Dubrovich, Anh-Minh Do, Paul Fuehrer, the Ghahremanians family, Kyoung Bae Kim, Chris PreJean, and Mimi Zarookian. For their unconditional support,

I am also deeply grateful to my parents, Dave and Jan; my sisters, Talia and Emily; and my wife, Lilia.

More generally, my research would not have been possible without support from the Armenians of Los Angeles. During the fieldwork, over one hundred Los Angeles Armenians agreed to share their life journeys with me and over one thousand agreed to participate in an original survey about the Armenians of Greater Los Angeles. While I am not able to list all these individuals by name, this book comes out of my experiences with them. And, as such, the Armenians of Los Angeles, particularly all of those with whom I interacted while collecting data for this book, are the reason it exists.

Note on Transliteration

When appropriate, I have transliterated Armenian words based on the Library of Congress system. As such, Armenian words have been transliterated according to the Eastern Armenian pronunciation and traditional orthography. In a few instances, I have adapted the transliteration to make pronunciation easier. For names, I have used the transliterations used by the speakers themselves. As a result, some phonetic variants of names follow Western Armenian based on the orthographical preferences of those named.

ETHNOPOLITICAL ENTREPRENEURS

INTRODUCTION

On a sunny afternoon in mid-February 2018, I sat outside Urartu Coffee, a popular Armenian-owned café on Artsakh Avenue in Glendale's pedestrian zone.[1] As I waited for a meeting to begin, I overheard the conversation of ten or so Armenian young people at a nearby table. From the University of Southern California sweaters several wore, I presumed they were undergraduates, most likely between eighteen and twenty-two years of age. They spoke with youthful exuberance and volume, the sort that made not overhearing their conversation impossible. I pondered code-switching as the discussion vacillated between Armenian and English without any consistency that I could discern. But then, at some point, one person announced to the others, "Guys, we should have a Vernissage here in Glendale! Can you imagine how many people would show up?" In all seriousness, another picked up this thread immediately: "Yeah, man! When I'm the mayor of Glendale, I'll definitely make that happen!" Vernissage, a large, open-air market in Armenia's capital city, Yerevan, offers an extensive collection of traditional Armenian art, books, carpets, jewelry, musical instruments, and many other crafts. It is a popular attraction among locals as well as tourists. These ambitious youth recognized the cultural and economic implications of bringing the market to their local suburban community. They seemed to articulate an entrepreneurial ambition, but not in the traditional way of operating commercial businesses. Rather, they wanted to empower and enrich their community as the future mayors of Glendale. I was struck that a group of young people would spend a Saturday afternoon brainstorming their future careers as local political entrepreneurs.

What I observed outside Urartu Coffee certainly could have several other interpretations. Perhaps the group's enthusiastic pronouncements reflected a flight of fancy instead of a rooted commitment to local politics. But I observed this interaction at the end of my fieldwork in Glendale, where I had lived for over a year. What I heard resonated with me and corroborated many of my personal experiences in Glendale, where I had participated in rallies, volunteered in local campaigns, shadowed Armenian political candidates, attended political fundraisers, and brainstormed Glendale politics with local friends—sometimes at that very same café! Indeed, as the youth at the next table formulated their future aspirations, I was waiting for a friend—another Glendale Armenian, not much older than they were—who had recently decided against a career in filmmaking and founded, instead, a political consultancy firm for aspiring Armenian elected officials in Glendale and Greater Los Angeles. For me, these young people embodied what had come to represent the distinct energy, optimism, and ambition of Armenians when they discuss their city, Glendale.

Given Glendale's recent history, the young people's seeming civic aspirations are especially striking. While Glendale now resembles several of California's bustling, multiethnic suburbs, this iteration of the city is relatively new. Only several decades before the interaction I observed at the Armenian café, Glendale was still adapting begrudgingly to rapid demographic changes, which began to take shape in the mid-1970s and early 1980s. It had long been a bastion of conservatism and prejudice. Headquartering the western region's American Nazi Party and hosting a chapter of the Ku Klux Klan, the "sundown town" was notoriously associated with bigotry toward ethnic and racial minorities. Even as recently as 2016, officials from the neighboring community of La Crescenta-Montrose had to remove signage identifying a green space as Hindenburg Park—named after Paul von Hindenburg, the German president who appointed Adolf Hitler chancellor of Germany in 1933.[2] Historically, the German American Bund and the American Nazi Party had used Hindenburg Park to host rallies and boycott Jewish products. In the face of vehement protest, city officials restored the park to its original name, Crescenta Valley Community Regional Park.[3] Nonetheless, the sign brought back to the surface the long, troubling history that Glendale and the San Fernando Valley have had with racism toward ethnic and racial minorities. In Glendale, these two realities coexist: exuberant, politicized immigrants, who have done much to transform practically every aspect of the city, and a history rooted in restrictions imposed on and prejudices acted out against minorities.

Before the 1970s, very few Armenians had ever heard of Glendale. Since then, however, a relatively rapid convergence of Armenians from all over the world has fundamentally reconfigured the city. They have established themselves in Glendale with a multitude of Armenian cultural centers, organizations, churches,

FIGURE 1. Armenian café Urartu Coffee on Artsakh Avenue in downtown Glendale, California.

restaurants, and businesses. More than two hundred thousand Armenians live in Los Angeles County, but Glendale has become particularly recognizable for Armenians worldwide.[4] On social media, Armenians in the diaspora and the Republic of Armenia often post satiric videos about the extravagances of Glendale and its Armenian residents. It also inspired a racy reality television series, *Glendale Life*. Even among non-Armenian Angelenos, the words *Glendale* and *Armenian* are practically synonymous.

Nonetheless, of the many ways Armenians have reshaped Glendale over the last few decades, their role in the city's political landscape stands out. When I collected data for this book between 2015 and 2018, Armenians made up about 40 percent of Glendale's two hundred thousand-plus population and yet accounted for nearly 70 percent of its elected officials. They served as its mayor, city council members, education board members, and in many other elected capacities. In nonelected positions, they also acted as Glendale's city manager and deputy city manager; in addition, Glendale Armenians constituted the majority of officials serving on the city's many boards and commissions.[5] This political mobilization has occurred rapidly, too—as of 2018, approximately 70 percent of the Armenian population consisted of first-generation immigrants. Local policies reflect the impact of Armenian political actors, who have increased subsidized housing (for the elderly), expanded park space, introduced Armenian/English dual-language immersion programs in public schools, established April 24 (commemorating the Armenian Genocide) as a public school holiday, passed legislation for and financed the creation of a state-funded Armenian American museum (in the city center), ensured city signage and city literature appear in Armenian, reclassified "Armenian" as a distinct "race/ethnicity" in city demographic data reports, and coordinated many other Armenian-interest initiatives.

When I began collecting data for this book, Glendale Armenians' electoral success and political influence confused me. Sociologists and political scientists typically assume that legal and social incorporation should occur sooner than political or electoral incorporation. But Glendale's Armenians consisted predominately of first-generation newcomers—many of whom had no previous experience living in representative democracies. Before I moved to Glendale, I had assumed that non-Armenians, by campaigning on the promise to advance Armenian-related issues in exchange for Glendale Armenians' votes, would primarily occupy the city's governmental positions. But what I found in Glendale proved that these assumptions were misguided. How then did a population with so few "social remittances" (Levitt 1998; Levitt and Lamba-Nieves 2011) conducive to political enfranchisement in the United States achieve this level of political influence and electoral success in such a short time—before, indeed, a great many had yet even acquired proficiency in English?

As my fieldwork developed, I found that this type of electoral success was not entirely unique to the Armenians of Glendale. As I looked more closely into immigrant political representation within other multiethnic suburbs in Greater Los Angeles, I found there existed several other places with oversized immigrant or co-ethnic political representation. For the Chinese in San Gabriel County, along with several others, this phenomenon proved particularly conspicuous. Despite the striking differences in terms of Armenian and Chinese immigrants' backgrounds, their stories follow overlapping trajectories (see chapter 2). Eventually, it became clear to me that what had taken place in Glendale pertained, in fact, to many of California's increasingly multiethnic suburbs—that is, that the political phenomenon I observed in Glendale related more to a statewide, structural evolution than to the specific dynamics taking place within one intra-ethnically diverse population. It was not, however, until I began preparing this book for publication in late 2020 and early 2021—during the aftermath of the contentious presidential election and the tense Senate runoff in Georgia—that I realized Glendale Armenians' political incorporation story is not merely about many of California's suburbs; rather, it is becoming a new chapter in US political history.

In the 2020 presidential election and the 2021 Senate runoff, suburban Asian American and Pacific Islander (AAPI) voters in Georgia's Gwinnett County captivated the public's attention. In the media, many journalists speculated that the fate of both elections ultimately came down to AAPI, Black, and Latino suburban voters.[6] Of Gwinnett's over nine hundred thousand residents, Asian residents made up about 12 percent of the population.[7] Nonetheless, during the period leading up to the elections, among the five commissioners on the county board, one, Ben Ku, was of Asian descent. In addition, Gwinnett has many AAPI organizations, community organizers, ethnic media outlets, and advocacy groups—such as the Asian American Advocacy Fund. In 2020, the most significant national increases in voter turnout occurred among AAPI voters.[8] A growing number of these voters live in multiethnic suburbs, such as those in Georgia's Gwinnett County. After a long, right-leaning history, Gwinnett voted Democratic in both the 2016 and the 2020 presidential elections.

Responding to questions about the role of AAPI voters in Gwinnett, the president of the New Georgia Project (NGP), Nsé Ufot, told media sources, "I will say that the demographic shifts are the fire and organizing is absolutely the accelerant. . . . Phone calls, text messages, knocking on their doors and postcards, as well as digital ads, all together."[9] Organizations such as the NGP, the National Coalition on Black Civic Participation, and Georgia STAND-UP registered thousands of new voters. And, in the 2020 and early 2021 elections, immigrants and other minorities not only ensured Georgia voted Democratic in the presidential election; they also secured a Democratic majority in the Senate by electing a Black pastor, Raphael Warnock, and a Jewish American, Jon Ossoff. In addition to the Black and Latino organizers' efforts, AAPI organizations, elected officials, and multimedia actors worked tirelessly to register voters. These initiatives played an important role in the election results. As Ufot's statement indicates, demographic shifts do not solely account for the mobilization of racial and ethnic minorities; rather, the strategies of local organizers play an equally significant role. Even Georgia, a traditional Republican stronghold with a long history of racism against Black and Jewish Americans, exemplifies the increasing prominence of not only suburbs but also the actors constructing voting blocs among ethnically diverse populations. Thus, in this book, I argue that, by creating unified voting blocs out of internally fragmented populations, suburban political actors launch and sustain political careers by driving immigrant political incorporation. And the incorporation of immigrants in multiethnic, multiracial suburbs is transforming the political dynamics of the United States, on local, state, and, increasingly, national levels.[10]

While this book is ostensibly about Armenians' rapid political mobilization in Glendale, it is also about the dynamics shaping the political destiny of the

United States. This new chapter in US political history is not without precedent: Irish, Italian, Jewish, and many other newcomers within immigrant-concentrated metropolitan US cities began changing the country's political landscape from the late nineteenth century onward; similarly, today Armenian, Chinese, Korean, Mexican, and many others are changing the country's political reality within its dynamic, multiethnic suburbs. The processes look distinct in these various suburban contexts, but the underlying narrative holds: large populations of new-comers are converging on the United States' dynamic suburbs, and, at the same time, ambitious political actors are building careers by spearheading co-ethnics' political incorporation. These political actors construct membership among intra-ethnically diverse populations and influence local institutions.

This book presents the story of a recently established population whose mem-bers stem from very diverse locations (Armenia, Iran, Lebanon, Russia, Syria, and many others), and who are internally fragmented and have little experience with the US political system, yet rapidly mobilized and remade a US suburban space in their own likeness.[11] As the intra-ethnically diverse Glendale Armenians them-selves manifest, this evolution has been driven by the actors constructing a voting bloc based not on a single political ideology but instead on a sense of shared ethnic membership and linked fates (see chapter 4). The emergence of these political actors—whom I label *ethnopolitical entrepreneurs*—and the political incorpora-tion among newcomers in contemporary US suburbs (or "ethnoburbs") explain significant shifts taking place in the country's elections and political culture.

Although certainly not the only important actors in this story, Glendale's ethnopolitical entrepreneurs had the vision, creativity, and ambition to identify the electoral potential of the internally diverse Armenian population. By tap-ping into rapid changes in local demography and concentrated ethnic networks, they seized the opportunity to transform a sleepy, prejudicial sundown town into a domain of ethnic political mobilization and newcomer incorporation. The presence and strategies of these entrepreneurs lie at the core of political incor-poration among newcomers in Glendale and, by extension, in several other pre-dominantly first-generation, multiethnic US suburbs. It is true that Glendale's ethnopolitical entrepreneurs exploited what was already in place—in particu-lar, co-ethnic demographic convergence on a single site and a strong sense of ethnic identity among this demographic concentration. But, by taking advan-tage of various other factors, they have fundamentally altered Glendale's politi-cal culture. While there exists scholarship on both ethnoburbs and immigrant political incorporation, researchers rarely connect the two—that is, ethnoburb scholarship rarely analyzes newcomers' political incorporation, and immigrant political incorporation scholarship rarely applies to suburbs (Kasinitz, Mollen-kopf, and Waters 2004; Rumbaut 2008a; Li 2009; Lung-Amam 2017). This book

FIGURE 2.   The brick storefront of Abril Bookstore in downtown Glendale.

attempts to connect these two scholarly models through a case study of the economically invested and politically mobilized Armenians of Glendale.

As a microcosm, Glendale Armenians' story is fascinating and untold. But this story is also important to gain an understanding of place making and political mobilization in diverse immigrant suburbs. This book demonstrates that, in many of these dynamic urban ecologies, elected officials arise directly from their own communities in order to broker ties between the ethnic populations and bureaucratic institutions. I also argue that this brokerage is the foundation of contemporary immigrant political incorporation in diverse suburban landscapes. While I use the term *ethnopolitical entrepreneur* to describe, largely, those who vie for political office, this term also applies to those with whom prospective suburban elected officials as well as community organizers work in constructing voting blocs and mobilizing internally diverse populations.

As a result of Armenians' political and electoral incorporation successes, Glendale provides a unique opportunity to make sense of not only the circumstances under which immigrant political incorporation takes place but also something more fundamental about the gradual evolution of US political history. Although US suburbs have long been considered separate from the United States' urban and rural realities, they now reflect and amplify them—both in terms of the country's ethnic diversification and its economic inequality (what Becky M. Nicolaides and Andrew Wiese call "suburban disequilibrium").[12] In terms of municipal politics, Armenians' disproportionate influence makes Glendale a successful case of immigrant political incorporation. Glendale, therefore, provides an opportunity to learn not only the necessary ingredients for immigrant political and electoral incorporation but also the reasons that other immigrant communities sometimes falter. And, as the 2020 presidential election made clear, the successful incorporation of suburban immigrants has significant political implications for the entire country.

US Immigrant Settlement into Suburbs

US suburbs emerged largely in response to nineteenth-century urban industrialization. As industry grew in several US cities, metropolitan centers often lacked sufficient urban planning or proper sewage systems. As a result, many city centers became hotbeds of pollution, congestion, disease, poverty, crime, and lower mortality rates. Those with the means sought to escape industrial cities' perceived vices; they built bungalow-style homes in manicured communities on the periphery of metropolitan areas. Public transportation further facilitated the expansion and diversification of these suburbs. As the epicenter of early US industrialization, northeastern cities, such as Boston and New York, spawned the country's first suburbs; however, by the early twentieth century, suburbs proliferated across the United States. The inhabitants of these new suburban landscapes were not merely seeking new residential areas in which to live; they were also fashioning governing institutions and municipalities. Often in response to lifestyles associated with dwelling in city centers, middle- and upper-middle-class white Americans created residential communities along their own ethical guidelines and prejudices (Nicolaides 2002).

In the early twentieth century, as automobiles gradually supplanted commuter trains and streetcars, the suburban alternative became more accessible for a larger swath of Americans (Nicolaides and Wiese 2006). In the 1930s, New Deal housing programs enabled an even larger number of Americans to purchase and own homes in suburbs. These policies, however, also institutionalized segregation by denying mortgages and loans to people of color, particularly Black Americans—a state-backed practice referred to as "redlining." Despite racist redlining practices, New Deal programs, such as the National Housing Act (1934) and the establishment of the Federal Housing Administration (1934), accelerated the growth of suburbia, particularly after the Second World War. In various regional contexts, suburbs manifested distinct variations—mixed or predominantly industrial, semirural, and commercial, among others (Teaford 2011). Even as suburbs grew, however, individual suburban dwellers doggedly fought to preserve their distinct characters and compositions.

As a result of the dynamism and diversity of metropolitan areas, scholars have struggled to provide a standard definition of *suburbs* (Forsyth 2012; Airgood-Obrycki, Hanlon, and Rieger 2021). This challenge relates, in part, to the lack of an official definition. For example, in the United States, the Office of Management and Budget has avoided defining *suburbs* in its classification system. As Whitney Airgood-Obrycki, Bernadette Hanlon, and Shannon Rieger (2021) argue, this has meant that individual scholars in different fields have had to develop their own definitions. And scholars, too, have not yet established a standard definition. In the last several decades, the term has undergone several critical reexaminations (Jackson 1987; Fishman 1987; Harris and Lewis 2001; Nicolaides and Wiese 2006). While scholars have traditionally understood suburbs as affluent and middle-class white US neighborhoods, which are located at a distance from where the residents work, this definition does not sufficiently factor the racial and socioeconomic diversity that contemporary US suburbs comprise (Fishman 2008; Orfield and Luce 2013). Some scholars have expanded static, dichotomous (city-suburban) understandings of suburbs and distinguished these residential communities on the basis of spatial and temporal considerations. This scholarship has reconceptualized city centers as bundles of concentric regions, which arise at different times and contain different population densities. Analysts distinguish inner cities from US suburbs built between 1950 and 1969, or "inner suburbs," and those built after 1969, or "outer suburbs" (Lee and Leigh 2007; Hanlon 2009; Mikelbank 2004; McManus and Ethington 2007; Park and Burgess 2019). Generally, inner suburbs are closer in proximity to inner cities than to outer suburbs.[13] In addition, inner suburbs often have higher population density and poverty rates as well as more ethnic and racial diversity when compared to outer suburbs. Despite their important differences, both inner and outer suburbs in the United States possess several commonalities—in particular, they both are fast becoming more ethnically and racially diverse. As Airgood-Obrycki, Hanlon, and Rieger argue, "Across all definitions, there are significant proportions of different racial and ethnic groups living in the suburbs. Recognizing that lots of different types of people reside in the suburbs is important as we think about ways to develop policies and plans to create more equitable metropolitan neighborhoods" (2021, 1281).

While I acknowledge the important distinctions within US suburbs, in this book I define suburbs as places outside the political boundaries of cities yet still within larger metropolitan areas—that is, peripheral to the city, but nonetheless still connected to it (Hamel and Keil 2015). This broad definition encompasses a diverse range of metropolitan land areas and includes a characteristic both common to contemporary suburbs in the United States and particularly important for the topic of this book—that is, their political autonomy.

Suburban Governance in the United States

Even though suburbs exist throughout the world, their political independence is a particularly important distinction in the United States. US suburban residents exercise relative autonomy in determining land use, homeowners' rights, taxes, educational systems, and many other regulatory policies. And suburban residents have fought tenaciously to maintain this independence. As Jon C. Teaford articulates, "The American suburb is not just a neighborhood; it is a distinct governmental entity with all the coercive power necessary to fashion its own destiny" (2020, x). Many white residents have long used this autonomy to promote racial segregation (McGirr 2001; Lassiter 2006). However, more recently, suburbs are also where immigrants fight for their right to belong and participate in the United States (Carpio, Irazábal, and Pulido 2011). A combination of shifting demographics and the system of government unique to US suburbs has made this fight possible.

Suburbs typically possess a consistent system of government—mayors, city councils, boards of education, and so forth—but some follow a more hybridized approach (Dahl 1961). In California and throughout the United States, many suburbs, including Glendale, follow a council-manager system of government. This system combines the political leadership of elected officials and appointed local government managers. Like suburbs themselves, council-manager systems first arose in the late nineteenth century. Progressive Era reforms sought to improve the efficiency and weaken local partisan politics. This system is intended to promote long-term community interests (such as attracting firms and investments) and innovation, while, simultaneously, constraining elected officials from pursuing political opportunism (Feiock, Jeong, and Kim 2003). Although, in theory, this system differentiates the workload of elected officials and management—the local power invested in the elected officials and the oversight of delivery of public services invested in the management—these two roles often overlap. In addition, city managers also play important roles in terms of city governments and residents' sense of inclusion in the polity (see chapter 5). Whether the system is council-manager or not, the distinctly self-governing nature of US suburbs plays an important role in explaining how immigrants are reconfiguring the US political landscape.

Immigrants in Suburbs

In the past several decades, immigrants have played an important role in defining and governing contemporary US suburbs (Walker 2018). Despite the country's history of discriminatory lending practices, which favored socioeconomically and racially segregated suburban areas (Wiese 2004; Sugrue 2014; Frasure-Yokley 2015; Rothstein 2017), ethnic and racial populations have long participated in the shaping and reshaping of these dynamic spaces (Saito 1998; Haynes 2001; Li 2009).

Over the past five decades, restrictive immigrant policies, which favor high-skilled newcomers, have changed the demographic profile and settlement trajectories of those coming to the United States (Tichenor 2002; Zolberg 2006; Kapur 2010). In addition, political turmoil in the last quarter of the twentieth century (and continuing into the twenty-first century) forced many established diaspora communities and immigrants to relocate to the United States. As a result, since the 1970s, skilled and affluent immigrants have significantly altered several aspects of US cities and suburbs. Whereas redlining policies kept suburbs racially segregated for much of the twentieth century, immigration policies have profoundly diversified and transformed many of these residential areas in the more recent past. As Willow Lung-Amam (2017, 4) contends, diversity has become more the rule of suburbs rather than the exception.

But what distinguishes contemporary multiethnic suburbs, or ethnoburbs, from other urban or suburban spaces? According to Wei Li, "Ethnoburbs are fully functional communities, with their own internal socioeconomic structures that are integrated into both national and international networks of information exchange, business connection, and social activity" (2009, 42). As ethnic community members acquire an increasing number of businesses and real estate properties, more co-ethnics swell the population of the preexisting residential clusters. This incremental ingress reworks the socioeconomic and demographic infrastructure of the suburb, thereby transforming it into an ethnoburb. This transformation does not take place seamlessly; the preexisting population, invested emotionally and economically, often responds with bitterness and, sometimes, violence. But the backlash in turn can increase newcomers' sense of cohesion (or "reactive ethnicity"), which can help facilitate the formation of ethnopolitical campaigns and the establishment of ethnic political representatives in office. These activities gradually lead to greater social and political integration into the host society's "mainstream."

The political shift in contemporary suburbs extends an existing tradition in the United States, but it also marks a novel trajectory. In the 1880s, the residents of New York City and Boston elected new mayors, William Russell Grace (1880) and Hugh O'Brien (1884), respectively. Both Grace and O'Brien were Catholic immigrants from Ireland. These elections marked a shift in US politics, for they confirmed that, in major metropolitan areas, "ethnically" distinct immigrants could organize in response to the existing political machines—such as New York's Tammany Hall—or as a result of the religious leadership around the communal nuclei of churches and Irish aid organizations. And, as social scientists later noted, metropolitan immigrant communities developed both local and diasporic orientations: while they engaged in the struggle to participate fully as US citizens, they cultivated identities as "outsiders" and members of an imagined, transatlantic nation (Glazer and Moynihan 1970).[14] Many US immigrants no longer settle solely (or even largely) in the country's metropolitan centers. However, smaller, concentrated populations, such as the Armenians in Glendale or the Chinese in Monterey Park (in the San Gabriel Valley), form plurality or majority voting blocs and significantly affect local institutions. Like the metropolitan Irish, Italian, and Jewish immigrants before them, immigrants in multiethnic suburbs are still engaging in the struggle to participate fully as US citizens while also cultivating bilocal (or transnational) identities.

Pioneering social scientists, such as Henri Lefebvre and Michel Foucault, long ago noted power hierarchies inherent in urban landscapes and how these landscapes reproduce systems of inequality, often based on race and ethnicity. Subsequent scholarship on US suburbs reaffirms these assertions, particularly as they benefit whites and marginalize minorities (Nicolaides and Wiese 2006; Boyles 2015; Anacker 2016). While this book does not undermine these claims, it explores another side of the same story. By neglecting immigrant political incorporation in suburbs, sociologists and political scientists have overlooked the political autonomy and transformative agency of many predominantly first-generation immigrants.

Terminology

In this book, I often refer to Armenians as an "ethnic" population. As with various other populations stemming from southern, central, and eastern Europe, Armenians are generally considered "white" (or "white ethnic") in the United States (Tehranian 2000; Craver 2009). For this reason, the designation "ethnic" may at first seem out of place. But, as Neda Maghbouleh (2017) argues about Iranians in the United States, Armenians' racial classification and self-identification as "white" do not necessarily align with their lived experiences, particularly in terms of how they are perceived and treated by many non-Armenians (see Chapters 2 and 5). Still, I follow Kanchan Chandra in defining ethnic identity as a "subset of categories in which descent-based attributes are necessary for membership" (2012, 9). A descent-based approach can include a wide range of categories or "attributes," such as race, religion, or language. Chandra's approach to ethnic identity allows fluidity, which will prove important for this book's analysis of ethnopolitical entrepreneurs (see chapter 4). In addition, I typically refer to Los Angeles's internally diverse Armenians as "Armenian" as opposed to "Armenian American." This designation is intended to capture the entire range of experiences among the predominantly first-generation Armenians of Glendale yet remain inclusive of later generations. In some cases, however, it is important to highlight countries of origin, particularly when interviewees emphasized their regional identities. For example, Iranian Armenian refers to an Armenian from Iran. Also, some interviewees use the Armenian word *Hayastanci* to refer to an Armenian from Armenia.

In addition, I consistently refer to "immigrant political incorporation" throughout this book. To make sense of this framing, however, I should clarify what I mean by *immigrant* and differentiate *incorporation* from other, related words such as *assimilation* and *integration*.

Immigrant refers to a broad range of persons and experiences. Different policy regimes exist for various subcategories of immigrants—legal, illegal, temporary, permanent, student, and many others (Joppke 2013); in addition, the term is unevenly applied to include newcomers as well as later generations (Levitt 2009; Jiménez 2010; Alba and Nee 2012; Waldinger 2015, 2016). As such, it is not always clear to whom "immigrant" does and does not apply. Legal status, contextual familiarity (social, cultural, linguistic, etc.), and transnational ties may be some phenomena that distinguish immigrants from nonimmigrants (Schiller, Basch, and Blanc 1995; Foner 1997, 2001; Eckstein 2006, 2009). This book follows the definition provided in Jennifer Hochschild, Jacqueline Chattopadhyay, Claudine Gay, and Michael Jones-Correa's *Outsiders No More? Models of Immigrant Political Incorporation*: "Immigrants [are] individuals or groups who have moved from their country of origin to a new country in which they plan to reside for a considerable period of time. They are most importantly identified by their legal status at entry" (2013, 13). However, in this book, I extend this definition to include later generations, who continue to feel a sense of connection with a specific cultural identity. In multiethnic suburbs, later-generation immigrants also participate in the political incorporation of the populations with which they continue to identify.

Assimilation typically refers to the "decline of an ethnic distinction and its corollary cultural and social differences" (Alba and Nee 2003, 11). This process explains how immigrants and their children become similar to those in the host society's "mainstream." As such, assimilation implies an eventual erasure of a population's cultural identity. In contrast, the scholarship refers to *integration* as a "parallel" cultural process—that is, one in which newcomers retain their cultural identity while also adopting that of the host society (Gans 1997; Portes and Rumbaut 2001). This scholarship sometimes distinguishes structural and cultural integration in unpacking institutional participation (Entzinger and Biezeveld 2003).[15]

Incorporation scholarship initially involved case studies of large, socioeconomically disenfranchised communities in inner cities. Rufus Browning, Dale Marshall, and David Tabb (1984) were among the first to analyze the political consequences of changing urban ecologies from three perspectives: the civil rights movement, increased federal aid programs, and party demographics. According to them, these factors facilitated the formation of liberal coalitions. Coalition members became, in essence, political entrepreneurs, as they sought to resolve collective problems among Black and Latino citizens in exchange for prospective constituents' votes. By changing public debates and reallocating state resources, political actors secured mayoral and city council seats. Their innovative initiatives, in part, disrupted preexisting political equilibriums and established new political norms. Browning, Marshall, and Tabb (1984) referred to the upshot of the three processes as "political incorporation." From different vantages, subsequent scholars have developed this framework. For example, they have introduced individual or collective models (Koopmans et al. 2005; Ramírez and Fraga 2008); attitudes and beliefs or opportunity structures (Segura 2013); outcomes or processes (Hochschild et al. 2013); inclusion or exclusion (Shefter 1986); immigrant demography or host society policies (Waldinger and Tseng 1992); and feedback loops and incorporative trajectories (Hochschild et al. 2013). While assimilation scholarship tends to focus on individual outcomes, incorporation research unpacks the outcome of individual and collective interactions with political institutions.

These institutional interactions are dynamic and evolving (Gerstle and Mollenkopf 2001; Hochschild and Mollenkopf 2009b; Mollenkopf 2013; Ramakrishnan 2013). For example, in Europe during the 1980s, policies often prevented newcomers (and the children of newcomers) from becoming citizens (Joppke 2013). As Michael Walzer (1981) argues, these policies, which often applied to guestworkers, not only blocked immigrants from political participation but also turned them into second-class citizens. This exclusionary approach eventually gave way to a new set of policies in Europe—namely, the sort that provided paths to citizenship (Soysal 1994). Citizenship enabled full political participation but, as Joppke argues, made immigrants "invisible" (vis-à-vis their respective national, ethnic, or religious populations). Eventually, political incorporation, in some contexts, began to take on a more multicultural dimension (Kymlicka 1995). In these spaces, political institutions began recognizing the cultural and religious practices not merely of the polity's citizens but of its members, too.

In the volume, *Outsiders No More? Models of Immigrant Political Incorporation*, several scholars provide more nuanced and rigorous definitions of immigrant political incorporation. For example, Xavier de Souza Briggs argues that "[Immigrant political incorporation] refers to the processes by which the foreign born or other noncitizens attain membership and the capacity for legitimate influence in a host country polity" (2013, 326). For Briggs, political incorporation pertains to the processes that enable immigrants to become influential members of the host country polity. In this book, I follow Briggs's approach to immigrant political incorporation, particularly as it relates to the capacity for immigrants to influence the polity. However, I also follow scholars whose conceptualizations of immigrant political incorporation include less formal (or institutional) domains (Voss and Bloemraad 2011). For example, in the same volume, Ewa Morawska argues that "existing research has almost exclusively focused on the 'external' measures of immigrant/ethnic group members' political involvement in the host society, such as taking up citizenship . . . , voting participation, and engagement in other public sphere activities. I opt for the understanding of the 'political' that besides its legal-institutional aspects also includes people's notions of the rights and duties of citizenship and a good (and bad) state and its operation, and their practical applications of these ideas in their everyday lives" (2013, 137). In describing political phenomena, Morawska extends the legal-institutional dimensions to describe practical applications and the everyday experiences of a host society's members. Similarly, in defining immigrant political incorporation, Gary Gerstle argues that "political incorporation is the process through which immigrants and their descendants come to think of themselves as members of a polity with political rights and with a voice in politics, should they choose to exercise it" (2013, 306). Like Morawska's definition, Gerstle's extends the political beyond formal institutions to include immigrants' self-perceptions of inclusion and participation. Similarly, Michael Jones-Correa defines immigrant political incorporation more broadly as "methods or tactics used, by individuals or groups, to make claims about the allocation of material or symbolic public goods" (2013, 177). This definition highlights the importance of the symbolic in processes of immigrant political incorporation. Taken together, these definitions emphasize institutional interactions through which newcomers engage and influence the polity as well as gain a sense of inclusion in it. In this book, I draw from all these definitions; however, I would only qualify that successful immigrant political incorporation does not necessarily result in newcomers' developing a sense of inclusion or belonging. Rather, highly successful immigrant political incorporation can exist in the absence of such feelings (see chapter 5). Furthermore, because this book focuses largely on how immigrants become politically incorporated by electing co-ethnic candidates, I use the terms political incorporation and electoral incorporation to describe parallel processes—with political incorporation referring to the immigrants and electoral incorporation referring to the candidates. As such, this book somewhat narrows the scope of political incorporation research in order to unpack more fully the dynamics of certain suburbs.

This book therefore provides an empirical study of contemporary immigrant political incorporation in multiethnic, multiracial US suburbs. I follow the definitions provided in *Outsiders No More? Models of Immigrant Political Incorporation*; however, to this research, I add a new dimension—namely, the politics of ethnoburbs. As domains of immigrant political incorporation, ethnoburbs offer insight into the evolving dynamics of US politics. This evolution is occurring, in part, because of the suburbs' changing demographic compositions—that is, by becoming more ethnically and racially diverse; however, demography alone does not lead to immigrant political incorporation in multiethnic suburbs. Rather, specific political actors have emerged in ethnoburbs to drive these processes. I refer to these actors as *ethnopolitical entrepreneurs*.

The *ethnopolitical entrepreneurs* model developed in this book derives from the political entrepreneurship scholarship. Mark Schneider and Paul Teske define political entrepreneurs as high-level, unelected leaders (such as city managers), elected politicians, interest group leaders, or creators of new groups who "develop new and innovative policies and galvanize an otherwise difficult-to-organize, dispersed citizens to support their policies" (1992, 741). These actors gain political "profits" by solving collective problems among otherwise politically disempowered populations. For Schneider and Teske, political entrepreneurs reallocate resources to achieve various policy goals. Entrepreneurs thus play influential roles in metropolitan areas by affecting the preexisting political and economic policies and institutions and replacing them with new ones (Riker 1986). In return, they receive the "profits" that result from their disruptive initiatives. As such, political entrepreneurs do not always act out of a sense of selflessness or the desire to uplift ethnic and racial minority populations; in fact, they often work with their own interests in mind. Nonetheless, given the competitive nature of local governments, political entrepreneurs perform an important role in institutionalizing policy innovation in various governmental milieus. Political entrepreneurs emerge when there exists a clear and rational incentive (Schneider and Teske 1992). Schneider and Teske argue that rapid population growth and racial diversity conduce to the emergence of new political entrepreneurs (744). Political entrepreneurs therefore emerge most conspicuously where concentrated, disorganized, or vulnerable populations need them the most.

Building on the political entrepreneurship model, which arose in urban city centers, I also argue that ethnopolitical entrepreneurs establish new bases of governmental authority in order to exercise new political powers and redistribute governmental funding (Mollenkopf 1983; Statham 1999; Orleck 2001; Soehl 2013); however, these actors do so on behalf of their specific co-ethnic populations in contemporary US ethnoburbs. In the 1990s, Philip Kasinitz distinguished between the "ethnicity entrepreneur" and the ethnic political aspirant, who "cannot afford to be tagged as the representative of one group exclusively" (1992, 238). But ethnopolitical entrepreneurs' success depends, in large part, on their association with and mobilization of co-ethnic constituents—indeed, on their ability to create constituents (see chapter 4).

The concept of *ethnopolitical entrepreneur* is not new to this book. Building on Pierre Bourdieu, Rogers Brubaker (2004, 10) identifies an ethnopolitical entrepreneur as one who makes a living by reifying ethnicity: "By invoking groups, they seek to evoke them, summon them, call them into being." According to Bourdieu, politics is the quintessential site in which operate "signs capable of producing social entities and, above all, groups" (1991, 249–250). As such, all forms of political mobilization involve group-making processes in which designated representatives receive "the power of creating the group" (Bourdieu 1991, 248). Brubaker exemplifies Bourdieu's analysis by highlighting the ways ethnopolitical entrepreneurs (as well as others) rely on ethnicity to create ethnic groups. And, as Brubaker (2004, 10) asserts, analysts should try to make sense of the powerful ways these forms of ethnic reification operate. By analyzing how suburban ethnopolitical entrepreneurs create voting blocs and influence political institutions, this book attempts to do just that.

Site Selection and Methods

For several reasons, Glendale proved an ideal site in which to analyze immigrants' and suburbs' evolving roles in the United States. When I collected data for this book, Armenian immigrants of Greater Los Angeles possessed a naturalization rate (80%) that was twice the national average (40%), and in Glendale, Armenians form a demographic plurality of the population. Glendale's Armenians consisted of multi-origin, first-generation immigrants (approximately 70% in 2018); in addition, most of the city's elected officials were Armenian (in 2018, Armenians occupied 70% of the city's elected positions).[16] These elected officials relied, largely, on co-ethnic voters and had passed a great deal of Armenian-oriented legislation. Given these considerations, Glendale embodies the rapid evolution of US suburban spaces and politics.

In collecting data for this book, I used mixed methods, including in-depth interviews, demographic data analyses, surveying, and archival research. From 2015 to 2018, I conducted over one hundred interviews in order to gain the diverse perspectives of Armenians and officials in Glendale. Between 2015 and 2016, I lived in Glendale. Even after I moved to another location in Los Angeles, I continued to collect data for this book during regular visits to Glendale. For fieldwork interviews, I relied on snowballing methods to generate a diverse sample. The interviews were open-ended, but, generally, I asked about migration, family/personal histories, integration experiences, and local political engagement. In addition, I partook of extensive participant observation, particularly during the time I lived in Glendale. For example, I volunteered on the campaigns of local Armenian political entrepreneurs and attended Glendale town hall meetings. These experiences brought me into close contact with various Glendale Armenians: businesspeople, politicians, commissioners, civil servants, educators, ethnic organizations, ethnic media outlets, and many others. Through these experiences, I was able to set up interviews and meet with diverse Glendale residents and also observe/participate in many city events.

Because Armenian elected officials publicly supported my research, I was able to gain access to a diverse range of participants. As a non-Armenian with relative fluency in the Armenian language, I was uniquely positioned to acquire in-depth perspectives. Given my familiarity with Armenian history, politics, and culture, I initially occupied the intermediate position of the quasi outsider/insider. However, as my fieldwork developed, so did my personal ties with the people whom I daily engaged. Not only did I speak with hundreds of people, but I also formed several significant friendships with Los Angeles Armenians. The nature of these friendships was quite in-depth. I attended several Armenian ceremonies (birthdays, engagement parties, funerals, and other events). I spent consecutive days with friends and their families. My relative proficiency with the Armenian language and familiarity with many social practices often made me something of an oddity among Armenian peers and their relatives. Despite my distinct positionality, the complex and shifting relationships that came out of this fieldwork often blurred the traditional insider/outsider and observer/observed dichotomies (Narayan 1993).

Interviews and personal ties also enabled me to develop a narrative of Armenians' historical immigration to and settlement of Glendale (see chapter 1). Because Armenians' history to Southern California had not yet been written, I relied on oral histories of Armenians who had lived in Glendale since the 1960s and 1970s. These interviews also provided many insights into the internal dynamics of the different subgroups. In order to gauge the generalizability of my interview data, I mined the Integrated Public Use Microdata Series (IPUMS) databases and scoured archival sources (such as old newspaper clippings). For contemporary statistics, I used census data from 2010. I did not rely on the more recent American Community Survey (ACS) data set, as the former contains a more representative 10 percent sample. For archival sources, I relied on Glendale Central Library's archives and microfilm collections.

Because fieldwork limited me to those with whom I spoke, I arranged a survey (the Armenian Angeleno Survey, or AAS) to test interview data generalizability (see the online appendix: https://ecommons.cornell.edu/handle/1813/113257). The survey generated 1,070 responses. For online distribution, prominent and visible Los Angeles–based Armenians posted the survey to their social media. But, because social media cater to a particular demographic, I also undertook extensive outreach to access offline demographics. The survey was distributed in person at several events and to various organizations. In addition, the survey's link appeared in Los Angeles Armenian news and media sources. Outreach for the survey also proved an important part of my fieldwork on account of the sheer number of people with whom I interacted while distributing it. The public support and use of diverse platforms enabled me to undertake broad-ranging data collection.[17]

Following this introductory chapter, chapter 1 provides an overview of the historical streams of the Armenian diaspora. It also explains the geopolitical events that have given rise to the convergence of multiple Armenian streams on Glendale. The first half of chapter 1 describes Armenians' long history in dispersion, while the second half shifts the narrative focus to the United States. The chapter then traces Armenian origins from the East Coast to the West Coast, first in Fresno and then in Los Angeles and, ultimately, Glendale. It contextualizes not only the rich history of the Armenian diaspora but also the intra-ethnic diversity of the Armenians of Los Angeles and Glendale.

Chapter 2 shifts the focus from movement to transformation and presents Armenians' influence in practically all sectors of Glendale. Employing Li's ethnoburb model, this chapter provides a demographic snapshot of Armenians' influences in the city. While Li's framing was originally intended to describe predominantly Chinese suburbs, this chapter builds on the model to describe Glendale Armenians' socioeconomic and political impact. Chapter 2 also analyzes the model's limitations, particularly in treating structural racial inequalities. This analysis highlights that the persistence of institutionalized forms of racism continues to make electoral and political incorporation in US suburbs far less realizable for some populations as compared to others. But chapter 2 also attempts to develop the ethnoburb model by emphasizing key aspects of Glendale's post-1970s transformation: interethnic antagonism and municipal politics.

Building on the historical and demographic accounts, chapter 3 unpacks how these factors have given rise to novel suburban political actors—ethnopolitical entrepreneurs. This chapter provides two sketches—Rafi Manoukian and Ardashes

"Ardy" Kassakhian. The chapter's goal is to outline the distinct dimensions of ethnopolitical entrepreneurs and their significance in the political incorporation of immigrants and other minorities. Developing this analysis, chapter 4 investigates how ethnopolitical entrepreneurs' campaigns actively convert internally fragmented, multi-origin immigrants into ethnic voting blocs. Given Armenians' internal diversity, political candidates cannot merely call on Armenians' shared "ethnonational" inheritance to conjure solidarity. Rather, the grassroots work they do while campaigning actively constructs a sense of solidarity and creates a voting bloc. By emphasizing specific attributes of ethnic membership, ethnopolitical entrepreneurs in Glendale have brought together internally diverse Armenians with limited exposure to US institutions and created a sense of linked, local fates among them. But these actors also reflect the dynamic spectrum that ethnopolitical entrepreneurs inhabit. This chapter thus identifies the important commonalities among ethnopolitical entrepreneurs, but it also highlights some important differences, particularly among first- and second-generation Armenian ethnopolitical entrepreneurs.

Chapter 5 broadens the focus beyond Glendale's elected officials to include municipal bureaucrats and the voters themselves. It explores three reasons ethnopolitical entrepreneurs' electoral successes do not always correlate with a sense of newcomers' political empowerment or feelings of inclusion. First, chapter 5 examines the role of the city's bureaucratic workforce in facilitating immigrant political incorporation. Because Armenian migration and political mobilization have been so rapid, the city has a peculiar disparity: while Armenians have saturated political and economic sectors, they remain largely absent from many of the city's civil services, its management, and its high-level bureaucracy. Next, the chapter unpacks how symbolic capital, which co-ethnic representation brings to many newcomers (and those whom they elect), can sometimes undermine voters' interests. Finally, the chapter analyzes how the electoral success of one ethnic population can limit the political incorporation of others. It ends by investigating the potential inevitability of one demographically large, politically mobilized ethnic population displacing not only previously established residents but also other newcomers.

Chapter 6 reflects on the key insights explored in the previous chapters' examination of suburbia as new domains of political incorporation among diverse immigrant populations throughout the United States. It seeks to extract from the study of Glendale's Armenians some of the most fundamental strengths, which could be applied in other suburban contexts. But it also reiterates the shortcomings of suburban ethnopolitical entrepreneurs. It ends by offering some suggestions about how the next generation of ethnopolitical entrepreneurs might consider overcoming these pitfalls.

Beyond introducing and explaining the important roles of ethnopolitical entrepreneurs in suburban immigrant political incorporation, this book also presents a novel immigrant story. While the United States' political climate is fraught
with polarizing animosities, the abuse of detained children and "illegals," and the
looming specter of weakening democratic institutions, this book reveals a more
optimistic side of US politics; it tells the story of immigrants who have worked
hard to overcome internal and external challenges. And, in the process of making
a place for themselves—despite the prejudicial institutions and attitudes they often
encounter—they have become influential participants in US political history. This
does not diminish the significance of those who suffer in their migrations from
Mexico, Honduras, Guatemala, and many other locations. But the story of Glendale's Armenians is a stirring reminder of the ingenuity of the talented, innovative
immigrants who overcome serious barriers to participate in and reconfigure their
suburban communities. In microcosm, these incorporation trajectories reflect
evolving US sociopolitical history. Or, as José Itzigsohn has urged, "The study of
immigrant incorporation is the study of American society" (2009, 197).

THE ARMENIAN DIASPORA
A Brief History

I met professor Richard Hovannisian in his office at the University of California, Los Angeles (UCLA). The room overflowed with books, papers, and peri-
odicals. They cascaded down the bookshelves and tables, which lined the
relatively cramped office space. Hovannisian asked me to move a stack of books
from a chair next to his desk to a nearby table and have a seat. He insisted we
meet in the morning, for, even in his mid-eighties, he had a full agenda—meetings
to attend, work to edit, and students to advise. Hovannisian is not only a preemi-
nent scholar of modern Armenian history, but he also plays an important role in
the Armenian diaspora as an advocate of Armenian Genocide recognition.

During the Armenian Genocide, Hovannisian's parents fled to the United
States from Ottoman Armenian localities near Harput in Turkey. Leaving behind
the destruction of the First World War and the Genocide, they relocated to California's San Joaquin Valley. He and his family were among many Armenians
who participated in the region's agricultural boom of the early twentieth century.
Nonetheless, they often found an unpredictable and unwelcoming host society
in California. Hovannisian came of age in the pre–civil rights era, a period in
which coercive "Americanization" strategies alienated ethnic minorities. Despite
Armenians' and other minorities' commercial successes in Fresno and its environs, they were often targets of discrimination and, sometimes, even violence.
Determined to overcome these challenges, Hovannisian's parents tried to preserve their traditions while also easing their children's integration into US society. Hovannisian's parents gave him an American-sounding name (his middle
name is Gable—after Clark Gable), and he did not learn to speak or read Armenian

until later in life. While Hovannisian's family held firmly to their Armenian roots, they tried to assist their children to succeed in an intolerant milieu.

In the 1960s, Hovannisian moved to Los Angeles to undertake his doctorate at UCLA. At the time, there already existed a scattering of Armenians in Southern California. He shared his first impressions with me:

> The community largely consisted of two parts. One was old, [the] Ottoman Armenian community. Some of them had come earlier, very early on, to LA. But others of [them] had gone to Fresno and bought farms. But then, during the Great Depression, they couldn't make their payments. So, they were foreclosed upon. And many of those people moved to LA and became small-shop proprietors, for the most part—mom-and-pop grocery stores, photo engraving, a number of other things. They were the bulk of the community. They got things moving here in Los Angeles. But there was also another part of the community that had come very early on, around the turn of the twentieth century, the so-called Russian Armenians, who came from the region of Aleksandropol (now called Gyumri) and Kars—for example, the Kardashian family came from the Karakal region of Kars, which doesn't exist anymore.[1] So, these people concentrated in East Los Angeles, and they were sort of exotic because they did Caucasian dances and all the other things that we have now become accustomed to. But, for us Western Armenians, it was quite different because we were more sedate than they were.

In Los Angeles, Hovannisian encountered Armenians at a historical crossroads. For the first time in centuries, Armenians of various diasporic strands, from the East and the West, converged on the same site (Sabagh, Bozorgmehr, and Der-Martirosian 1990; Waldinger and Bozorgmehr 2006). While each population had gleaned vague ideas of the other from books in Armenian history and accounts of extended relatives, they remained, for a long time, uncertain how to engage or make sense of one another.

While Armenians come to Los Angeles with a robust sense of ethnic identity, they also understand what it means to be Armenian in very different ways. As such, it falls on leaders, such as ethnopolitical entrepreneurs, to create cohesion among them. And the work they do in creating this sense of cohesion has significant electoral and institutional implications. To appreciate how Armenian ethnopolitical entrepreneurs have created a group (or voting bloc) out of the internally diverse and fragmented Armenians of Glendale requires some understanding of this population's history of being scattered around the world. This chapter therefore provides a brief history of the Armenian diaspora and the distinct streams that, in the second half of the twentieth century, converged on

Los Angeles and ultimately gave rise to one of the largest, most hybridized concentrations of Armenians in a thousand years of dispersion.

"Diaspora"

According to Robin Cohen (2008), the study of diaspora has gone through four distinct stages: (1) During the 1960s and 1970s, the classical association of the Jewish diaspora (or Diaspora) was extended to include African, Armenian, Greek, and Irish dispersions; like the Jewish diaspora, these other populations understood their dispersion as resulting from a traumatizing event (or series of events).[2] (2) From the 1980s onward, scholars began conceptualizing diaspora as a "metaphoric designation," which captured the experiences of diverse individuals (Safran 1991). Khachig Tölölyan has summed up this shift, stating that "the term that once described Jewish, Greek, and Armenian dispersion now shares meanings with a larger semantic domain that includes words like immigrant, expatriate, refugee, guestworker, exile community, overseas community, ethnic community" (1991, 4). (3) In the mid-1990s, scholars sought to remove some foundational elements, which previous researchers had relied on in conceptualizing diaspora. In particular, scholars largely stopped assuming that dispersion resulting from a catastrophe, such as war, genocide, or the slave trade, was requisite in creating a diaspora. Instead, they began factoring other considerations—such as economic deprivation in the homeland—to be ample causes for dispersion and the formation of a diaspora. Through a postmodernist lens, scholars also began to conceive of deterritorialized, socially constructed collective identities in radically novel ways. (4) Diaspora scholarship from the turn of the century onward has, largely, accommodated the social constructivist perspective; however, it has also become increasingly preoccupied with the proliferation of the term (Dufoix 2008, 2017; Faist 2010; Brubaker 2005, 2017; Cohen and Fischer 2019). Because of this proliferation, more recent scholarship has struggled to establish clear boundaries that provide consistent and coherent meaning. In response to these challenges, according to Cohen, this fourth stage has sought to reestablish some analytic boundaries by reaffirming the "diasporic idea, including its core elements, common features, and ideal types" (2008, 2). For example, recent scholarship identifies six features that distinguish diaspora—namely, dispersal (or immigration), location outside a homeland, a sense of community, orientation to a perceived homeland, transnational circulations, and a group identity (Grossman 2019, 1264). These six features give the term some parameters to understand how scholars conceptualize diaspora at the time of this writing. Rather than attempt to contribute to the long-standing theoretical debates on how to define *diaspora*, following Stéphane Dufoix (2008), I believe it is more useful to try to understand the complex ways different dispersed peoples construct and imagine their relationships with their perceived homelands as well as themselves.

For many Armenians, the concept of "diaspora" is not merely a matter of intellectual debate; it has become a significant ontological aspect of a cultural vocabulary and identity (Pattie 1997; Tölölyan 2000, 2005). Until the nineteenth century, Armenians used the term *gaghut* (or *gaghtojakh*)—that is, "forced exile"—to describe their condition. After the Genocide, however, the term *spyurk*—that is, "dispersed"—became the popular parlance. The Ottoman Armenian writer Yervant Odian used the word *spyurk* (or "diaspora") in 1920, but it became common in 1958 with the Lebanese Armenian Simon Simonian's weekly, *Spyurk*.

These evolving linguistic distinctions highlight the discursive changes in how Armenians have understood their dispersal. As with the scholarship on diaspora, however, the term generates several confusions and contentions among Armenians, too. Some of these confusions and contentions relate to countries or regions of origin. As James Barry has pointed out regarding the term *diaspora*:

> In reality, the term is much more problematic as the Armenian homeland, or Historic Armenia (*patmakan hayastan*), stretches from the Euphrates to the Caspian from west to east, and from the Caucasus to Lake Urmia from north to south. Additionally, the Samatskhe-Javakheti region of Georgia, which has an Armenian majority, is also often considered part of Historic Armenia and its residents are therefore not in diaspora. Even Armenians living away from Historic Armenia at times reject the term. Istanbul Armenians, for example, do not regard themselves as part of the Diaspora since they have never left their homeland; instead the borders have moved. (2019, 19–20)

But the complexity of these debates is by no means limited to geographical identity. Tölölyan, who has played an integral role in diaspora studies since founding the journal *Diaspora* in 1991, asks the following:

> But what is an Armenian identity? Who made the template, who fashioned the model, who holds the copyright, who gets to judge what is proper Armenian identity and behavior? That's a question posed by many angry Armenian American teenagers to their parents every day, when they are accused of not living as "real" Armenians. In countries like the contemporary US or France, where there is no indiscriminate persecution of Armenians to serve as glue for communal identity, can we say that there is a single Armenian diaspora?[3]

Tölölyan's important questions highlight the theoretical and ontological challenges Armenians confront in understanding themselves as members of the Armenian diaspora. These questions also begin to explain the internal complexity of the global Armenian diaspora. To give the reader a better understanding of this complexity, the rest of the chapter sketches the long, fraught journey of the internally diverse Armenian people in an effort to explain the sequence of events that would, ultimately, give rise to their concentrated settlement in Southern California.

A History of the Armenian Diaspora before the Genocide

The northern boundary of the ancestral territory of the Armenian people ran along the southern slope of the Pontus Mountains, which line the southern shore of the Black Sea, and extended eastward along the southern border of what is now the Republic of Georgia. This territory extended west to the Euphrates River, south to the headwaters of the Tigris River, and east to what is now northernmost Iran and Azerbaijan. At its most extensive, Armenia once included parts of several modern countries, such as Iraq, Iran, and Azerbaijan. But the single largest part of historic Armenia is in contemporary Turkey. In terms of Armenians' origins, they are a blend of the peoples who inhabited these historical territories, variously known as the Urartians, the Nayirian confederation, and the Hye, Hay, or Khay, living north of the Assyrians and east of the Hittite Empire.

The Greek historian Hecataeus of Miletus provided the first textual reference to Armenia in 525 BCE (Chahin 2001). In its origins, an early Armenian "culture" consisted of diverse practices and beliefs. As Tölölyan has observed of Armenians' cultural origins, "Their cultural identity evolved slowly at first, through the syncretic amalgamation of indigenous beliefs and practices with those of Zoroastrian neighbors and Hellenistic conquerors" (1996, 36). In 301 CE, Armenia became the first state to adopt Christianity—more than a decade before Rome.[4] This conversion signaled a significant shift in Armenian cultural identity and would shape, largely, the history of the Armenians thereafter. In 405, the medieval Armenian linguist and priest Mesrop Mashtots created an Armenian alphabet and, with the assistance of his students, translated the Bible into Armenian. With these tools Armenians would then form the Armenian Apostolic Church, another cornerstone of early Armenian cultural heritage.

Between the seventh and tenth centuries, conflict between Arabs and Byzantines triggered Armenian migration out of Greater Armenia. In the eleventh century, Seljuk invasions intensified this migration. The Seljuks, nomadic Turkish warriors from central Asia, defeated the Byzantines at the battle of Manzikert in 1071 and established control of the Armenian homeland. In response to the Seljuk invasions, many Armenians dispersed out of Armenia in the eleventh century. These Armenians consisted of several noble families. Some of these families, consisting of merchants and skilled artisans, went north to Georgia or moved into the heartland of the Byzantine Empire, while others, members of the landed aristocracy accompanied by their retinues of fighting men, moved south-west and became established in chaotically governed territories between the empire and the Arab lands—that is, the Taurus Mountains and the Mediterranean Sea (Panossian 2006, 63). Among these dispersed Armenian nobles, Ruben, who had most likely served as a military commander in the medieval Kingdom of Armenia, ultimately declared the independence of Cilicia (now in southern Turkey) from the Byzantine Empire in 1080, thereby establishing the Rubenian dynasty—nominally Byzantine but enjoying de facto independence (Ghazarian 2018). In 1199, the Rubenian prince Levon helped elevate Armenian Cilicia from a princedom into the Armenian Kingdom of Cilicia, becoming its first king.

Over three centuries (1080–1375), the history of Cilicia was shaped by several historical power dynamics: Byzantine, European, Mamluk, and Mongolian. Cilicia thus depended on its leaders' ability to balance politically these disparate forces. In addition, although Armenians made up the ruling class in Cilicia, they were a plurality of the population, and probably never formed an absolute majority. Rather, consisting of Armenians, Greeks, Syriac Christians, Jews, Muslims, and Europeans, Cilicia had a demographically diverse population. In this dynamic and precarious milieu, Cilician Armenians founded institutions to preserve their culture, language, religion, and power, while maintaining links to their homeland in the eastern Anatolian plateau. As Tölölyan has posited regarding the formation of Cilicia, "A mixture of immigrants and diasporans actually founded a new state on land that had been alien to them, as in Cilician Armenia from 1071 to 1375 AD" (1996, 12). From a slightly different perspective, Razmik Panossian has also argued of Cilicia: "It was the beginning of an organised diaspora far away from the homeland" (2006, 65).

The Cilician Armenian population consisted of many clerics (including the Catholicos, the head of the Armenian Church), nobles, knights, and serfs. The gentry intermarried with Crusader nobility in Jerusalem, Antioch, and Edessa. This prosperous diasporic node endured as an autonomous region and then an independent state until 1375, at which time it fell to Mamluk invaders. While most Armenians fled and formed new diasporic nodes (in places such as Cyprus and Italy), many remained in the region until the twentieth century—for example, survivors from Cilicia would later constitute the Armenian diaspora communities of Syria, Lebanon, and Palestine.

Smaller Armenian diaspora communities also emerged under varying conditions—such as those formed in eleventh-century Egypt and the Crimean Peninsula. The latter merchant diaspora proved a pivotal springboard for other Armenian diaspora populations, which subsequently formed in eastern Europe, such as the one established in fourteenth-century Polish Lvov (today Lviv in Ukraine). Relying on their trading networks and mercantile prowess, politically powerless Armenians proved indispensable "middlemen" in creating wealth through trade in growing European cities (Bonacich 1973). The Armenians of Lvov continued to thrive into the seventeenth century. This population grew and spawned several other communities throughout Europe. As in Cilicia, the elite fostered ties with the homeland and developed identity-preserving institutions, such as churches and, later, printing presses. During this period, a more global and interconnected sense of diaspora began to emerge, as clerical elites from the homeland traveled to Lvov and, in turn, Polish Armenians toured other Armenian communities (Tölölyan 2005).

As Polish Armenian mercantile trade networks expanded, other populations emerged in the region. Armenians established themselves in contemporary Ukraine, Moldova, Romania, Transylvania, Hungary, and Venice. In addition, the Celali rebellions in the Ottoman Empire (ca. 1595–1620) and Ottoman-Persian wars (1517–1639) devastated Armenia, leading to the creation of the Armenian diaspora communities of Istanbul and the western Ottoman Empire and, in 1603–1604, to the emergence of the Isfahan / New Julfa ("Nor Jugha") diasporic node in the Persian Empire. These communities supported the homeland financially and provided resources in the cultural development of all Armenians in both homeland and diaspora. These resources often included books (in Armenian); by 1750, Armenian printing presses had produced over five hundred books.[5] The distribution of commissioned books and the growth of printing presses in Armenian script helped Armenians in the diaspora as well as in the homeland maintain a strong attachment to their cultural heritage (Aslanian 2014).

In addition to mercantile activity, military conquests also catalyzed the formation of new Armenian diasporic nodes. When the Ottomans conquered the Byzantine capital of Constantinople in 1453, there was already an Armenian presence in the city—in fact, several Byzantine rulers had Armenian roots. Ottomans replenished this population by recruiting Armenians (and, after 1492, Jews) to relocate and develop the empire's commercial sectors. Many of these Armenians were already in Ottoman-controlled territories, such as those in Crimea and in what is Romania today. Furthermore, the Ottoman-Persian wars between 1514 and 1639 led Armenians to flee their ancestral territories. Many of these refugees settled in the Ottoman Empire, where they formed Armenian communities in Bursa, Kutahya, Smyrna, Constantinople, and other cities. In time, these communities would develop and prosper.

On the other side of the Ottoman-Persian wars, Shah Abbas I (1588–1629) first began transplanting thousands of Armenian merchants and their families from Julfa (present-day Azerbaijan) and the Ararat Valley to towns scattered throughout Persia—along the Caspian Sea and the Elburz Mountains and throughout central and southern Iran (Barry 2019). Abbas settled many wealthy artisans and merchants near his Safavid capital, Isfahan. The part of Isfahan where Armenians concentrated became known as New Julfa. This forced migration to Persia took place, largely, throughout the first decade of the seventeenth century. Shah Abbas hoped Armenians would bring economic growth to his new capital. But this forced migration proved a tragic event for many Armenians. On the basis of the available sources, Vazken Ghougassian (1998, 31) estimates that, of the several hundreds of thousands of Armenians deported to Persia (between three hundred thousand and four hundred thousand) approximately one hundred thousand perished en route. Despite the tragic losses of this migration, the community quickly took root and thrived as a minority population with relative autonomy in internal affairs because the shah allowed Armenians to govern themselves and maintain their own institutions.

Over the next century, New Julfan Armenians became quite prosperous. As Panossian points out, "Armenian traders of New Julfa were among the richest merchants in the world, living opulent lives, as they handled a substantial component of Persia's foreign trade, including that with India, Russia and Europe" (2006, 79). These merchants organized the silk trade to Europe and the Indian subcontinent (McCabe 1999). Sophisticated Julfan merchants expanded their trading networks into India, Burma, Tibet, Malaysia, Singapore, Indonesia, the Philippines, China, Russia, the Ottoman Empire, Venice, Amsterdam, France, England, and elsewhere (Herzig 1996; McCabe 1999; Tölölyan 2005; Aslanian 2014). And New Julfan Armenian merchant activities catalyzed the formation of new communities as trade networks expanded. With the growing presence of printing presses and the charitable contributions of Julfan merchants, Armenian global interconnectivity (and Julfan influence) also increased (Ghougassian 1995).

In many of the relevant eighteenth-century documents published in Europe and India, a strong sense of Armenian solidarity and global connectivity are often articulated. Tölölyan (2005, 39) argues that late eighteenth-century Armenians began to see themselves increasingly as a coerced, dispersed, and polycentric population. Out of this sense of coerced dispersion, Armenian intellectual elites called for a unified, proto-national culture (as reflected in the formation of a distinctly Armenian canon)—based on the European model of the eighteenth century—and for liberation from the Muslim "yoke" in the ancestral homeland and a return thereto (with Echmiadzin at the religious center of the homeland).

Armenian merchants commissioned Catholic Armenian monks—the Mekhitarist Order or Brotherhood—to help form a canon. Despite the central role Armenian elites placed on the Apostolic Church, these Catholic monks, imbued with the intellectual vigor of the Enlightenment, would, remarkably, produce the secular canon necessary in the continuation and preservation of Armenian letters. Since 1717, the Mekhitarist Order has lived on a small island in Venice, San Lazzaro. In the eighteenth century, this intellectually prolific order produced the first Armenian dictionary; a history of the Armenian people (in three volumes); the first vernacular manual and classical Armenian grammar; literary translations from Italian, French, German, Greek, and Latin; and textbooks on various topics. Financial elites of the diaspora (such as those in India, Isfahan, and Constantinople) funded not only the production but also the circulation of these publications (Nichanian 1999; Aslanian 2014).

In the eighteenth century, a new imperial agent swept Armenian-inhabited lands and created new diasporic nodes. As the Romanov czars gradually expanded to the Black Sea, the Caspian Sea, Siberia, central Asia, and the Pacific Ocean, Armenians from Persian-occupied ancestral territories often joined the Russians in the hope of a Christian "liberation" of their homeland in the Muslim-controlled Caucasus. By the late eighteenth century, Russia had conquered much of the easternmost region of Armenian ancestral homelands. Russian officials sought and sometimes coerced Armenian migrants from Crimea and the Kingdom of Georgia to settle newly acquired territories in the Don steppes. With migration from Crimea and the Persian and Ottoman Empires steadily increasing, Armenians in Russian-controlled territories continued to grow in number into the nineteenth century. New diasporic nodes arose in Astrakhan, Moscow, Nor Nakhichevan, and St. Petersburg. Between 1801 and 1828, Russian imperial territory grew to encompass the Transcaucasus, which includes the lands of today's Republics of Armenia, Azerbaijan, and Georgia.

In these territories, Armenians already resided. In Georgia, they lived largely in cities (in the capital, Tbilisi, Armenians constituted three-fourths of the population in 1801), whereas in Armenia, they lived among Turkic and Tatar populations in more rural settings (Suny 1993). Tölölyan (2005, 41) characterizes the Armenian diaspora of the Russian Empire as an "intrastate diaspora"—that is, geographically distinct Armenian communities living under the rule of the same state. Armenian communities formed in various sites under Russian control, such as those of Georgia, Baku (the capital of Azerbaijan), the Crimea, Rostov na Donu, and Moscow. In these diverse spaces, Russian was frequently the sec-

THE ARMENIAN DIASPORA 31

ond, if not the first, language of the intellectual elite. While Armenia's capital, Yerevan, was a city of only sparse habitation and significance to Armenians in the nineteenth century, cultural and financial centers for the Armenian diaspora in this period concentrated in Tbilisi, Baku, Moscow, and St. Petersburg.[6] As before in New Julfa and India for global Armenian communities, Armenian elites in these city centers financed the construction of Armenian institutions (particularly churches) in other locales scattered throughout the Russian Empire. During the nineteenth century, the polycentric Armenian diaspora developed along two distinct lines and centered in two distinct metropolises—in the Ottoman "West," Constantinople, and in the Russian "East," Tbilisi.

Governing the Armenian confessional community, or millet, in the "West" was the state-recognized patriarch, the head of the Apostolic Church in Ottoman lands, who had a nonstable relationship with the patriarch of Jerusalem, which, at the time, was also in Ottoman territory. Because Ottoman officials divided populations into these millets on the basis of religious affiliation, and because most but not all Armenians were members of the Apostolic Church, religion and ethnicity were nearly indistinguishable until 1848, when the sultan created a Catholic millet in which Armenian Catholics joined all other Catholic minorities of the empire. Within the Ottoman Empire, elite Armenians prospered in several commercial sectors; they worked as an essential "middleman minority" both economically and politically (Bonacich 1973). In state affairs, Ottoman Armenians often worked as translators and officials in Constantinople. In the mid- and late nineteenth century, however, Ottoman officials sought to reform and democratize practically every level of the empire's administration. These reforms granted millets considerable self-governing agency. Ottoman Armenians developed the empire's first civilian hospital, a seminary, orphanages, churches, a network of elementary and secondary schools (including several for women), a theater, and press media. In these media, the Constantinople-based vernacular version of Armenian was used and reformed to become Western Armenian, the formal language of the news, the schools, and the arts. The conservative Muslim opponents of the sultans resisted, however, and, after Abdülhamid II became sultan in 1876, they reversed many of these reforms.

From the eighteenth century and on to the final transition, Ottoman Armenian elites (or *amiras*) played important and diverse roles in the empire: at first they acted primarily as moneylenders, but in the period of their greatest prominence in the first half of the nineteenth century they became financiers and taxation specialists. The class was enlarged over the decades by the extending of the title *amira* to notable Armenians who carried out other major functions in the Ottoman Empire, such as the director of the Ottoman mint, the manager of Ottoman gunpowder production, and others (Barsoumian 1980). Richard Antaramian describes the important functions they served in the following way: "*Amiras* used the wealth produced by their investments in Ottoman governance and economy, particularly tax collection, to patronize their own community. Philanthropy was political. The *amiras'* roles—financier, technocrat, and philanthropist—provided them with a strategic location in the politics that obligated state and provincial elite to one another" (2022, 325).

At the same time, Armenian intellectuals in Tbilisi and elsewhere in the Russian Empire developed their own identities and their own vernacular (Eastern Armenian).[7] This intellectual elite of the Russian Empire produced prodigious literature, art, and political writings. In 1890, three Armenian intellectuals— Christapor Mikayelyan (1859–1905), Simon Zavarian (1866–1913), and Stepan Zoryan (1867–1919)—founded the Armenian Revolutionary Federation (ARF), or Dashnaktsutyun. Other parties that emerged during this period included the Armenakan Party (1885), the Hnchakian Party (1887), and the Ramgavar Party (1921), which developed a close association with the Armenian General Benevolent Union. While the Ramgavars sought to counter the ARF authority after 1923, the latter remained more influential (especially in the diaspora). In its origins, the ARF sought to mobilize Armenians in the eastern part of the Ottoman Empire. In the nineteenth and early twentieth centuries, the Ottoman and Russian Empires fought several wars. Antagonism between these two empires limited interaction between Eastern and Western Armenians (and between the homelands and the diaspora). In the West, this interstate antagonism made Armenians, who prospered on both sides of the division, a subject of Ottoman suspicion. The ARF responded by sending members to Ottoman territories to organize Armenian peasants into self-defense groups. Ultimately, these efforts usually fell on deaf ears, and any resistance only intensified Ottoman officials' suspicions about their Armenian subjects. Like the Catholic Mekhitarist Brotherhood, the eastern and western pre-Genocide diaspora populations produced an impressive linguistic, literary, and artistic oeuvre in the period after the European uprisings of 1848 and the start of the First World War. Despite their limited communication, Armenian commercial elites and industrial artisans on both sides of the divide continued a long-established history of productivity, prosperity, industry, and creativity. For example, in the czarist Russian Empire, from approximately 1860 to 1918, Armenians, in part, staffed and led the Baku oil industry (Suny 2019).

To be sure, most pre-Genocide Armenians in various diasporic nodes, cut off from their ancestral homelands, did not think of themselves as belonging to a diaspora. Rather, most Armenians settled permanently in their host societies with the intention of sustaining themselves and their families. These newcomers had diverse backgrounds: some came as refugees from border regions, others as members of a labor diaspora; another segment came from the centers of imperial prosperity, such as those in Constantinople (later Istanbul) and Izmir. But tracing the intellectual trends helps clarify the roots and routes of the Armenian people in their long, storied journey around the world.

The Armenian Diaspora after the Genocide

In 1908, the Young Turks brought down the Ottoman sultan, Abdülhamid II. While Ottoman Armenians initially supported the Young Turks and what the latter purported to offer—namely, the restoration of a liberal constitution and legal protection for non-Muslims—Turkish nationalism soon became the guiding force of the ruling faction, the Committee of Union and Progress (CUP). Increasingly, Armenians became targets of hostility and suspicion among CUP officials, because, as Ronald Grigor Suny argues, "the Sublime Porte saw Armenians as a more seriously subversive element, since European powers, most importantly Russia, promoted their protection and used the 'Armenian Question' as a wedge into Ottoman internal affairs" (2021, 4). In the years leading up to the First World War, the Ottoman government endured one loss after another in Bosnia-Herzegovina, Bulgaria, Crete, Albania, and Libya, among others. In response, Turkish nationalist fervor came to supplement and then replace efforts to maintain the crumbling Ottoman Empire. When a group of Young Turk leaders—Ismail Enver Pasha, Ahmet Cemal Pasha, and Mehmet Talat Pasha—seized the government in 1913, Turkish nationalism became the governing ideology, one that would have catastrophic consequences for Armenians, Assyrians, and other minorities.

From the outset of the First World War, Armenians inhabited an increasingly precarious position in the Ottoman Empire. They had long proved a scapegoat for Ottoman shortcomings. But animosities intensified in 1914, when the Young Turks sought to compensate Ottoman territorial losses and strengthen the empire by joining Austro-Hungary and Germany to fight against France, Great Britain, and Russia.[8] In the Caucasus campaign of eastern Anatolia and Russia during the winter of 1914–1915, Armenians, who were subjects of both the Ottoman and czarist Russian Empires, fought on both sides of the conflict. After having some initial success, the Ottoman army, led by war minister Enver Pasha, suffered a major defeat in the Battle of Sarikamish. Incurring major losses in this humiliating defeat, the Ottoman military was ultimately forced back. Enver attributed defeat by claiming that Armenians had betrayed the empire; he did so in a manner similar to the German claim *after* the First World War that

Jews had "stabbed Germany in the back" (Schleunes 1970). Made on the heels of a calamitous defeat during the war, the claim intensified already rooted suspicions and facilitated Enver's and Talat's subsequent genocidal plans regarding the Ottoman Armenians (Rafter and Walklate 2012; Suny 2021).

Shortly after their crushing defeat in the Battle of Sarikamish, the CUP leaders began the deportation and mass murder of Armenians, first in the east and, after, throughout the empire. On April 24, 1915, officials rounded up, deported, and eventually murdered Armenian intellectuals in Constantinople. Missionaries and foreign officials witnessed the death marches of the Armenians in eastern Anatolia. Most of the Armenians, suffering starvation and dehydration, died in these one-thousand-mile desert convoys. In addition, Armenians were consistently attacked and murdered not only by the Ottoman soldiers and irregular Turkish combatants but also by various other groups, such as Kurds and Circassians. These events culminated in the Armenian Genocide, or the systematic attempt to eliminate the Armenians (Hovannisian 1998, 2009; Suny 2021). Up to 1.5 million died during the Armenian Genocide (Kévorkian 2011). These events nearly wiped out the Ottoman Armenians' presence in their traditional homeland as well as centuries of culture and civilization. The Armenian Genocide proved to be one of the greatest crimes against humanity the world had witnessed to date (Dadrian 2003).

Those who survived did so in the Arab Middle East or fled to Europe, the Americas, or the Russian Empire. Approximately half of the survivors found refuge in the Russian Empire's Armenian provinces. In 1918, the Republic of Armenia would comprise these provinces. That year, the Republic of Armenia declared its independence. Fittingly, independence was announced from the diaspora in Tbilisi (Tölölyan 2005). Only two years later, Vladimir Lenin's armies returned to reclaim what was lost following the end of czarist Russia. In December 1920, Armenia thus became one of the federated socialist republics of the Soviet Union.

Following the Genocide, the dispersal of Armenians led older communities to grow and new communities to form. For example, of the Armenian refugees in Europe and the Near East, approximately 30 percent (or sixty-five thousand) fled to France (Mandel 2003). French authorities relied on refugee labor to rebuild the country's war-devastated economy; they put many Armenians to work, at least initially, in coal mines and textile factories. When the United States implemented strict immigration policies in 1924, this egress to France and other European outposts further intensified. As Maud Mandel (2003) notes, by 1931, 11 percent of France's labor force consisted of foreign-born immigrants and refugees. Or, even more substantially, nearly 240,000 survivors fled to the Middle East, where half ended up in bondage, forced to convert to Islam, or disappeared (Tölölyan 2005). Joining the millions of other displaced persons in the wake of

FIGURE 3. Turkish soldiers marching Armenians out of Harput.

the First World War, Armenian refugees settled in Egypt, Iran, Iraq, Lebanon, Syria, and other countries. While the pre-Genocide diasporic Armenians typically brought wealth or skills to varied host societies, these dispossessed and uprooted refugees came to the Middle East in a state of near ruin. Nonetheless, with the financial help of international organizations, the Armenian churches, and wealthy Armenians in the West (often in the form of compatriotic societies), new Armenian communities emerged in Aleppo, Amman, Baghdad, Beirut, Damascus, Mosul, and elsewhere. In addition, existing communities in Cairo and Alexandria were enlarged. While these were initially considered temporary resettlements, the Treaty of Lausanne (1923) shut Armenians off from the prospect of returning to their ancestral homeland.[9] Beginning in poverty, Middle Eastern and European Armenians first survived (1923–1945) and then adapted and attained a measure of prosperity in their new homes.

The case of Lebanon vividly reflects this rapid transformation. Some Armenians have inhabited what is today called Lebanon since the seventeenth century. By the end of the eighteenth century, Catholic Armenians had established a monastery and patriarchal see. By the end of the nineteenth century, however, an influx of Apostolic Armenians entered as merchants and students. While the initial waves of Armenians came voluntarily, many Armenian refugees arrived from the Ottoman Empire as survivors of pogroms and the Genocide. The French High Commission settled Armenian survivors in various refugee camps throughout

Lebanon and other former French colonies (Nalbantian 2013). Initially, the French Mandate conferred citizenship to Armenian refugees and, later, the Lebanese government. Thousands of survivors were sheltered in tents or shanties. To prevent the spread of disease and infection, authorities quarantined many of these newly arrived Armenians. Between 1920 and 1922, the French retreated from Cilician Armenia, and, in 1938–1939, more Armenian refugees poured into Lebanon, first when the French surrendered the last surviving portions of Cilician Armenia to Turkey and then when the French transferred Syrian Sanjak of Alexandretta to the Turks (Abramson 2013). With support from the Armenian Catholic Church, the League of Nations, Armenian relief organizations, and the Lebanese authorities, the newly arrived Armenians in Lebanon raised money to purchase property and build homes for themselves. Thus, Armenian population centers—most conspicuously Bourj Hammoud—had already begun to emerge by the 1930s on the sites of refugee settlements.

From the 1930s onward, the Lebanese Armenian community's transformation proved rapid and dramatic. Lebanese Armenians quickly became highly influential as artisans, merchants, intellectuals, and other professionals. In fact, some scholars have claimed that Armenian commercial successes of the middle twentieth century in Lebanon exceeded the economic accomplishments of most other prosperous historical diasporic nodes (Hewsen 2001). In addition to rapid material development, the Lebanese Armenians proved successful in gaining political representation. Taking advantage of Lebanon's confessional mandate, Lebanese Armenians have participated in national parliament since 1934. While several political parties have existed in Lebanon, the ARF has proved the most consistently influential among them. Lebanon has suffered from chronically weak governmental institutions (Acemoglu and Robinson 2020), but Armenian political representation ensured that Armenians' schools, churches, and ethnic identity not only survived the Genocide but also flourished. While the Lebanese case is particularly striking, Armenians throughout the Middle East adapted and acquired a distinct yet privileged status in their respective post-Genocide host societies.

Dikran, who came to the United States in 1977 from Iraq, met me in a café in one of San Fernando Valley's most affluent neighborhoods—La Cañada Flintridge. He owned a home a couple of blocks down the street. Of the distinct role Armenians had played in Iraq, he explained:

> Since [Iraqi Armenians] were educated, they couldn't stand difficulties, and sometimes—it happened to me also and to others—they were forcing you to go into the Islamic religion classes. Some people didn't like it. Some people didn't care. But most of us over there were more like,

FIGURE 4. A narrow street in Bourj Hammoud, Lebanon.

because of the religious difference, I mean, it was not acceptable to comingle to do something with the [Muslims]. We were living together on the same street, but my mom and dad never let us play, interact with them. It was very interesting. I think religion and nationality played a very strong reason why. However, they forced you to go into the army, because it was mandated. . . . It wasn't officially the government versus Armenia. In fact, we were very trusted people. Even Saddam's [Saddam Hussein] chef was Armenian. Saddam's babysitter was Armenian. Because he did not trust anyone else. . . . Christian minorities are different.

Dikran explained to me the complicated role Armenians (as well as other non-Muslim minorities) played in their respective Middle Eastern host societies. Armenians had a distinct status in each diaspora: in Lebanon and Iran, they were incorporated into the state and guaranteed seats in their respective parliaments; in Turkey, they were allegedly "protected" under the Lausanne Treaty; in Egypt, they enjoyed no form of state-granted sociopolitical privilege but were economically successful. Autocratic leaders often relied on members of these "trusted" religious minorities simply because the latter lacked a sufficiently large power base with which to oppose them. In addition, Armenians could be counted on not to become part of Muslim political factions. The privileged status of Armenians in the Middle East in the second half of the twentieth century reflects, in part, the remarkably rapid transformation of the post-Genocide Armenian Ottoman refugees.

While post-Genocide Middle Eastern Armenian communities quickly rebounded and prospered, regional turmoil would, yet again, reconfigure the Armenian diaspora in the final decades of the twentieth century. A great many Genocide survivors sought refuge in North America, South America, and Western Europe, but these numbers paled compared to the deluge of migration resulting from the Lebanese Civil War (1975–1990), the Iranian Revolution (1979), the Iran-Iraq War (1980–1988), and the collapse of the Soviet Union (1991).[10] As Armenian populations in the Middle East and Soviet Union shrank in number, those in Western countries expanded exponentially. Seismic political shifts in the Middle East from the late 1960s onward have significantly expanded the Armenian populations of Australia, Canada, France, Germany, and many other countries. Among these more recent expansions, the United States, and in particular Greater Los Angeles, would eventually become the most conspicuous (Takooshian 1986; Mekdjian 2009).

Armenian Migration to the United States

Although sparse and scattered, Armenians' settlement in the United States extends back to the colonial period.[11] The first person identified as Armenian in the New World came, most likely, in 1618 or 1619 (Malcolm 1910, 50). Referred to as "Martin the Armenian," this early Armenian immigrant is mentioned in the available records several times until 1624, at which point, presumably, he returned to England with the tobacco he had grown in Virginia (Malcolm 1910). Several other Armenians followed Martin to Virginia, and their contributions are recorded in various spheres from the mid-seventeenth century onward. By the seventeenth century, Armenians had become well known for their silk-weaving production (Aslanian 2014), and early colonial entrepreneurs sought their expertise in this area starting around 1653 (Mirak 1983). John Ferrer eulogized one of these Armenians, "George the Armenian," in poetic verse:

> His two Armenians from Turky sent
> Are now most busy on his brave attempt
> And had he stock sufficient for next yeare
> Ten thousand pound of Silk would then appeare
> And to the skies his worthy deeds upreare. (Quoted in Mirak 1983, 36)[12]

Despite their numerical insignificance, the handful of early Armenian settlers, as Robert Mirak eloquently articulates, played a "mythological role for a later generation of immigrant Armenians . . . to feel a part of American history; like Yankee bluebloods, they too possessed deep roots in America" (1983, 36).

Following the Genocide, most early Armenians docked in New York (although others docked in Boston, Philadelphia, and, outside of the United States, in Mexico, Canada, and elsewhere). Many from this wave settled throughout the Northeast. However, a small number came directly to California as well. Those reaching Californian ports often had come from Japan or China, traveling via Russia (LaPiere 1930, 160). In the northeastern United States, Armenians typically worked in factories (with the largest concentrations in industrial cities in Massachusetts, such as Worcester, Boston, Watertown, Lynn, and Lowell). However, they also settled in various other places and became involved in various industries: they worked in silk in Rhode Island and New Jersey, railroads and electricity in New York, coal mines in Pennsylvania, iron and steel in Illinois, automobiles in Michigan, slaughter yards in Illinois, furniture in Wisconsin, agriculture in Northern California, steel and cement in Southern California, and many others elsewhere (Heitman 1987). Thus, Armenians began planting roots and forming communities in various US cities from the beginning of the twentieth century.

Fresno

While most Armenian newcomers worked in manufacturing and industrial capacities, some brought with them talent in farming and viniculture. Although they lived in various places throughout California from the late nineteenth century onward, the most concentrated and significant settlement first arose in Fresno. Mirak documents this settlement in his book *Torn between Two Lands* (1983). He chronicles the auspicious timing of ambitious Armenians who moved to Fresno just as the fallow fields blossomed into a prosperous agricultural center on account of irrigation and the railroad (Mirak 1983, 111). The first Fresno Armenians arrived in the 1870s. Consistent with the entrepreneurial spirit associated with other early settlers, these Armenians were often talented business owners. For example,

FIGURE 5. Armenian women in a rubber factory in Watertown, Massachusetts.

the Seropian family came with the hope that the climate might improve the health of the family's patriarch, John Seropian. Once settled, they opened a general store in the 1880s (Bulbulian 2000, 22). During their time in Fresno, the Seropians dabbled in the fruit industry, coffee shops, grocery stores, dried fruit packaging, goods shipment, real estate speculation, and several other enterprises. Their business ventures brought them attention not only among other Fresno residents but also among other Armenians scattered throughout the United States. Seeing the opportunities available in Fresno, Armenians followed the Seropians west. The Seropians and other early Fresno Armenian settlers, such as Stepan Shahamirian, Melkon Markarian, and Krikor Arakelian, laid the groundwork for a larger community to develop (Bulbulian 2000).

Like the Seropians, most early Armenian settlers migrated to Fresno from other parts of the United States. According to Richard T. LaPiere (1930), 84 percent of early Armenian settlers had moved to Fresno after living 5.7 years (on average) in some other US city. By 1904, Armenians farmed more than ten thousand acres of land that they owned (Bulbulian 2000, 55). While farming was not the only work they did, Fresno Armenians gained the most prominence in this occupation. By the outbreak of the First World War, ten thousand Armenians were estimated to reside in Fresno—making up about 25 percent of the county's minority population (Mirak 1983, 113). Outbidding competitors, newly settled Armenians acquired lands to cultivate grapes, melons, figs, and other fruits. And their prominence came not only from landholding but also from capital gains: prior to the Eighteenth Amendment's prohibition on alcohol consumption in 1919, prices for raisins soared and Armenian viticulturalists began to amass great wealth. With this wealth, they purchased more property and expanded their business ventures. Although these ventures plummeted in the 1920s, Armenians had already established themselves as a powerful influence in the thriving agricultural scene of Fresno and the surrounding area.

Fresno proved a land of opportunity for many Armenian farmers, not only those involved with the cultivation of grapes and raisins. The first and only US-based Armenian community, Yettem—about forty miles southeast of Fresno—developed a commercial pistachio orchard; the first Armenian millionaire in California, Krikor Arakelian, also known as the "Melon King," led melon production; and the Markarians cornered a substantial portion of the fig market—20 percent of US production (Bulbulian 2000, 73). This early period proved truly fecund in Armenian economic prosperity. Even after the farming industry began to decline, post-Genocide Armenians, who settled in and around Fresno, continued to acquire and cultivate land. While the fortunes of these later waves were often less than those of their predecessors, farming in Fresno continued to be one of the most conspicuous areas of Armenian influence. That agriculture did not require thorough familiarity with the local institutions, practices, or language also favorably oriented many newly arrived Armenians to farming.

These early Fresno Armenians overcame adversity and prospered in the face of unfamiliarity, prejudice, and competition.[13] As Mirak argues, "Because of their business abilities, work ethic, frugal living, and good management, all in a generally prosperous economic climate, the Armenians in and around Fresno achieved considerable success before World War I" (1983, 119). Their success is reflected in the number of local institutions they created—churches, schools, newspapers, restaurants, and others. This impressive population established a precedent of achievement for the California Armenians who came after them.

Building on Armenian successes in Fresno, other communities quickly sprouted in the environs of this fertile soil. Even today, there are Armenian churches not only in Fresno but also in Yettem, Fowler, Reedley, and Wahtoke. Although these smaller communities have gradually declined, they testify to the geographical breadth of Armenian settlement and ambition in the early twentieth century.

Throughout this period, Armenians had already begun to reside in Southern California; however, they remained a comparatively small, scattered population in the early part of the twentieth century. No one would likely have anticipated that, shortly after the Second World War, the central node of Armenian diasporic activity would shift so rapidly to various sites throughout Los Angeles—Pasadena, Boyle Heights, Montebello, Hollywood, and, most conspicuously, Glendale.

Los Angeles

While the growth of Los Angeles's Armenian population is largely associated with political tumult in the Middle East and the Soviet Union in the second half of the twentieth century, Armenians, in smaller numbers, have inhabited the city for a much longer period. Among the first to settle in Los Angeles were artisans, who set up carpet shops in Los Angeles and Pasadena. Just as the Seropians had perceived in Fresno a more salutary climate, these entrepreneurs, such as the Pashigian brothers of Pasadena, typically moved westward for mercantile opportunities in established communities in the late nineteenth century. And, as in Fresno, these were trailblazing and ambitious individuals.

Some of the first settlers—the so-called Russian Armenians—came to Los Angeles at the turn of the century. Their history is aligned with that of the Russian Dukhobors and Molokans. These religious minorities had been persecuted in Russia in the late eighteenth century (Hardwick 1993). In 1895, Czar Nicholas II persecuted the Dukhobors residing in the Caucasus for their refusal to serve in the royal military (Mirak 1983, 57). Among those targeted, approximately four thousand were forcibly relocated to Armenian and Georgian villages. After living near Armenians for several years, they forged social ties. In 1898, after securing financial and political relief (from the likes of Count Lev Tolstoy and others), many sailed ultimately for Winnipeg, Canada. Transnational circulations, such as letters, eventually resulted in the chain migration of other Dukhobors, as well as their Armenian neighbors, to Canada. From Canada, many Dukhobors relocated to Los Angeles. And when the Russian Armenians arrived in Canada, several followed the Dukhobors (Mirak 1983, 58). In addition, economic hardship and growing conflict (in the Russian Revolution of 1905 and the Russo-Tatar Wars of 1905–1907) increased Russian Armenian migration from the Caucasus to the New World, and ultimately to Los Angeles, in the first decade of the twentieth century. This small population of Russian Armenians was among the first in Greater Los Angeles (most prominently in Riverside).

Several of the original Russian Armenians settled in the ethnically diverse neighborhood of Boyle Heights. This neighborhood attracted diverse new settlers on account of its streetcars, which gave commuters access to downtown Los Angeles (Wilson 2013). Its ethnic diversity earned it the moniker "the Ellis Island of the West Coast." In addition, wealthy landholders subdivided their estates and began renting them to recent immigrants at relatively affordable rates (Luce 2013, 28). Boyle Heights' population expanded considerably in the opening decades of the twentieth century; this expansion included Russian Armenians (and Russian Molokans) as well as Jews, Mexicans, and Black Americans. The growth of Boyle Heights reflects that of Los Angeles. Indeed, Los Angeles's population doubled

FIGURE 6.   Montebello Genocide Memorial, Montebello, California.

(from 577,000 to 1.24 million) in the 1920s alone (Tygiel 2001). It was in these settlement pockets that something resembling an Armenian community began to emerge.

Hollywood

In 1965, the US Congress passed the Hart-Celler Act (or Immigration and Nationality Act). Before that, immigration had been restricted largely to those from Western Europe. However, the Hart-Celler Act led to an unprecedented diversification of the United States; it opened the borders to migrants from Asia, Africa, the Middle East, and Southern and Eastern Europe. Many of these immigrants and their children inculcated civil rights values and challenged conventional perceptions regarding race and ethnicity. As Gary Gerstle has argued, "Immigrant groups, both old and new, quickly adopted a similar stance in regard to their own

FIGURE 7. Street sign in Little Armenia, Los Angeles.

ethnic cultures, thereby broadening and intensifying the effort to locate America's vitality in its ethnic and racial diversity" (2013, 315). Thus, post-1965 immigrants reoriented the US mainstream, both demographically and ideologically. Americans' aggressive, pre-1960s assimilationist attitudes were confronted by an increasing sense of ethnic and racial empowerment.

It was in this dynamic period that Armenians began coming to Southern California in much larger numbers. And the countries from which they came were also undergoing profound internal upheavals. Armenians came to Southern California in distinct waves and in response to several international events, such as the Lebanese Civil War, the Iranian Revolution, the Iran-Iraq War, the collapse of the Soviet Union, the subsequent economic crash of the Republic of Armenia, and others.[14] In response to these events, several pieces of US legislation would further facilitate Armenians' migrations to the United States, particularly out of the former Soviet Union and Iran. These included the Jackson-Vanik Amendment (1974), the Lautenberg Amendment (1989), and the Specter Amendment (2004).[15] These events and policies substantially increased the size of the Armenian population throughout Greater Los Angeles.

Before Glendale, Hollywood was home to the greatest concentration of Armenians in Los Angeles. Hollywood Armenians concentrated in sufficient numbers to resemble an "ethnic enclave"—that is, a residential or business district with high ethnic concentration, a distinct cultural identity, and salient economic footprints (see chapter 2). To this day, Hollywood Armenians' contributions are pervasive: restaurants, shops, schools, and churches suffuse the main arteries. In the 1960s and 1970s, newcomers from several locations in the United States as well as many from Iran, Lebanon, Soviet Armenia, and elsewhere came to Hollywood to join their Armenian families and friends. A second wave occurred in the 1980s and continued with the fall of the Soviet Union (and with the establishment of an independent Republic of Armenia). This neighborhood became the ultimate destination for many post-Soviet Armenians (as well as others), who brought a distinct set of cultural and political orientations.

Hollywood Armenians concentrated their energies in several fields, many of which expanded considerably over the twentieth century. Areas of salient contribution included commerce and automobiles. Vahe Karapetian is one vivid example of the Hollywood Armenians' contributions. Born in Lebanon in 1940 to Armenian Genocide survivors, Karapetian had a turbulent youth. At the age of five, he and his family moved to Soviet Armenia during a period of widespread "repatriation" from the diaspora (Pattie 2004). He undertook his schooling and university training in Yerevan. By 1968, Karapetian had moved to Hollywood. At that time, he spoke no English. He began working at a gas station but networked quickly. In 1971, he had designed an early model of the food truck. As these mobile kitchens became increasingly popular in subsequent years, Karapetian's business expanded—from selling approximately 50 units per year in the 1970s to over 250 per year by the 1980s. And he sold food trucks all over the world—Japan, Germany, China, and elsewhere. As Mark Vallianatos has argued regarding food trucks in Southern California, "the modern, self-propelled, 'cook-aboard' food truck, as it is known in many communities and celebrated in popular culture was born in, evolved in, and reached its apogee in the LA region" (2017, 68). Karapetian's design played an important role in the growth of the food truck industry not only in Los Angeles but throughout the world.

Armenians' pride in their contributions gave rise to a district gaining the name, although perhaps a bit anachronistically, Little Armenia, in October 2000. Seeing the district named Thai Town, a Hollywood Armenian, Garo Keurjikian, who owned an automotive shop, complained to then city council member Jackie Goldberg. Goldberg urged Hollywood Armenians to procure ten thousand votes in favor of the name. Through grassroots outreach, the signatures were acquired and the designation of Little Armenia was approved. Even as Hollywood Armenian population waned, the designation marked Armenians' imprint in this part of the city.

While Glendale and San Fernando have more recently become the main centers of Armenian habitation, most Armenian commercial franchises or chains

FIGURE 8. Over one hundred thousand people fill East Wilson Avenue in Glendale, California, during the 2015 March for Justice.

originated in Hollywood: the popular restaurant chain Zankou Chicken and the franchise grocery outlet JONS, for example, began in Hollywood. Armenian automotive work has also become quite prominent in Hollywood, and, to this day, Armenians own a substantial portion of local car shops. Proximity to Los Angeles's city center also led Hollywood Armenians to adopt urban practices entirely absent elsewhere in the diaspora, such as the first version of an Armenian street gang, Armenian Power. While the gang began initially to protect siblings and friends from other street gangs, it gradually adapted to harsh inner-city realities and began dabbling in money laundering, extortion, and other forms of criminality.

Like other ethnic enclaves, such as those of the Chinese in Chinatown, the Japanese in Little Tokyo, or the Koreans in Koreatown (K-Town), Hollywood's Little Armenia is an important part of Los Angeles's cultural and historical "mosaic" (Wilson 2013). And, similar to the Chinese, Japanese, and Koreans, Armenians have largely migrated to the suburbs. For Armenians, this demographic shift has been particularly pronounced in Glendale and other suburbs throughout the San Fernando Valley. Nonetheless, Hollywood's Little Armenia represents an important part of Armenian history in and contribution to Los Angeles.

The Armenians of Glendale

Armenians' spontaneous settlement of Glendale may at first seem surprising. Up until the 1960s, Glendale was home to relatively few Armenians. In addition,

Glendale's local ordinances were notoriously prohibitive and discriminatory. Through the 1960s, Glendale was a sundown town—that is, a community in which minorities were prohibited after the sun had set. The police would often escort non-"white" people in sundown towns to the city limits lest their presence provoke the local residents. By the mid-1960s, Armenians' "whiteness" may not have been as contested as it had been several decades before (Tehranian 2000; Craver 2009). Nonetheless, Armenians continued to face discrimination (see chapter 2). One Glendale resident reportedly said of the community in the 1960s, "Hispanics and people of Arabic and Armenian descent were tolerated, but only if they lived in areas in the part of town bordering Los Angeles, not in the 'upper' part nearer the hills."[16] Armenians' rapid, concentrated settlement of Glendale in the 1970s and 1980s may therefore seem a bit peculiar. Armenians had already established themselves in other nearby locations. Hollywood's growing Armenian population had already begun to take definite shape by midcentury. It seemed as though this area would grow into Los Angeles's Armenians' main hub. Nevertheless, by the early 1980s, the momentum had clearly shifted to Glendale.

Among some of the first Armenians to settle in Glendale were members of the Jamgochian family. Avedis Jamgochian purchased property and built a home in Glendale by 1913, after moving to Southern California in 1911. Jamgochian became active in the Near East Relief Committee. With this organization, he spearheaded initiatives to assist Armenians left destitute in the wake of the Genocide. A local judge and manager of the Southern California Armenian Relief Committee, H. N. Wells, also participated in the Armenian drive of 1918 and 1919. Wells had spent time in Syria and Turkey, where he experienced firsthand the atrocities Armenians suffered. In his appeal, he wrote passionately on behalf of Armenians and the necessity to aid them in a time of acute distress. He invoked Glendale residents' civic duty to aid Armenians, stating, "It does not seem conceivable that the response to the appeal for funds to help the destitute Armenians will not be answered doubly. Every cent contributed will be sent to the relief of the 4,000,000 known to be starving, to the 400,000 orphans who are actually crying for something to eat. This community [Glendale] will have an opportunity to do its share."[17] Wells's appeal and Glendale's response ultimately proved among the most successful in Greater Los Angeles. Thus, Glendale's earliest Armenian inhabitants (and others) undertook intensive outreach on behalf of displaced Armenians. According to the *Glendale Evening News*, Glendale "went over the top in the Armenian Drive" and raised $2,144.58 (approximately $38,576 in 2022 dollars) to contribute to the cause.[18] As the same article observes, "In view of the fact that returns are lagging in Los Angeles and many other communities . . . it is cheering to know that this city [Glendale] has oversubscribed and helped that much in making good deficiencies elsewhere." This is among the first recorded outreach efforts between Glendale and Armenians.

According to a thesis written in 1923, about five families, or approximately twenty Armenians, lived in Glendale during the first two decades of the twentieth century (Yeretzian 1923, 38).[19] The *Glendale Evening News* distributed an article in 1922 entitled "'Taxi Nish' Secures Citizenship Papers." In the article, Nushon (Nish) Bader Parsekian is identified as a resident of Glendale. A native of "Ban [Van], Armenia," Parsekian is described as a self-reliant taxi driver, whose father was "killed in a rebellion against Turkey."[20] Parsekian moved to the United States in 1909 and settled in Glendale around 1918. The article identifies his residence at 119 West Broadway. A more recognizable early Glendale resident was Paul Robert Ignatius (the grandson of Avedis Jamgochian), who ultimately served as the secretary of the navy between 1967 and 1969, as well as assistant secretary of defense during the Lyndon Johnson administration. Ignatius wrote a memoir, *Now I Know in Part*, in which he describes his upbringing in Glendale. While Jamgochian, Parsekian, Ignatius, and others like them are an important part of Armenians' history in Glendale, they were exceptional. Only after the 1960s did Glendale begin to receive a steadier stream of Armenian newcomers.

In 1976, one of Glendale's local newspapers spotlighted the city's burgeoning Armenian population. In the article, the author asked, "But why Glendale?," and answered, "The consensus among Armenians interviewed is that Glendale has become a center for their nationality because it is considered a peaceful, conservative town and therefore a good environment for people who strongly believe in traditions."[21] While this assessment was likely true in a general sense, it does not provide a concrete explanation for why, out of several peaceful suburbs, Glendale has become perhaps among the most densely concentrated Armenian populations outside of Armenia. In fact, neighboring Pasadena fits a similar description and has been a site of Armenian habitation since the opening years of the twentieth century. Even more strikingly, Pasadena granted Armenians protected minority status in 1985. By including its Armenian population in affirmative action policy, Pasadena recognized Armenians officially as a minority, a status shift that is interpreted along different community lines (Chahinian and Bakalian 2016).[22] Two early court decisions—*In re Halladjian et al.* (1909) and *United States v. Cartozian* (1925)—granted Armenians the right to naturalization on account of their determined "whiteness" (Alexander 2005; Craver 2009). Pasadena therefore provided prospective Armenian immigrants a way to participate in local institutions more readily than neighboring communities. Nonetheless, Glendale proved the most significant destination for a large number of globally migrating Armenians.[23] And, by the late 1980s, when President Ronald Reagan increased the quota of Soviet Armenian immigrants to the

United States, local conversations among Glendale elected officials had shifted to how to fund and integrate the influx of coming Armenian students in need of teachers and residents in need of low-income housing.[24]

Alice Shirvanian hosted me at her home in one of northern Glendale's more affluent neighborhoods. She invited me to sit opposite her at the recently renovated kitchen island, where she presented a delicious array of Armenian and American foodstuffs. As we snacked, Alice regaled me with stories about her family's history. In Iran, her grandparents interacted with Seventh-Day Adventist missionaries. Her grandfather, ultimately, became an Adventist minister. In 1955, Alice and her family moved to Los Angeles, where her parents founded and operated what would become one of the city's largest solid waste companies—Western Waste Industries.[25] The company's commercial success enabled Alice's family to choose where and how they lived. After commuting from a neighborhood near Hollywood, Los Feliz, her parents decided to settle in Glendale. They chose Glendale because the Seventh-Day Adventist academy was in the city, and they wanted her to attend an Adventist school.

Alice grew up in Glendale but, as a young adult, moved to the San Francisco Bay Area. Later, however, she returned to Glendale. When I asked her why she moved back to Glendale, she succinctly replied:

> That was the time when there was plenty of property to buy and build. We bought this and that and the one next door. We wanted the corner, so we took the corner. Then another friend from the Bay Area, who is the architect of most of our homes, said, 'Hey, all of my friends are down there. They are not opening an Armenian school [in the Bay Area]. You've opened one down in LA, so we're coming. I have kids. I want them in an Armenian school.' And see how it works—it's who you know . . . and how close can you be with them. As I said initially, clean community, upper-middle at the time, all white, great schools, and, to boot, they had just started the Armenian Church and the school.

As Alice explained to me, Armenians' rather rapid settlement of Glendale related to various factors, such as the earlier settlement of Glendale by some noteworthy Armenians—particularly well-to-do families and students from Iran in the 1950s and 1960s; the city's demographic composition ("all white") and its socioeconomic position ("upper-middle"); and the establishment of Armenian institutions, such as an Armenian church and school, by the mid-1970s.

Among the first Armenians to settle in Glendale during the second half of the twentieth century, Iranian Armenians, like Alice and her family, made up a large portion of the population. In fact, Iran had been sending students to the United States even before the passage of the Hart-Celler Act. After years of boycotting

Iranian oil, the United States reopened trade once the shah had been restored in 1953. The resumption of oil revenue and aid to Iran bolstered its economy significantly. As Mehdi Bozorgmehr and Georges Sabagh explain, "The oil revenues increased 16 times from $34 million in 1954–55 to $555 million in 1963, and more than doubled to $1.2 billion in 1970–71" (1988, 10). This revenue led to state-sponsored industrialization and modernization initiatives. Despite the inflow of money, Iran lacked the educational facilities and human resources to generate specialists to operate the machinery. The shah's government therefore invested in education by sending Iranian students abroad in large numbers. The shortage of space in Iran's universities along with the difficulty of entrance exams most likely led to exponential increases in Iranian and Iranian Armenian student visitors coming to the United States—from 18,000 in 1963 to 227,497 in 1997 (Bozorgmehr and Sabagh 1988, 10). Since Iranian Armenians had already settled in Glendale, it proved an attractive option for many students who entered in the 1960s.

Glendale also suited many Iranian Armenian students socioeconomically. Those who arrived during the 1950s and 1960s often had the resources to travel and study abroad. They therefore represented a relatively affluent segment of Iranian society. Unlike traditional immigrants who arrived with fewer resources and settled in urban centers, Iranian Armenians came with financial means. Iran's economy had boomed, and those from this socioeconomic stratum of society profited from that boom. According to Homa Katouzian (1981), Iran's oil revenues increased from $4.4 billion to $17.1 billion in the mid-1970s alone. Many of the first Iranian Armenians to settle in Glendale were the beneficiaries of these new revenue flows, whether directly or indirectly. Early Iranian Armenians, particularly those whose migrations predate the shah's demise, could afford to buy homes in relatively well-off neighborhoods. Compared to Hollywood or other urban locations, Glendale's affluent residential neighborhoods presented an appealing alternative for these student visitors, their relatives, and others from their social networks. And their selection conditioned their settlement patterns. Like the Taiwanese in Monterey Park or first-wave Cubans in several areas in Florida (Eckstein and Berg 2009), early Iranian Armenian settlers "leapfrogged" socioeconomic impecuniousness and settled in suburban comfort shortly after their arrival. While a much larger and more socioeconomically diverse stream of Iranian Armenians as well as several other Armenians would later expand Glendale's Armenian population, the Armenian newcomers between the 1950s and the 1970s consisted of a relatively elite demographic cluster.

In fact, some early Iranian Armenians became quite prominent in Glendale both commercially and politically. For example, Larry Zarian came to Glendale in the early 1950s. After completing high school in Massachusetts, he moved to Los Angeles. He initially moved to Hollywood but relocated to Glendale soon thereafter. Still a teenager when he settled in Glendale, Zarian spent most of his life in the city. As a family member explained to me, "A friend told him how great Glendale was and how nice Glendale College was, so he hopped a ride with some guys and came out to California by car from Boston." Zarian moved to Glendale in 1953 and joined a handful of other Armenian students. Afterward, he worked as a businessman for many years but eventually became interested in public office. After an unsuccessful bid in 1967, he won a seat on Glendale's city council in 1983. He was the first Armenian in Glendale to hold political office. Zarian, a moderate conservative, was active in Glendale politics for sixteen years—from 1983 to 1999. He eventually became Glendale's first Armenian mayor. Quite popular among non-Armenian residents, Zarian did not need to rely on Armenian voters. In fact, very few Armenians voted before the late 1990s. Thus, Zarian achieved and maintained electoral success in Glendale without co-ethnic support. He served four terms as mayor, in 1986–1987, 1990–1991, 1993–1994, and 1997–1998. Although he passed away in 2011, his influence remains in the city. For example, the Glendale Transportation Center is dedicated to him. In addition, Zarian's visibility as a public official (and public personality) attracted Armenian newcomers to Glendale and influenced a later generation of Armenian elected officials (see chapter 3).

In addition to Zarian, the Shirvanians were among the early Iranian Armenians to settle in Glendale. Alice Shirvanian was a part of this family. The Shirvanians chose Glendale not only because of the family's strong ties to the Adventist Church, which was in Glendale, but also because of their ties to the Republican Party—Glendale was a Republican headquarters before Armenian political activists helped shift the city's political orientation in the late 1990s and early 2000s (see chapter 3). By investing in trash collection, the Shirvanian family amassed a great fortune, establishing Western Waste Industries in 1955. Their Iranian Armenian network and the visible success among several of those who had settled in Glendale explain several subsequent Armenians' migrations. Perceiving trouble afoot in the shah's regime, friends of the Shirvanians left Iran and settled in Los Angeles. In fact, many of the first Iranian Armenians who purchased homes in Glendale's hills came directly from overlapping social and family networks.

In addition to people coming to Glendale from abroad, the city was also experiencing several sociopolitical changes, which facilitated its demographic diversification. By the 1960s, Glendale had begun to take on a more progressive character. Just as migrants from Cuba, Iran, Korea, and elsewhere began settling in Glendale, several city ordinances made new ethnic settlement possible. While many traditions persisted—such as housing discrimination, which targeted Black Americans through the early 2000s—the civil rights ethos that had been altering national legislation also became a mainstay of local suburbs. For example, native Glendale residents protested the presence of the neo-Nazi headquarters in 1964 (Arroyo 2006). A new generation of Glendale residents sought to oust these racist and fascist organizations. In the 1960s, Glendale government officials created new bodies and organizations that sought to safeguard minority rights. Although Armenians would not enter the scene with demographic prominence until the mid-1970s, the 1960s laid a foundation that would enable new ethnic members of the city to participate in Glendale's development.

This foundation included an increasingly prosperous commercial sector. Responding to economic downturn in the 1950s and 1960s, Glendale city officials sought to attract prospective consumers by constructing new shopping malls and creating new business opportunities. City officials incentivized large companies by waiving business license fees as well as payroll and corporation taxes.[26] For many businesses, Glendale also proved less chaotic than the frenetic downtown area. Nestle, DreamWorks, Disney, Whole Foods, and other corporations established offices in Glendale and, in turn, enriched the local economy. These new businesses also generated employment opportunities for newcomers. In addition, conservative city ordinances related to housing, interestingly, created more opportunities for multiethnic immigrants. Among the new business clientele that entered Glendale were several commercial real estate developers. As Glendale natives moved out, developers came in to build large apartment complexes. This profit-driven scheme provided spaces in which less affluent immigrants could settle. Developers purchased the property of landowners and built several new multiunit apartment buildings (Arroyo 2006). For Armenians coming to Southern California from places such as Iran, Iraq, and Jordan, Glendale's apartment units were affordable and offered family-oriented housing options in a quiet, peaceful suburban neighborhood. These commercial changes provided a foundation on which Armenians could establish a more visible presence in the city.

The tenor of official city discourse also began changing with the emergence of increasingly visible ethnic populations, including Armenians, Cubans, Filipinos, and Koreans. In 1974, the city launched its most ambitious infrastructural and commercial initiative to date: the construction of Glendale's massive shopping mall, the Galleria. The first wing of the Galleria opened in 1976, and it continued to grow through the early 1980s. At the time of its construction, it was among the largest malls in the United States.

National legislation and local socioeconomic changes overlapped with Armenians' multipolar arrival to Los Angeles. As more Armenians moved from abroad or Hollywood to Glendale, the community's presence in the city had become quite distinct by the 1980s. Only a couple of decades after people like the Shirvanians and Zarian entered the homogeneous sundown town, Glendale began to emerge as the most demographically concentrated Armenian habitation throughout the Americas.

As the population expanded, Armenians established several important organizations and institutions, which made Glendale more visible and accessible to more Armenian newcomers (Vassilian 1995). These included St. Mary's Armenian Apostolic Church, a branch of the ARF party, the Iranian Armenian Society, the Homenetmen, the Scouts, and the Armenian Education Foundation. Over time, the number of Armenian-owned and Armenian-operated establishments expanded: Armenian shops, restaurants, banquet halls, grocery stores, bakeries, and delis began to populate every major artery throughout the city. Armenian businesspeople began to own and operate many of the non-Armenian establishments as well.

Despite these contributions, for some Glendale residents, Armenians (as well as other newcomers) played a disruptive role in the city. As the Armenian presence increasingly pervaded the city, some established, typically white, Glendale residents reacted with hostility (see chapter 2). The growing resentment appeared in newspapers, city hall meetings, and interpersonal interactions. Backlash against Armenians occurred in various sectors of the community: the more established population responded harshly to wealthy Armenians in the north for the elaborate designs of their homes ("mansionization") and the less affluent Armenians for their dense concentration in the south. Development in Glendale also became (and, in some respects, continues to be) negatively associated with the Armenian population.

But the backlash, in turn, only helped create its own backlash—that is, an increased sense of ethnic cohesion among an otherwise internally diverse and fragmented population. And, for the internally fragmented population of Armenians in Glendale, the result of feeling targeted as a single ethnic group would have significant implications for several political aspirants among them. As Rogers Brubaker (2004) argues, ethnopolitical entrepreneurs employ ethnicity for group-making projects to achieve distinct ends. Indeed, Armenians, who had been considered politically insignificant throughout the 1980s, emerged in the late 1990s as a dominant political force.

THE ARMENIANS OF GLENDALE

An Ethnoburb in Los Angeles's San
Fernando Valley

While conducting fieldwork in Glendale, I frequented many Armenian cafés, restaurants, and shops. Whenever possible, I spoke with the owners and learned about their personal histories. In many of these establishments, I also attended formal events and arranged fieldwork interviews. But these were also spaces in which I cultivated existing friendships and established new ones. The method of making new friends in restaurants and banquet halls was fairly consistent: my Armenian peers would inevitably discover other friends or relatives who happened to be patronizing the same establishment. We would then merge groups until yet another person from our expanding friendship circle recognized someone else at a different table. This pattern would repeat until, eventually, it seemed as though all the individual tables had fused into a single social group. One popular establishment that I visited several times was Carousel Restaurant on 304 North Brand Boulevard.

Carousel was founded by a family of Lebanese Armenians, the Tcholakians, who immigrated as a result of the Lebanese Civil War (1975–1990). Like many other Armenian newcomers in the last two decades of the twentieth century, the Tcholakians settled in Hollywood in the late 1970s. After dabbling in several food-related industries, Krikor and Vartouhi Tcholakian opened the first Carousel Restaurant in 1984. Eventually, the first Carousel became a prominent home-style restaurant among Hollywood's ethnic eateries. Its success enabled the Tcholakian family to expand to Glendale, where they opened a second Carousel in 1998. This expansion was led by Krikor and Vartouhi's son, Mike. Mike told me why he and his family decided to open the Glendale restaurant when they did: "We saw that Glendale was the city that was growing in Armenian population, and we thought that it needed a nice, upscale family dining experience." With Armenians' presence in Glendale growing in the 1990s, the Tcholakians introduced a more complete and upscale Armenian culinary experience. This more embellished version of the restaurant offers a rich range of food offerings. In 2014, *Los Angeles Magazine* reviewed the restaurant; the article's author (and chef), Patric Kuh, appetizingly summarized the menu's wide-ranging meze-style dining options:

> Here all is variety, the antithesis of the austere single-page modern menu in which the entries read like an MFA's poem in a lit journal. It's as though the family was reluctant to leave out a single option. You can savor the French influence on Beirut—once called "the Paris of the Middle East"—in the battered frog legs *provençale* or a trio of quail in a citrusy amber lacquer that tastes like a sumac-jacked sauce *à l'orange*. There's not just one tabbouleh but two: In the more Lebanese version, chopped tomatoes, parsley, lemon juice, and olive oil are all the moisture that's needed to give the cracked wheat—the essential starch in many preparations—its trademark short-of-soft texture; the more Armenian version gets its deep red hue from a *sofrito* of tomatoes and onions and gains a whole other dimension when mixed with a spoonful of tahini-radiating *baba ghanouj*.[1]

Its multilayered offerings and festive atmosphere have made Carousel one of Glendale's most popular restaurants. Carousel offers both familiarity and novelty for multilocal Armenian and non-Armenian patrons. Mike told me that the Armenian restaurant caters to a broad clientele: "Having a diverse business with diverse clientele in Hollywood, we knew that we would be able to expand that, especially from a prime downtown, bedroom community, safe neighborhood like Glendale." While Mike acknowledged that Carousel is an important site for local Armenians, he stressed that the restaurant's main objective is "going broad and catering to all ethnicities and not just concentrating on your own." Although Carousel is an Armenian restaurant, it forms a part of Glendale's mainstream. Carousel is just one example of the wide-ranging contributions Armenians make to Glendale in practically every sector of the city.

Ethnoburbs

In chapter 1, we learned about Armenians' diverse, global history in dispersion. This chapter shifts the focus to Glendale and provides a demographic snapshot of

FIGURE 9. The storefront of Carousel Restaurant in Glendale, California.

the internally complex Armenian population. In order to present Armenians' demographic complexity, the chapter situates Glendale in discussions of "ethnoburbs." While much of the data presented in this chapter are continually changing, they highlight one salient feature of an ethnoburb—namely, the large concentration of a socioeconomically diverse co-ethnic population. Glendale Armenians are internally diverse based not only on their countries of origin but also on their educational attainments, vocational fields, and socioeconomic profiles.

While the scholarship on ethnoburbs typically applies the term to Chinese and other Asian immigrant populations (Lin and Robinson 2005; Chang 2010; Oh and Chung 2014), Glendale proves that the ethnoburb model fits in a broader field of investigation. Each ethnoburb possesses its own specificity; however, fundamental commonalties link populations and spaces in California as varied as the Chinese of Monterey Park, the Vietnamese of Westminster, the Filipinos of Daly City, the Koreans of Irvine, and the Armenians of Glendale.

In part, ethnoburb scholarship corrects a problematic narrative that has long persisted in the US imaginary about immigrants: poor, disenfranchised immigrants settle in urban centers and form ethnic enclaves, such as a Chinatown, Little Armenia, or Koreatown (K-Town). These hardworking, urban-dwelling immigrants own small shops in downtown districts. They push their children to work tirelessly in the pursuit of higher education and professional careers. These children become integrated into US mainstream society, attend universities, attain professional success, intermarry, and settle into predominantly white suburbs. In these suburbs, they form a small minority of assimilated ethnic peoples. According to this narrative, the marginalized and poor inhabit ghettos, the marginalized and ethnic inhabit enclaves, and the upwardly mobile and privileged inhabit suburbs. Despite its persistence in the collective imaginary, this problematic narrative glaringly oversimplifies the habitation of urban spaces (Coon 2014; Lung-Amam 2017).

Even before the post–civil rights era, immigrants and other minorities were participating in the formation of many US urban ecologies. But new modes of urban habitation have become especially apparent since the 1960s. To unpack the significance of these new modes, scholars have posited several important theoretical frameworks. Wei Li's ethnoburbs model is one such example. According to Li, "Ethnoburbs are suburban ethnic clusters of residential and business districts within large metropolitan areas. They are multiracial/multiethnic, multicultural, multilingual, and often multinational communities, in which one ethnic minority group has a significant concentration" (2009, 29). These ethnoburbs replicate aspects of both the ethnic enclave and the suburb. Li's model offers the conceptual tools to understand the evolution of many urban US spaces over the past several decades.

Li's framework stems from her study of a specific type of urban settlement in a particular place. As Li claims, "The establishment of the Chinese ethnoburb as a new type of ethnic settlement in the San Gabriel Valley [part of the Greater Los Angeles metropolitan area] has occurred within a framework of global, national, and place-specific conditions" (2009, 79). Subsequent scholarship has expanded this model to include various other aspects of international Chinese immigrant populations (Chang 2010; Li, Skop, and Yu 2016; Robertson et al. 2022). The Chinese of Monterey Park are themselves internally complex and diverse. However, their immigration to and settlement of the San Gabriel Valley have come out of a series of shared global, national, and local events, movements, and policies. Armenian migration pathways to the United States closely resemble those of the Chinese as well as other immigrants. These immigrant populations also arrived on account of a combination of global geopolitical factors, and their migrations are transforming several urban spaces throughout the United States.

In the 1950s and 1960s, relatively affluent immigrants moved into suburban neighborhoods and formed "small-scale residential clusters" (Li 2009, 41). These clusters of individuals bought homes, sent their children to the local schools, and worked in local businesses. While this migration did not transform the more foundational ecology, the suburban clusters these immigrants formed served as proto-ethnoburbs.

With the passage of the Hart-Celler Act in 1965, new streams of socioeconomically diverse immigrants came to the United States in much greater concentration (Portes and Rumbaut 2006; Massey 2008). These immigrants sought reunification with friends and family, several of which had formed the earlier residential clusters and "leapfrogged" inner-city settlement. This proved true in both the San Gabriel Valley and the San Fernando Valley, with large concentrations of newcomers settling in Monterey Park and Glendale. As with the Chinese in Monterey Park, Armenians' concentrated settlement of Glendale in the 1980s and 1990s led to the community's beginning to restructure economically, socially, and politically. As both commercial and political entrepreneurs became successful, these demographic clusters increasingly developed into magnets for further co-ethnic migration. In addition, the growing co-ethnic populations caused spillover in surrounding areas. For example, Armenian presence in the San Fernando Valley expanded out of Glendale to include Burbank, North Hollywood, Tujunga, Calabasas, and La Cañada Flintridge. In San Gabriel, Chinese immigrants expanded out of Monterey Park to Alhambra, Arcadia, Rosemead, and San Marino. Beyond Glendale and Monterey Park, suburban demography in the US underwent significant changes: in large metropolitan areas, the share of ethnic and racial minorities making up suburban residents increased from 47 percent to 59 percent between 1990 and 2010 (Frey 2011; Diamond and Posey-Maddox 2020). By 2010, immigrants comprised a majority—59 percent—of suburban residents in large metropolitan areas (Suro, Wilson, and Singer 2011).

Taking advantage of concentrated co-ethnic settlement and intergroup antagonisms, new political actors have arisen to mobilize internally diverse populations in the country's evolving suburbs. Given their relative political autonomy, US suburbs—or ethnoburbs—have become particularly suitable sites in which this political mobilization can take place. But what specific characteristics make an ethnoburb distinct from other urban ecologies?

According to Li (2009), an ethnoburb is a relatively new type of urban ecology; it combines features of the ethnic enclave and the suburb. She distinguishes ethnoburbs from ghettos and ethnic enclaves along the following four lines: (1) "dynamics"—ethnic residents own a large portion of the local businesses in ethnoburbs and also "participate in the globalization of capital and international flows of commodities and skilled, high tech, and managerial personnel"; (2) "geographical locations and density"—ethnoburbs exist in larger geographical areas (this may include several municipalities and unincorporated areas) and in lower demographic density as compared to inner-city ghettos and enclaves; (3) "internal stratification"—the ethnic population of ethnoburbs typically manifests internal diversity, financially, ideologically, and generationally, and these differences can cause stratification and conflict/tension; and (4) "functionality"— ethnoburbs act as new "ports of entry," with residents gaining access to mainstream society and its institutions (46–47). As Li frames this last point, "Given this mixed environment and daily contacts with people of different backgrounds, ethnic minority people in ethnoburbs are both inward and outward looking in their socioeconomic and political pursuits" (47). Ethnoburb residents are thus more likely to become involved in local political activities than co-ethnics in downtown enclaves, such as Chinatown, Little Armenia, or Koreatown. According to Li, these are the basic elements that distinguish an ethnoburb from ethnic enclaves and ghettos.

In addition to complicating imaginaries regarding the habitation of US urban spaces, Li's ethnoburb model also challenges classical theories of assimilation. Concentrated migration into suburban US cities reconfigures spaces and redirects movements of capital. To diverse suburbs, highly skilled immigrants bring both tangible and intangible resources, such as money, skills, and global networks. These resources facilitate the settlement patterns of immigrants. Their global networks and resources enable them to acquire properties and transform the physical spaces in which they live. These transformations involve the establishment or acquisition of local ethnic institutions (such as schools and churches), political and social organizations, businesses, real estate, and restaurants. As the community evolves and as new co-ethnics move in, the integration trajectories of newcomers change, too. While such trajectories do not resist assimilation permanently, they provide many newcomers with the conditions to preserve ethnic practices for an extended period of time.

In framing ethnoburbs, Li and others have a distinct region and population in mind—particularly the Chinese of San Gabriel Valley. And, as such, they have created a model that defines Chinese migration of a specific sort. Scholarship has expanded the conceptual forcefulness and regional variety of the ethnoburb model; however, it remains most often associated with Chinese migration and suburban habitation. While there are some exceptions (Wen, Lauderdale, and Kandula 2009; Schneider 2014; Phillips 2016), the generalizability of the model has not been sufficiently demonstrated. As a result, its status as a model remains somewhat in question. The next section of this chapter tests the generalizability of the model by applying Li's four distinguishing features to a culturally distinct population—Glendale's intra-ethnically diverse Armenians.

Glendale Armenians and Monterey Park Chinese follow similar settlement trajectories: (1) From the late 1950s until the early 1970s, Glendale began to receive a scattering of newcomers. Following the growth of suburbanization throughout the United States, Armenians (as well as others) began moving to Glendale in small numbers. (2) Between the mid-1970s and the early 1990s, an increasingly large number Armenians settled in Glendale. Unlike those Armenians preceding them, these newcomers were far more multilocal in origin. They came from Egypt, Iran, Iraq, Lebanon, the Soviet Union, and other locations. These newcomers were also far more socioeconomically mixed than their comparatively wealthy predecessors. During this period, Glendale began to become a significant port of entry for Armenians. (3) From the 1990s until today, Glendale has become a global symbol of the Armenian diaspora. It now attracts Armenians from every corner of the world and from every economic stratum.

Glendale

With Armenians' growing influence, Glendale's local economy and institutions have altered in many significant ways. Armenian businesses and political entrepreneurs have established channels through which an expanded "ethnic" economy has developed. In addition, Armenian residents have sought recognition for their traditions and beliefs. For example, schools in the Glendale Unified School District have established April 24 as a holiday in recognition of the Armenian Genocide, and Armenian/English dual-language immersion programs exist in several of Glendale's public schools. Also, local Armenians' real estate ventures have enabled Glendale's housing market to grow. For an ethnoburb to emerge, an ethnic business and residential sector must converge on one site. And this is precisely what has taken place in Glendale. However, as with other newcomers in different ethnoburbs, by leapfrogging into more affluent middle-class suburbs, Armenians have also threatened the preexisting, typically white, residents' sense of normalcy. In turn, many from the "old guard" have responded with backlash or decided, instead, to leave Glendale altogether.[2]

Demographic/Residential Profile

The San Fernando Valley occupies a large geographical area. Glendale itself is one of the largest cities in Los Angeles County. The geographical density, as compared to the older settlement in Hollywood, a neighborhood in the city of Los Angeles, is considerably lower. Armenians' concentration in Glendale has led to significant spillover in the communities of Burbank, Tujunga, Calabasas, and North Hollywood. In addition, Armenians own and operate many businesses in these communities. But the only site forming a demographic plurality is Glendale, where Armenians' presence can be observed by the ubiquity of signage in the Armenian script, the concentration of services and stores that cater to the

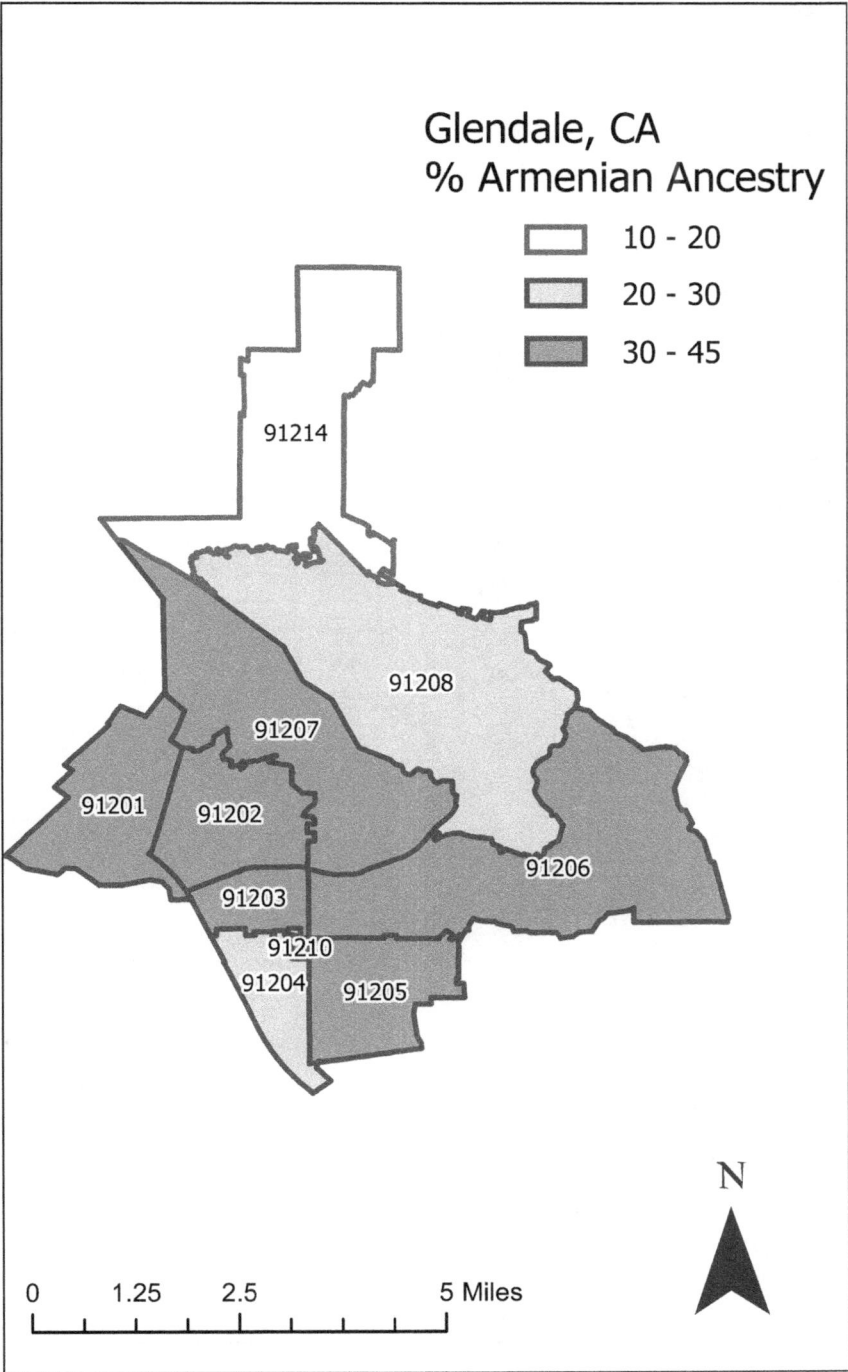

FIGURE 10. Armenians live in much denser concentration in Glendale's southern districts. Source: Diana Ter-Ghazaryan. Data source: US Census Bureau, 2015 ACS five-year data.

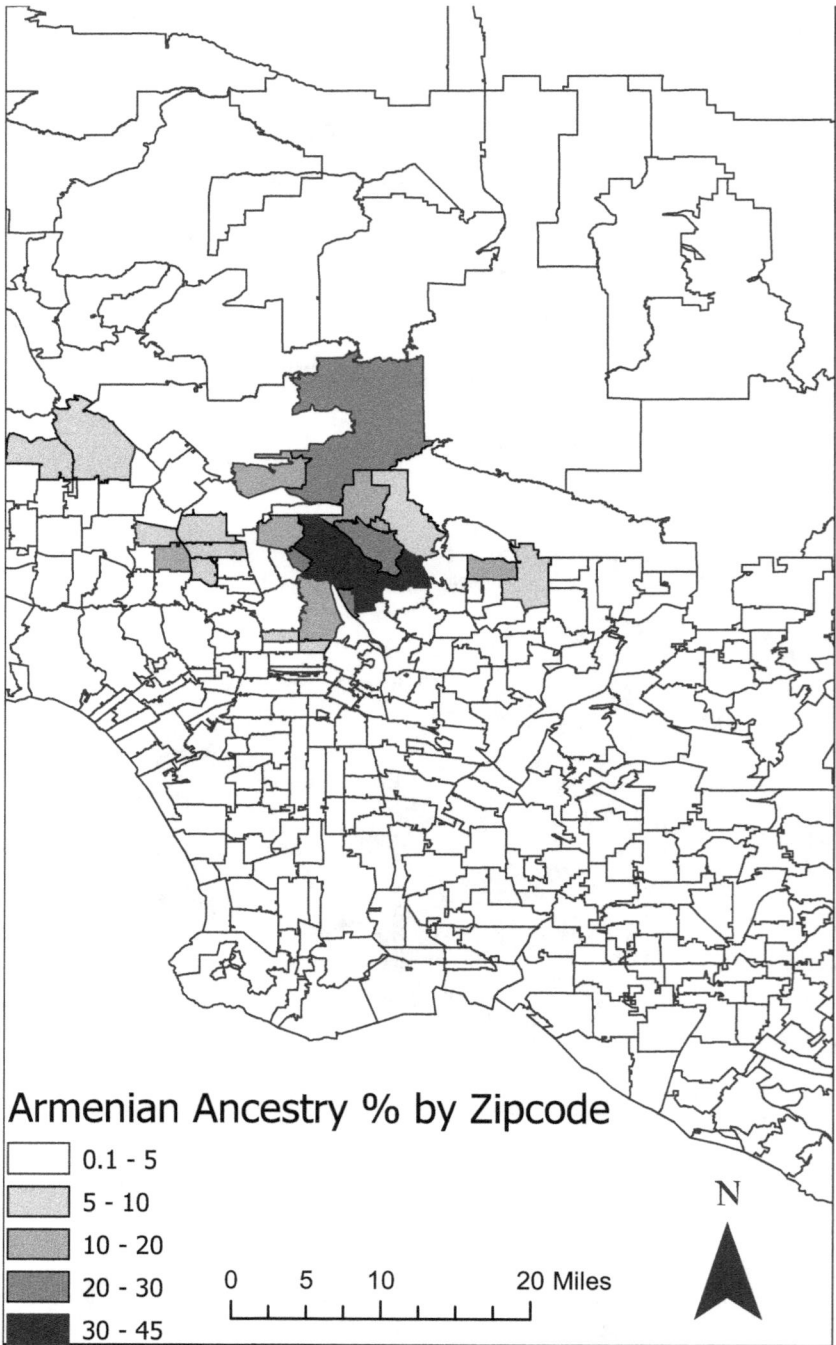

FIGURE 11. While Armenians are heavily concentrated in Glendale, other populations have developed in several neighborhoods throughout not only San Fernando Valley but also Greater Los Angeles more generally. Source: Diana Ter-Ghazaryan. Data source: US Census Bureau, 2015 ACS five-year data.

TABLE 1. Glendale's population growth, 1990–2010

	1990 (IDENTITY/ORIGIN)	2000 (IDENTITY/ORIGIN)	2010 (IDENTITY/ORIGIN)
Iran	13,404 (17,126)	18,853 (25,123)	22,405 (27,480)
(Post–)Soviet Union	7,549 (8,432)	16,327 (18,313)	28,616 (29,503)
Lebanon	2,114 (3,043)	2,540 (4,364)	2,094 (3,313)
Iraq	982 (1,284)	1,595 (2,280)	1,975 (2,811)
Syria	900 (1,266)	1,384 (1,796)	557 (1,583)
California	2,576 (54,561)	7,932 (58,385)	15,364 (60,773)
All countries (self-identifying)	29,996 (17% overall population)	52,249 (27% overall population)	74,511 (39% overall population)

Sources: US Census, 1990, 2000, and 2010.

Armenian population, the number of publicly advertised specialists with Armenian surnames, and even the use of Armenian language on several city streets.

Since 1970, Glendale's overall population has grown at a rapid rate. Even as many established residents moved out, newcomers have far outpaced the rate of those leaving. Unlike surrounding towns, whose populations increased more gradually, census data for Glendale report a city population of 132,664 residents in 1970, but 191,719 by 2010. While these newcomers consisted of various other ethnic populations, the Armenians grew the most visibly. Because of Armenians' multilocality and categorization as "white" in official data sources, they are an especially elusive population to track demographically. Nonetheless, the data do afford some sense of Glendale's evolving demography.

Table 1 shows the multilocal character of the internally diverse Glendale Armenian population. The countries included are not exhaustive. Armenians have come to Glendale from various other countries in smaller numbers (France, Egypt , Jordan, Turkey, among many others). In 2010, the American Community Survey (ACS) reported that self-identifying Armenians listed over sixteen countries as their birthplaces. The countries in table 1, however, are the most numerically significant. They represent approximately 92, 93, and 95 percent, respectively, of all reported Glendale Armenians in each census report. Later migrations reflect geopolitical events in Armenian host societies, such as Iraq and Syria. In addition, Armenian migration from Armenia and the former Soviet Union grew between the 1980s and the 2010s. These latter flows diversified Glendale's predominant Iranian Armenian population. But the numbers are not static; they fluctuate depending on various factors, such as political upheavals and immigration policies. Post-Soviet Armenian migration has also increased in locations near Glendale, such as Burbank, Tujunga, and North Hollywood. In addition, table 1 shows internal Armenian migration to Glendale. These internal migrants previously lived in diverse locations throughout the United

States. The highest concentration of internal migrants occurs within California—an increase from 2,576 in 1990 to 15,364 in 2010. This stream reflects the growing visibility of Glendale as a distinct hub or, as Li articulates, "port of entry" for newcomers and later-generation Armenians alike. Table 1 includes both the numbers of those who self-identified as Armenian and the sites from which Armenians immigrated to Glendale. These numbers set up different interpretations. For example, between 18,853 and 25,123 Iranian Armenians were living in Glendale by 2000. For 6,270 who reported Iranian origins, it is difficult to determine what percentage self-identifies as Armenian (Glendale has a relatively small Iranian population). Nonetheless, the table indicates that Armenians represented at least 39 percent of Glendale's population in 2010.

Armenians are not the only ones to diversify Glendale's population. Glendale also has relatively large concentrations of non-Armenian migrants. As of 2010, the largest populations included Mexicans (10,609), Koreans (9,708), and Filipinos (9,663). About 55 percent of Glendale's population at that time was foreign-born.[3] These ethnic populations have also contributed significantly to Glendale's cultural diversity and economic prosperity.

Socioeconomic Profile

Glendale Armenians exist in practically all of the city's socioeconomic and professional sectors. According to the Integrated Public Use Microdata Series (IPUMS) ACS sample 2010 data, 47 percent of Glendale residents with an undergraduate degree were Armenian and 29 percent of those who had obtained a graduate degree were Armenian. Glendale Armenians, therefore, obtain undergraduate and graduate degrees at higher rates than the national averages (39.7% and 14.3%, respectively).[4] Glendale Armenians also participate in every sphere of the local economy. Their business and cultural influence is omnipresent. Armenians own many prominent businesses that serve the local economy, such as Carousel, Eden on Brand, Famous Bar, Karas, Khinkali House (formerly Tumanyan Khinkali Factory), Lahmajune Factory, Lord Bakery, Massis Kabob, Pacific Food Mart, Paradise Pastry, Raffi's Place, and Tavern on Brand, among many others. Table 2 presents some occupational trends in Glendale.

Given their socioeconomic and educational diversity, Glendale Armenians are visible in both high-skilled and low-skilled professions. They are especially prominent in managerial and high-tech positions. Glendale also hosts several Armenian-founded international organizations, such as the software company ServiceTitan and the Kradjian Importing Company. In addition, Armenian real estate and business ventures have contributed to Glendale's thriving economy and created jobs for Armenians and non-Armenians alike. These investments enrich Glendale

TABLE 2. Armenians in selected occupations, Glendale, 2010

OCCUPATION	ARMENIAN REPRESENTATION (%)
Chief executives and public administrators	32
Computer systems analysts and scientists	33
Drivers (truck, delivery, tractor, bus, and taxi)	52
Laborers (construction and otherwise)	42
Managerial positions	36
Physicians	32
Salespersons	40
Subject instructors (high school / college)	37
Supervisors	32
Teachers	23

Source: US Census Bureau, 2010 IPUMS ACS.

with resources both locally and internationally. Local Armenian companies and businesspeople are thus participating in the globalization of capital flows as well as the enrichment of the local economy.

But the Armenians of Glendale are an internally diverse population. Some subgroups gravitate toward specific occupations more than others. Table 3 provides an overview of Glendale's three most prevalent Armenian subgroups by occupation and birthplace: Armenians from Armenia or the former Soviet Union, Iranian Armenians, and California Armenians. According to the 2010 ACS, Glendale's Armenian population comprised 28,616 Armenians from Armenia or the former Soviet Union (38%), 22,405 Iranian Armenians (30%), and 15,367 California Armenians (about 20%). These three made up 88 percent of the overall Armenian population in Glendale.[5]

Of the populations specified, each has its own reporting habits. Those not reporting their occupations were as follows: California Armenians, 12,332 out of 15,367 (80%); Iranian Armenians, 9,518 out of 22,405 (42%); and Armenians from Armenia or the former Soviet Union, 8,486 out of 28,616 (29%). Despite the disproportionately low rate of reporting among California-based Armenians skewing their occupational representation, some general work-related distinctions can still be gleaned. For some occupations, there was a clear majority: Iranian Armenians formed a majority among engineers, whereas Armenians from Armenia or the former Soviet Union formed clear majorities among financial managers, physicians, registered nurses, and nursing aides. But, for many other occupations, the distributions were fairly evenly divided among the different subgroups. The difference among teachers and customer service representatives, for example, was negligible. As such, the data do show clear occupational groupings

TABLE 3. Origins of Armenians employed in selected occupations, Glendale, 2010

OCCUPATION	ARMENIA AND FORMER SOVIET UNION (%)	IRAN (%)	CALIFORNIA (%)
Customer service representatives	47.0	53.0	—
Drivers	63.0	37.0	—
Engineers	40.0	60.0	—
Financial managers	54.3	9.6	28.3
Nursing aides	76.0	17.0	6.0
Physicians	71.0	29.0	—
Registered nurses	77.0	23.0	—
Teachers	49.0	39.0	—

Source: US Census Bureau, 2010 IPUMS ACS.

among Armenians from different countries. They also show areas in which Armenians were absent. For example, Armenians represented small fractions among several industries in the public service sector, such as the police force and the fire department (although census data indicate that they represent most of those in the "protective services"). According to the City of Glendale's (2018) report *Workforce Demographics, 2003 through 2016*, Armenians made up 10.1 percent of the police department and 7.1 percent of the fire department as of 2016. Also, that Armenians represent a majority of all elected offices in Glendale but only about 15 percent of school principals reflected (as of 2018) the uneven demographic distribution in civic positions (see chapter 5).

Political Profile

One of the areas in which Glendale Armenians are the most visible is in electoral politics. Before 1999, only one Armenian, Larry Zarian, had ever been elected to public office in Glendale. Zarian proved a formidable local politician, serving in various capacities over a long career in city government (see chapter 1). By the end of his political career, however, a new generation of Armenian political actors launched a series of campaigns that transformed this bastion of conservatism into a far more Democrat-leaning polity. From the end of Zarian's tenure until the present, Armenians have nearly taken over electoral politics. Their initiatives and reforms have led to more park spaces throughout Glendale, greater opportunities for businesses, and increased housing for the elderly. In addition, they sit on over 50 percent of all commissions and boards.[6]

Tables 4 and 5 reflect the extent to which Armenians have become an integral part of city government. The Armenians of Los Angeles have high naturalization

TABLE 4. Makeup of Glendale boards, commissions, and committees, 2018

	ARMENIAN	NON-ARMENIAN
Arts and Culture Commission Board	4	1
Audit Committee	2	3
Building and Fire Appeals Commission	3	2
Civil Service Commission	4	1
Commission on the Status of Women	3	2
Community Development Block Grant Advisory Committee	4	1
Design Review Board	5	0
Glendale Housing Authority	1	1
Glendale Oversight Board (dissolved in 2018)	2	5
Glendale Water and Power Commission	1	4
Historic Preservation Commission	1	4
Metropolitan Water District	0	1
Parks, Recreation, and Community Services Commission	2	3
Planning Commission	3	2
Transportation and Parking Commission	3	2
Vector Control District	0	1

Source: City of Glendale, https://www.glendaleca.gov/government/departments/city-clerk/boards-and
-commissions. Current makeups are available at this website.

TABLE 5. City of Glendale's electoral seats, 2018

	ARMENIAN	NON-ARMENIAN
City council	4	1
Board of Education	4	1
Glendale Community College Board	3	2
City clerk	1	0
City treasurer	1	0

Sources: City of Glendale, https://www.glendaleca.gov; Glendale Unified School District, https://www.gusd
.net; Glendale Community College, https://www.glendale.edu. Current posts are available at these websites.

rates (80%, or twice the national average) and vote at relatively high rates in Glendale (Barreto and Garcia 2011). While Glendale Armenians' high-level of educational attainment encourages political engagement and voter turnout (Bueker 2005), their mobilization also results from the joint efforts of various actors, such as co-ethnic elected officials, ethnic organizations, and ethnic media. Even "unauthorized immigrants" (Cook 2013) become involved by participating in civic life—town hall meetings, demonstrations, and other venues. Relying on a highly mobilized population, Armenian candidates have organized campaigns and, with support from ethnic media, ethnic organizations, and financial donors, have successfully secured a majority of elected seats. As subsequent chapters bear out, electoral success is a particularly salient aspect of Glendale's Armenian population (see chapters 3 and 4).

Glendale and Monterey Park

The commonalities between the ethnoburbs of Monterey Park and Glendale are noteworthy. Just like the early Taiwanese immigrants of the San Gabriel Valley (Monterey Park), Iranian Armenians came with more financial and educational resources and sought out a middle-class community in which they could leapfrog into a comfortable suburb. In addition, like the Chinese in Monterey Park, Armenian immigrants in Glendale disrupted the previous residential and commercial sectors (Fong 1994; Horton 1995; Zhou 2009). They engaged in real estate acquisition, thereby driving up the value of property and building multiunit complexes. These developments, as before, created residential spaces for more newcomers and led to higher levels of density in certain districts. Both the Chinese and the Armenians became visible business owners in several economic sectors, with commercial merchandise and signage that clearly catered to co-ethnics (Li 1998, 2009). And, just as subsequent waves of migration significantly diversified the intra-ethnic diversity of Monterey Park's Chinese population, Glendale Armenians splintered along several fault lines as political upheavals brought new Armenians from Armenia, Iran, Iraq, Lebanon, and the former Soviet Union into the same site in subsequent decades. This surge of Armenian and Chinese residents undermined the previous dominance of white ownership and control—economically, commercially, and politically. These expansions were responded to with vehement backlash and resentment from the old guard (see "The Dialectics of Suburban Backlash" in this chapter). This vehemence manifested itself in local newspapers, city council meetings, and everyday interactions. And both communities experienced backlash over the establishment of houses of worship (Li 2009). Also, like the Chinese in the San Gabriel Valley, who spread from Monterey Park to adjacent communities such as Alhambra and Hacienda Heights, Glendale Armenians have spilled over into the San Fernando Valley in places like Burbank, Tujunga, and North Hollywood, with the most affluent settling in the highly exclusive community of La Cañada Flintridge (just as the more affluent Chinese settled in San Marino). In addition to the demographic shifts, Glendale Armenians and Monterey Park Chinese thus confirm Li's assertion about the socioeconomic stratification of an ethnoburb. Even the pattern of initial entrance into political office reflects similarities between the two cases: Glendale's first Armenian politician, Larry Zarian, took office in 1983; Monterey Park's first Chinese elected official, Lily Lee Chen, was elected mayor in 1983. These quite distinct populations share strikingly parallel histories in terms of their suburban integration. Given the foregoing analysis, the Chinese San Gabriel Valley model that Li has introduced can be expanded to include a distinct population—the multilocal Armenians of Glendale. This suggests that the ethnoburb model need not be confined solely to Asian American populations, but can be applied among others as well. While each community manifests its own distinctions, the ethnoburb model proves a particularly suitable framework to describe their similarities.

This analysis therefore situates Glendale into discussions of ethnoburbs: (1) Its internal "dynamics" reflect a distinctly Armenian consumer market, yet one that is integrated into international economic markets. In addition, Glendale Armenians play key roles in globalizing capital and international flows of commodities and personnel. The concentration of Armenians maximizes their ability to create social, political, and financial networks. (2) Glendale has the "geographical locations and diversity" of the ethnoburb insofar as it exists in a suburb of large geographical area and lower density than that of the inner city. It is also surrounded by several unincorporated areas within the San Fernando Valley. In addition, Armenians' presence has transformed local residential and business aesthetics and practices. This concentration of Armenian organizations, churches, businesses, and residences suffuses all parts of Glendale, so much so that marked spillover has occurred throughout the San Fernando Valley. And, as such, its boundaries are porous and arbitrary. Also, (3) tables 1–5 reflect the internal stratification of Glendale's Armenian subgroups. Armenians occupy every socioeconomic and professional stratum. Their internal differences create distinct residential and economic strata in the north and south of Glendale. The establishment of Glendale's Armenian cluster in the 1970s and 1980s led to a significant increase in its population. These replenished numbers strengthened their socioeconomic influence in the city. Finally, Glendale's (4) "functionality" is that of an ethnoburb inasmuch as it now operates as a port of entry. Glendale's Armenian population has gone mainstream, particularly in certain sectors such as local politics, in which it represents a clear majority of elected officials. As such, Glendale Armenians might be characterized as both "inward and outward looking in their socioeconomic and political pursuits" (Li 2009, 47). Glendale Armenians engage with multiethnic populations and contribute to the prosperity of the city without sacrificing a sense of loyalty and commitment to their own ethnic identity. And, as Li reflects of the Chinese's fight for solidarity in Monterey Park, the same holds for Glendale Armenians: "Although there are class differences and conflicts within the ethnic group, the group often unites in solidarity to fight for their rights whenever those rights are threatened. Cul-

tivating an ethnic consciousness leads to growth and prosperity" (47). Consequently, Glendale can comfortably be situated in the ethnoburb model.
Armenians' inclusion expands discussions of ethnoburbs and proves the generalizability of the model.

Despite the overlapping experiences of the Armenian and Chinese populations in their respective ethnoburbs, there are a couple of important differences.
The first relates to transnational business ventures and the globalization of capital. To be sure, Armenians participate in several industries that globalize capital. They also participate in the international circulation of high tech and
personnel. Armenians also contribute with their own companies. But Armenians
come to the United States under very different circumstances compared to those
from mainland China, Taiwan, or Hong Kong (Ng 1998). Dispossessed of their
historical homelands and without a financially stable home country economy,
Glendale Armenians simply do not have the same sort of transnational economic
relationship with a home government or its financial institutions (Gomez and
Hsiao 2004). This difference in scale does not take away from their business contributions to non-Armenian corporations and banks, but it warrants reference.
The second qualification pertains to size. Armenian numerical representation
worldwide is difficult to determine; however, it most probably does not exceed
11 million. In contrast, the global Chinese population exceeds 1.4 billion. This
disparity signifies differences in scope in terms of transnational transactions,
migratory trajectories, and potential replenishments.

Apart from these two qualifications, the ethnoburb model captures well the
overlapping experiences of internally diverse co-ethnic populations such as the
Chinese of Monterey Park and the Armenians of Glendale. Li's ethnoburb model
provides scholars with the tools for understanding why certain urban centers
have undergone such significant changes in the past few decades. This model
could apply in other contexts as well, such as the Koreans of Irvine, the Vietnamese of Westminster, and the Filipinos of Daly City, among many others.

Some Limitations of the Ethnoburb Model

While the ethnoburb model captures a broad range of immigrants' experiences
in contemporary multiethnic, multiracial suburbs, it also possesses several limitations. One limitation relates to duration. What does the snapshot gleaned of
these dynamic and prosperous suburbs tell us about their futures? Suburban immigrant populations negotiate and interact with various institutional and demographic factors, which yield varied results. Even though the ethnoburb model

presents an important and dynamic analysis of how urban ecology has changed over the past several decades, it does not help us understand in what direction these communities are evolving.

Also, while Armenians may fit well within the ethnoburb framework, in some ways the parallels between the Chinese and the Armenians also point to another shortcoming of the model—namely, distinguishing the experiences of different racial and ethnic populations. Ethnoburbs create opportunities for immigrants to mobilize economically and politically, but they also reinforce the same ethnic and racial prejudices witnessed throughout the United States. Asian Americans are often grouped together and referred to as "honorary whites" (Gans 1999; Tuan 1999; Bonilla-Silva 2004) or a "model minority"—a problematic overgeneralization that associates intra-ethnically diverse Asian communities with higher-than-average levels of economic success, social acceptance, and educational attainment (Zhou and Xiong 2005; Chao et al. 2013; Zhou and Bankston 2020). Similarly, Armenians are often classified as "white" or "white ethnic"—a term typically applied to those who claim ancestry from Southern, Eastern, or Central Europe or the Caucasus. As in several other traditional case studies, such as those of the Irish, Italian, and Jewish, Armenians are not always identified as ethnically or racially distinct from mainstream white Americans.[7]

Although these problematic overgeneralizations disregard the many challenges ethnic and racial minorities continue to face in the United States, they do point to the different ways minorities are perceived and treated. Given these considerations, is the ethnoburb model equally achievable for all populations regardless of ethnicity or race? Race continues to play a very important role in multiethnic suburbs; these factors lead to some very uneven trajectories among Armenian, Chinese, Latino, and Black American populations (Cattacin 2009; Albarracín 2016). In this way, the ethnoburb model may run the risk of overlooking institutional factors, which make it less achievable for some populations throughout the United States.

Nonetheless, as Daniel T. Lichter, Domenico Parisi, and Michael C. Taquino have demonstrated, resettlement patterns, such as those observed in ethnoburbs, "have made some places more racially homogenous while others became more diverse" (2015, 845). While Black-white and Black–non-Black segregation remains a consistent occurrence among US urban and suburban spaces (Rogers 2006, 2009), the redistribution of populations and the reconfiguration of suburbs in the first two decades of the 2000s have existed alongside greater racial and ethnic integration, particularly among Latinos, Asians, and, in the case of Glendale, Armenians. While rooted racial injustices and hierarchies continue to manifest political resistance against certain minority populations—particularly Black Americans—several ethnoburbs facilitate greater diversity in US cities and suburbs (Lichter,

Parisi, and Taquino 2017). Armenian and Asian ethnoburbs manifest important demographic redistributions and political realignments among the country's evolving urban ecologies; however, research on Black suburbs highlights a very different reality (Clerge 2019). While the United States' growing ethnoburbs are helping to facilitate more racial integration among some, these spaces also reinforce racial segregation and inequality.

Despite the very real limitations that institutionalized racism continues to impose on several minority populations in the United States, ethnicity and race remain powerful phenomena through which political actors construct and mobilize groups. As Rogers Brubaker asserts, "Ethnicity, race and nationhood are fundamentally ways of perceiving, interpreting, and representing the social world. They are not things in the world, but perspectives on the world" (2004, 17). As such, the ethnoburb model is a particularly useful lens through which to study immigrant political incorporation. As contemporary election cycles show, US suburbs no longer cater solely to white US political prerogative. Rather, they play an increasingly important role in determining the results of local and national elections. And ethnoburbs play an integral role in this recent shift. More specifically, ethnoburbs present the conditions under which new political actors arise. In the context of diverse ethnoburbs, these new political actors help integrate newcomers by mobilizing intra-ethnically diverse populations and, in the process, they create co-ethnic voting blocs. For these suburban political actors (or ethnopolitical entrepreneurs) to emerge, Li's four features for ethnoburbs all play important roles. Ethnoburbs also often contain another key element, one that pertains to conflict between different ethnic and racial populations. As Li argues, "Ethnic people in an ethnoburb also have interactions with other groups, but these conflicts between groups tend to enhance ethnicity" (2009, 45). But conflict or interethnic antagonism within ethnoburbs not only "enhances ethnicity"; it also has particular significance for the political mobilization of internally diverse populations.

The Dialectics of Suburban Backlash

In ethnoburbs as elsewhere, newcomers often disrupt the preexisting status quo and generate conflict with the already established residents. Prior to the 1960s, newcomers to the United States were pressured to assimilate, but in the politically charged, post–civil rights era, many racial and ethnic minorities have made a concerted effort to push back against discrimination and strengthen ethnic cohesion and solidarity (Bakalian and Bozorgmehr 2009). For internally diverse and fragmented populations, this interethnic antagonism can even sometimes prove useful in terms of creating a common cause around which internally fragmented co-ethnics unify.

In terms of interethnic antagonism, a rich social scientific scholarship exists that treats two, related phenomena: (1) the seeming inevitability of competition and conflict occurring when distinguishable populations—in particular, ethnically and racially distinguishable populations—encounter one another and (2) the extent to which interethnic conflict can strengthen pan-ethnic solidarity among targeted populations (Young 1932; Park 1950; Steinberg 1981; Bakalian and Bozorgmehr 2009; Zepeda-Millán 2017). As far back as 1908, Georg Simmel argued, "Conflict may not only heighten the concentration of an existing unit, radically eliminating all elements which might blur the distinctness of its boundaries against the enemy; it may also bring persons and groups together which have otherwise nothing to do with each other" (1955, 98–99; quoted in Bakalian and Bozorgmehr 2009, 10). Subsequent sociological and social psychological scholarship has further developed the connection between external antagonism and internal cohesion among ethnic populations (Coser 1956; Tajfel et al. 1979; Bakalian 1993; Waldinger and Fitzgerald 2004; Olzak 2006; Abrams and Hogg 2006). In describing what scholars refer to as "reactive ethnicity," Rubén G. Rumbaut argues: "This process of forging a reactive ethnicity in the face of perceived threats, persecution, discrimination, and exclusion is not uncommon. It is one mode of ethnic identity formation that highlights the role of a hostile context of reception in accounting for the rise rather than the erosion of ethnicity" (2008b, 110). In contemporary ethnoburbs, this interethnic antagonism (or the reactive ethnicity it generates) has powerful political implications.

While Armenians' rapid and concentrated settlement of Glendale generated considerable backlash, the interethnic antagonism has evolved. In the 1970s and 1980s, many Glendale residents overtly targeted Armenians. As the former mayor of Burbank, Will Rogers, who also worked as a writer in the 1970s and 1980s, shared with me:

> [Armenians] were coming up against such hatred you wouldn't believe. . . . The hatred was so strong. I remember we had a reporter at the newspaper whose name was Tanya Soussan, and people would see that as "Soussanian" or assume she changed it. And all of us would get calls virtually every day. But she would get the nastiest calls. "You're one of them. And I can see you just wrote this story to help them. You didn't mention the robber in this was Armenian . . . wasn't it?! Wasn't it?!"

In later years, these overt forms of antagonism became more nuanced and institutionalized. For example, in the late 1980s and early 1990s, the City of Glendale passed a series of ordinances that restricted multifamily residential development throughout the city, particularly in hillside areas. This push to limit residential development specifically affected Armenians and other newcomers, who were involved in construction projects to build apartment buildings and multigenerational family homes. To check Armenians from developing large, multistory houses (or "McMansions") and apartments, Glendale council members imposed several restrictions. What Willow Lung-Amam has argued regarding white residents' responses to Asian newcomers' houses in Fremont (in California's San Francisco Bay Area) applies to the restrictions imposed on Armenians in Glendale as well: "They tended to privilege extant suburban landscapes and their embedded ideals while also naturalizing and normalizing older, typically White residents' sense of place. At the same time, they disparately impacted Silicon Valley newcomers who did not share the same norms of housing and landscape design" (2017, 140).[8]

As Glendale's population swelled in the 1980s and 1990s, several developers—many Armenian—responded to accommodate the increasing demand for housing. In the 1980s, developers built multifamily residential units throughout the city. White Glendale residents responded vehemently with calls to limit this development, particularly in the city's more affluent, northern districts. To put a stop the city's aesthetic, cultural, and demographic changes, these residents called on elected officials to impose moratoria. Because so many of Glendale's newcomers were not registered to vote and lacked political representation, the more established voters influenced elected officials to freeze hundreds of projects already underway and prevent new developments. In 1988, Glendale officials established a moratorium on moderate and high-density residential construction projects. In addition, officials enacted a hillside moratorium, which limited development to single-family homes. This backlash continued into the early 1990s, when the city approved residential down-zoning programs, which capped the number of building permits issued. A report prepared for the City of Glendale Planning Division states, "As a result of the moratoria and downzoning, the number of residential projects constructed between 1990 and 2000 was relatively few" (City of Glendale, South Glendale Historic Context, Historic Resources Group 2014, 109). These restrictions sought to obstruct Glendale's demographic growth and development changes, which its increasingly diverse population introduced.

In addition to restrictions imposed on residential development, Armenian places of worship were also targeted. For example, in the mid-1990s, Armenians sought to modify St. Mary's Armenian Apostolic Church. Among other changes, they attempted to replace the church's roof with a dome. Domes are an important part of Armenian churches and Armenian architectural history.[9] Glendale officials made a concerted effort to prevent this proposed redesign. Armenian church officials established St. Mary's in 1975, and shortly thereafter, in 1977, the church was added to a list of historic (and therefore protected) sites in the city. In 1985, Armenian church officials purchased the building, but six months after this purchase, the city enacted a historic preservation ordinance.[10] The ostensible purpose of the law was to preserve the city's history and architecture.[11] As such, Glendale's Historic Preservation Commission, whose members were appointed by the city council, had to approve any changes to St. Mary's beforehand. Even before the plans for the dome were made, the commission had already manifested strong opposition to any other changes; it had rejected proposed projects for installing stained glass windows and painting the exterior.[12] Although several Armenians in Glendale attempted to remove St. Mary's from the list of protected sites, city officials ultimately enforced the historic preservation ordinance and prevented the dome's construction.

Assisting the Historic Preservation Commission was the Glendale Historical Society. Founded in 1979, the society has sought to create "awareness of Glendale's history and architectural heritage and the need to preserve this rich legacy through advocacy, outreach and education."[13] While the historical society has no direct political authority, as an elected official in Glendale told me, its members consist of "many single-family homeowners from very influential neighborhoods, where the voter turnout is much higher than other parts of the city." This elected official added, "If you look at who within city is donating [in local elections], many of the folks from the historical [society] donate to campaigns." For more than four decades, the Glendale Historical Society has proved to be an influential group in Glendale. In 1995, a member of the historical society justified her opposition to the dome, saying, "We just want the city to stand by its historic preservation policy. There is a common good that comes from retaining these buildings. It gives us a sense of our past."[14] This "common good," however, targeted and marginalized Armenians as well as other newcomers. Although framed in neutral terms, this language articulates for whom, according to the society member, the community is intended ("sense of our past") and, implicitly, those for whom it is not.

As Anny Bakalian argues, once a specific demographic threshold has been met, Armenians in the diaspora usually establish a church for the community in which they have settled (1993). St. Mary's Armenian Apostolic Church helped Armenians establish a permanent place for themselves in Glendale. However, beyond symbolic attachment, the church structure itself also plays a significant role in Armenian place making. And the dome is one of the most visible features of an Armenian church. By policing an imagined past, the Historic Preservation Commission and the Glendale Historical Society sought to impose their values and standards on Armenians and other newcomers by way of regulating how they

FIGURE 12. St. Mary's Armenian Apostolic Church in Glendale, California.

participated and influenced the city's urban design and planning. While Lung-Amam has unpacked the backlash in urban design and planning that Asian populations have experienced in multiethnic US suburbs, the same findings apply in the context of Glendale's Armenians: "By establishing design standards, guidelines, and review processes that reinforce hegemonic norms about housing's proper form and function, regulations can signal to newcomers that their values and preferences are not welcome" (2017, 142). The rhetorical benignity of "just wanting the city to stand by its historic preservation policy"—a policy enacted, at least in part, to combat and neutralize newcomers' contributions—embedded a starker reality, one in which Armenians and other immigrants were made to feel unwelcome and unwanted.

Beyond neutralizing aesthetic and architectural contributions, city officials also attempted to prevent both Armenian commercial and cultural impact. By the late 1990s, several Armenians had bought restaurants throughout Glendale and converted them into banquet halls. Banquet halls formed (and continue to form) an integral part of Armenians' social and cultural experience in Southern California. Armenians meet at banquet halls to celebrate, socialize, commemorate, and reify their ethnic identities. But these banquet halls threatened the white, non-Armenian residents of Glendale. Labeling them a "public nuisance,"

Glendale city council passed several ordinances that specifically targeted banquet halls. These ordinances stipulated that banquet halls needed to provide more parking than restaurants and could not be within two hundred feet of residential areas. Relatedly, another ordinance established a 70/30 rule, which meant a private party could not take up more than 30 percent of a restaurant's serving area.[15] Following these ordinances, city officials also banned outdoor grilling at restaurants and banquet halls. All these laws sought to check Armenians' growing commercial and cultural influence in the city.[16] Like the residential moratoria and the historic preservation ordinance, these laws sought to maintain the more established population's sense of place and order. In this case, however, Glendale voters passed restrictive ordinances that not only diminished Armenians' impact on the city but also provided a pathway to criminalize Armenian cultural practices. Nonetheless, in response to these restrictions, several Armenian banquet hall owners joined efforts and formed the Restaurant and Banquet Hall Owners Association. They spoke out vociferously. The association's outcry (and its strong financial backing) helped ensure that most of these ordinances were ultimately not enforced or taken off the books.

Bernd Simon and Bert Klandermans (2001) argue that politicized collective identities often develop out of the struggle between groups for power, especially where there exist shared grievances and an adversary (or "other") to whom such grievances can be attributed. While the intra-ethnically diverse Armenians had already developed a strong sense of ethnic and cultural identity before coming to Glendale, the discriminatory ordinances they faced—that is, to "naturalize and normalize older, typically White residents' sense of place" (Lung-Amam 2017, 140)—helped energize an otherwise politically and socially fragmented co-ethnic population. And, for the internally diverse Armenians in Glendale, the backlash they received, in part, helped generate a sense of ethnic cohesion and solidarity (or reactive ethnicity), and it also motivated a cadre of political aspirants to create a voting bloc out of Glendale's intra-ethnically diverse Armenians. Furthermore, these political aspirants received some policy assistance from specific legislation. For example, President Bill Clinton's Personal Responsibility and Work Opportunity Reconciliation Act of 1996 gave only citizens access to welfare, and, as such, many immigrants were incentivized to become citizens, which, in turn, empowered them to vote for their own representatives. Indeed, Armenians, who had been disregarded as politically insignificant throughout the 1980s and much of the 1990s, emerged in the late 1990s as a dominant political force.

GLENDALE'S ETHNOPOLITICAL ENTREPRENEURS

A New Chapter in US Politics

Sociologists have noted the powerful implications of actors who "create" groups for political purposes.[1] For example, in *Ethnicity without Groups*, Rogers Brubaker reminds scholars to pay close attention to ethnopolitical entrepreneurs:

> To criticize ethnopolitical entrepreneurs for reifying ethnic groups would be a kind of category mistake. Reifying groups is precisely what ethnopolitical entrepreneurs are in the business of doing. When they are successful, the political fiction of the unified group can be momentarily yet powerfully realized in practice. As analysts, we should certainly try to *account* for the ways in which—and conditions under which—this practice of reification, this powerful crystallization of group feeling, can work. (2004, 10)

Rather than merely criticize them for instrumentalizing ethnicity, Brubaker encourages scholars to make sense of the powerful implications of ethnopolitical entrepreneurs. In the past several decades, ethnopolitical entrepreneurs inside many suburbs across the United States have reified ethnicity and created voting blocs (or groups of constituents) out of internally diverse co-ethnics. And, in the 2020 presidential election and the 2021 senate runoff, the implications of this "powerful crystallization of group feeling" were on full display.

In several news outlets from 2020 and 2021, election analysts shifted their discussions from large urban centers to multiethnic suburbs. As Willow Lung-Amam reports in a Bloomberg op-ed, "At first, the nation could barely take its eyes off of Detroit, Philadelphia, Atlanta, Phoenix and Milwaukee, as their record number of votes were carefully tallied. . . . But in the torturous five days after the election, people also learned how to pronounce Gwinnett County—one of America's most diverse suburbs—after having watched Black, Latinx and Asian Americans wait in hours-long lines to vote outside strip malls in Georgia."[2] Multiethnic suburban voters, such as those in Gwinnet County, proved pivotal in determining the election results. What the media accounts often did not include, however, were the political actors behind the suburban voter turnout. These ethnopolitical entrepreneurs undertook extensive outreach and registered thousands of new voters.

Ethnopolitical entrepreneurs are not the only actors involved in reifying (or "summoning") ethnicity. For example, in Glendale, backlash from non-Armenians helped create a common cause among this intra-ethnically diverse immigrant population—that is, reactive ethnicity also created a sense of cohesion among the Armenians of Glendale. In turn, several prospective Armenian political candidates were able to take advantage of this imposed sense of unity that the backlash generated. Still, while demographics and reactive ethnicity may help create opportunities for ethnopolitical entrepreneurs to arise and mobilize co-ethnics, simply invoking ethnicity does not guarantee their success. There exist many suburbs where ethnic and racial majority or plurality populations, who suffer from discrimination and racial profiling, do not generate large voter turnout or co-ethnic political representation (Pincetl 1994). Rather, there is often an arduous learning curve for ethnopolitical entrepreneurs, who must identify the most effective uses of ethnicity to mobilize co-ethnic populations and win political elections. This learning curve is something with which Armenian political aspirants in Glendale are quite familiar.

By 1989, Armenians may not yet have reached a demographic threshold or sufficient rate of citizenship to determine local elections on their own, but they did make up a sizable enough percentage of the population (17.4%) to at least influence local elections. Berdj Karapetian recognized the political potential of Armenians' rapid concentration in Glendale. Born in Armenia, but raised in Azerbaijan and France, Karapetian came to the United States with his family in 1970. Like most Armenians at that time, Karapetian's family settled in Hollywood. He attended college at California State University, Los Angeles. In 1980, Karapetian was selected to participate in the California State Fellowship Program; he spent nearly ten months in Sacramento, where he worked for a state senator, Robert B. Presley, on legislation to fund toxic cleanup in Southern California. As a fellow working with the governor's office, he also sat in on several meetings among senior state officials. From these experiences, he gained firsthand insight into legislative processes at the state level of government. Subsequently, Karapetian returned to Los Angeles, where he began working for an influential Armenian grassroots organization, the Armenian National Committee of America (ANCA).

As Heather S. Gregg notes, the "ANCA traces its origins back to the American Committee for the Independence of Armenia (ACIA), the organization that lobbied on behalf of the ARF-governed Republic of Armenia, beginning in 1918" (2002, 10). The ACIA was founded by Vahan Cardashian, a former counselor to the Ottoman Embassy in Washington, DC, and, after, to the Ottoman Consulate General in New York City. Affiliated with the Armenian Revolutionary Federation (ARF), the ACIA originally pursued an independent Armenia, particularly a "Wilsonian Armenia," as established by the Treaty of Sèvres (1920) after the defeat of the Ottoman Empire in the First World War. Headquartered in New York City, the ACIA soon expanded to include many regional offices across the United States. In 1941, the ACIA changed its name to the ANCA after it had altered some of its key objectives, especially related to promoting Armenian Genocide recognition among local and national governments. Since the mid-twentieth century, the ANCA has expanded not only across the United States but also all over the global Armenian diaspora. It has extended its outreach efforts to include Armenian Genocide instruction (in schools), voter registration, and political candidate sponsorship. The ANCA plays an influential role in contemporary Armenian American politics. In addition to Armenian Genocide recognition, the ANCA's objectives include support for Artsakh/Nagorno-Karabakh, sanctions against Turkey, and lobbying for economic relief for Armenia. Headquartered in Washington, DC, the ANCA has two regional branches (in New York City and Los Angeles) and over fifty local chapters throughout the United States. Representatives from the ANCA regularly meet with non-Armenian elected officials on city, county, state, and federal levels of government. ANCA representatives encourage these elected officials to support Armenian-related initiatives. In California, some elected officials who have worked closely with the ANCA to promote Armenian-related causes include county supervisor Kathryn Barger, state senator Anthony Portantino, and congressman Adam Schiff. Operating on five continents, the ANCA is the largest Armenian grassroots political organization in the world.

Working with the ANCA, Karapetian helped organize several events, particularly related to Armenian Genocide recognition and commemoration. While working with the ANCA, he connected with congressman Matthew Martinez (of Montebello). Martinez invited Karapetian to work with him in his Washington, DC, office. Karapetian accepted the offer and relocated to the nation's capital, where he spent nearly four years. In addition to working with Martinez, Karapetian helped establish an ANCA office in DC and worked on promoting Armenian Genocide recognition. By 1986, Karapetian had returned to Los Angeles, where he continued working with the ANCA at its Western Region office, located in Glendale. Drawing from the insights gleaned during his time in Sacramento and DC, he decided to run for Glendale's city council in 1989.

By the late 1980s, Armenians had become the targets of several city ordinances related to housing (see chapter 2). This backlash inspired Karapetian to run for office. As he told me: "I knew a lot of these developers and builders who were caught in that moratorium, and they could not move forward with construction. And I felt it was not just, it was not fair, the way the city was handling it. And I thought I would try to run to bring about a change. Over 80 percent of the individuals who had projects caught in the pipeline were Armenian. So something was not fair." While the internally diverse Armenians of Glendale may have identified strong differences among themselves based on country of origin or socioeconomic background, the backlash they received from non-Armenians—in this case, regarding housing and development—helped create common cause around which all Armenians in Glendale could unify. In this way, non-Armenians played a quite important role in creating a sense of ethnic cohesion (or reactive ethnicity) among the intra-ethnically diverse Armenians of Glendale. Karapetian concisely articulated the benefits of reactive ethnicity that the backlash triggered: "The feeling was, whether you were an Armenian living on the hillsides, wealthy, or an Armenian living in an apartment, they saw that there was a discrimination against them. So that helped."

Taking advantage of the specific factors that come together in an ethnoburb (see chapter 2), Karapetian felt confident he could secure office. However, as stated, for suburban ethnopolitical entrepreneurs to realize their goals, they must also develop successful strategies to politically incorporate internally diverse populations. Fearing that there were not enough registered Armenian voters in Glendale, Karapetian opted for a strategy that attempted to appeal to both Armenians and non-Armenians. But this approach targeted too broad a prospective voting base. In addition, two other Armenians, Joe Ayvazi and Richard Diradourian, also ran in the same election. The fact that three Armenians ran in the same election worked against all of them, for they divided the limited number of Armenian votes they received. In addition, the election was happening at a time when Armenians were increasingly targeted. During his campaign, Karapetian was consistently harassed by Glendale residents; some even painted swastikas on his car. When Larry Zarian had initially obtained office in Glendale, the number of newcomers was still quite meager. By the late 1980s, public attitudes had shifted significantly.

Thus, several factors worked against Karapetian on his campaign. These included mounting hostility toward Armenians, the strategies relied on in running the campaign, and the rate of citizenship among Armenians and other newcomers.

For these reasons, Karapetian (as well as the other two Armenians in the race) did not obtain enough votes to win office.[3] Prospective Armenian ethnopolitical entrepreneurs in Glendale would continue struggling until the late 1990s—at which time the city had reached a demographic threshold of eligible voters and the ethnopolitical entrepreneurs themselves had devised a successful set of campaign strategies—to begin taking advantage of this ethnoburb's powerful political potential. These shifts would fundamentally change Glendale's political culture.

The rest of this chapter attempts to illustrate these powerful changes that took place in the late 1990s. The chapter relies on two examples of Glendale-based Armenian elected officials, Rafi Manoukian and Ardashes (Ardy) Kassakhian. Manoukian, a native of Beirut, Lebanon, represents a particular sort of entrepreneur. In 1975, he came to the United States as a seventeen-year-old. He went to college and served in the US military. Since then, he has served as Glendale's mayor, treasurer, and city council member. Kassakhian, by comparison, represents another example of a successful ethnopolitical entrepreneur. Apart from a brief period overseas during his childhood, Kassakhian was raised in the United States. Kassakhian has worked in Glendale as the mayor, the city clerk, and a city council member. Manoukian and Kassakhian represent different ends on a spectrum of ethnopolitical entrepreneur experience as well as the evolving roles of ethnopolitical entrepreneurs in ethnoburbs. Manoukian's native fluency in the Armenian language and immigrant background enable him to connect with Glendale's majority Armenian immigrant population, whereas Kassakhian's non-native Armenian language, second-generation status, and his non-Armenian spouse can, at times, introduce some stumbling blocks. However, Kassakhian's familiarity with US institutions and his background experiences provide him the resources to run for political office beyond Glendale. Their career trajectories reflect the political evolution in US ethnic suburbs.

Glendale's Ethnopolitical Entrepreneurs

As I sat waiting for Adrin Nazarian to arrive in the reception area of his office within the bleak Van Nuys State Building, his secretary informed me that Mr. Nazarian had just called to apologize for running late; he was on his way. Only having arrived a few minutes before, I did not think Nazarian was running late at all. In fact, in doing fieldwork, I had grown quite accustomed to meetings and events happening on *haykakan zhamanak* (Armenian time)—that is, beginning and ending when they begin and end rather than at predetermined times. As a result, I barely registered how much time had elapsed. However, even before the secretary had finished the sentence, Nazarian rushed through the main doors. Distractedly, he escorted me into his office. His spacious office seemed somewhat drab and vacant, as though he had only recently moved into it. And, indeed, on entering his office, Nazarian explained that because he spent so much time in the state's capital, Sacramento, and because he had so little free time, he had not gotten around to moving into the Van Nuys office. As the representative of California's Forty-Sixth State Assembly District, Nazarian had a busy life. Every week, he shuttled between Sacramento and Los Angeles to represent his nearly half million constituents. Since he seemed rushed, I told him my questions should not take up too much time. Noticing my concern, he asked me if I had any lunch plans and suggested we move our meeting to Raffi's Place—an Iranian Armenian restaurant in central Glendale—where we could speak in a more relaxed manner.[4]

In Raffi's Place's semi-open dining space, Nazarian became my culinary guide and provided a detailed review of the menu's food options. What constitutes "Armenian food" can often prove elusive, especially since the answer frequently is "it depends"; apart from a few distinct staples, Armenians have adopted and adapted the cuisines of their host societies, such as those of Georgia, Iran, Lebanon, Syria, and Turkey, among many others. In Glendale, Armenians' internal diversity is made evident by the international cuisine associated with and familiar to the Armenian palate. Thus, while Nazarian, an Armenian born in Iran, represented California's Forty-Sixth State Assembly District (in North Hollywood), it seemed appropriate to meet in Glendale, for it was here that he undertook some of his earliest ethnopolitical entrepreneurial work to incorporate all the different strands of the multilocal Armenian population.[5] Moreover, founded in 1993 by Iranian Armenians, Rafik and Gohar Bakijanian, Raffi's Place was an appropriate location for Nazarian to tell me about his background and how he first became involved with political outreach in Glendale.[6]

As tensions grew during the Iran-Iraq War (1980–1988), Nazarian and his mother fled Iran and came to the United States. At the time, he was only eight years old. He attended Holy Martyrs Ferrahian High School in Encino and then the University of California, Los Angeles (UCLA). After graduating from UCLA in 1996, Nazarian worked as an aide to congressman Brad Sherman. In 1999, governor Gray Davis appointed him special assistant to the California Trade and Commerce Agency. He also worked as the chief of staff to an Armenian American, Paul Krekorian, from 2006 until 2010, when Krekorian served as the California State Assembly member of the Forty-Third District; Nazarian continued in this capacity from 2010 until 2012, during the first two years of Krekorian's time as a member of the Los Angeles City Council for the Second District. Between 2012 and 2022, Nazarian served as a California State Assembly member for the Forty-Sixth State Assembly District. As a California State Assembly member, he spearheaded several important pieces of legislation, many of which promoted Armenian-related initiatives.

Nazarian vividly exemplifies the important role personal characteristics play in determining elected officials' position-taking behavior (Burden 2007; Jones 2009; Baumann, Debus, and Müller 2015); even though relatively few Armenians live in Nazarian's district, he has authored several successful, Armenian-oriented bills. For example, in 2014, governor Jerry Brown signed into law Nazarian's Armenian Genocide Education Act (Assembly Bill [AB] 1915); this law requires the inclusion of Armenian Genocide instruction in California school curricula. Then, in 2019, governor Gavin Newsom signed into law the third iteration of Nazarian's Divestment from Turkish Bonds Act (AB 1320); this law restricts boards of the California Public Employees' Retirement System and the California State Teachers' Retirement System from acquiring new or renewing existing governmental bonds owned or controlled by the government of Turkey. And, in 2022, Governor Newsom signed Nazarian's Genocide Remembrance Day bill (AB 1801); this law established the 24th of April as Genocide Remembrance Day, a state holiday in California. While AB 1801 commemorates all Californians whose families have been affected by genocides, the publicly funded holiday is commemorated on Armenian Genocide Remembrance Day.[7]

Beyond these and other pieces of legislation, Nazarian also played a key role in the political mobilization of Los Angeles Armenians. Between the late 1990s and the early 2000s, Nazarian and several other ethnopolitical entrepreneurs organized campaigns for Los Angeles–based Armenian political candidates and registered thousands of Armenian voters. These initiatives began with Rafi Manoukian's 1999 Glendale City Council campaign. Despite the daunting odds they faced, Nazarian and his colleagues helped secure Manoukian's victory. Nazarian explained to me the surprising success of the 1999 campaign:

> We started going to apartment buildings, and south Glendale became a big hub for that. We registered almost three thousand new voters. By Election Day, we got almost six thousand out to vote, which almost tripled the highest performance in an election prior to that in Glendale. Rafi [Manoukian] ended up winning. He got a total of, I think, seventy-two hundred votes. I think it was a complete shock to the community . . . [Armenians] voted. They got the result. So they were like, this is not like the old country. This isn't like Lebanon, where we're duking it out with Maronites. This isn't Iran, where we just stay quiet and go about our way. . . . It's not Armenia, where government is never at your door to help. . . . So [it] was this sense of, "Wow, we can actually do this."

Helping run Manoukian's campaign, Nazarian and other ethnopolitical entrepreneurs targeted Glendale's densely concentrated southern districts, where a plurality of prospective first-generation Armenian voters lived. Nazarian understood that Armenians come to Glendale with a strong sense of ethnic identity. For example, according to AAS data, in response to the question "How important is the preservation of your Armenian identity to you," 86.1 percent of AAS respondents chose "very important."[8] Even when disaggregating the data based on subpopulations, this strong sense of ethnicity recurs. Despite Armenians' strong sense of ethnicity, Nazarian also understood that he could not take ethnic solidarity for granted. Indeed, Glendale Armenians had previously tried and failed to win office by rallying co-ethnic support. Rather, he and his team would have to employ creative strategies to unify an otherwise internally fragmented population. And Nazarian recognized that creating a cohesive voting bloc among such internally diverse voters in Glendale would prove a difficult task. Still, much to their own surprise, these ethnopolitical entrepreneurs, eventually, accomplished the task and launched a model that would become the basis of Glendale Armenians' political and electoral incorporation. Indeed, Manoukian's campaign was the first time an Armenian was elected in Glendale based almost exclusively on voter support from other Armenians.

Rafi Manoukian

The city treasurer's office was a short walk from my apartment in central Glendale. While living in Glendale, I often visited the city's administrative buildings, where I met with elected officials and city staff. On one of several visits to the office of the treasurer, I asked Manoukian about his motivation to become involved in local politics. His answer (and the vehemence with which he expressed it) surprised me:

> I'm Armenian. I served in the air force. . . . I was an FOB [fresh off the boat] from Lebanon. I had a green card. I wasn't a citizen. They weren't going to let me work on their jet engines. "You're welcome, Mr. Foreigner, to our top secret engines." I didn't understand that until much later. Other immigrants told me about their experiences in the military. But my thinking was, "Here I am, I shoveled shit for your country for four years. Even if I'm not a citizen, I joined the air force with a green card. You're not going to tell me, just because I only have a green card, I don't have any rights!" We would go to these events, and there would be people walking around collecting signatures. And they would say, "Oh, are you a citizen?" And I'd say no, and they'd completely blow me

off. . . . It would just piss me off. So I became a citizen! The reason I ran was Glendale was overtly Armenian at that time. Even some of the politicians, they would say [Armenians] don't vote, just ask money from them. And they would completely ignore the Armenian community.

The dismissive and exclusionary attitudes Manoukian experienced firsthand both enraged and motivated him. He lived in an increasingly ethnic suburb (where he and his multilocal co-ethnics constituted a plurality) and yet felt ignored and belittled by the city's political leadership. Furthermore, by the 1990s, white residents had long targeted and marginalized Armenians in Glendale (see chapter 2). Like Karapetian nearly a decade before him, Manoukian was motivated to seek political office in Glendale by his feelings of indignation. Along with a cadre of other activist-minded Armenians, he took action, first becoming a citizen and then, in 1999, securing political office.

Although an Armenian immigrant, Larry Zarian, had held office in Glendale between 1983 and 1998, a paradigmatic shift in terms of campaigning did not occur until Manoukian ran for city council. As such, Armenian immigrant political incorporation markedly accelerated during the 1999 campaign. In fact, Manoukian told me that he deliberately launched his campaign the year Zarian stepped down. While other Armenians had attempted to hold office, it required the vision and shrewdness of a small cadre of ethnopolitical entrepreneurs— aspiring elected officials, political analysts, ethnic organizations, and ethnic media—to seize emergent opportunities (such as demographic concentration and interethnic antagonism / reactive ethnicity) and launch new immigrant-centered strategies in Glendale.

Unlike Zarian, Manoukian was the first Armenian elected official in Glendale to successfully run on the basis of co-ethnic support. He explained to me that Glendale's uninspiring voter turnout galvanized him into action: "Before 1999, we got involved in a lot of the elections. And some council members got elected with something like fifty-five hundred votes. And I thought to myself, that's nothing for a population of over two hundred thousand people. And, in general elections, I [knew] turnout was very low. . . . At that point I decided to run." Glendale's Armenian political incorporation began, in part, with a few ambitious ethnopolitical entrepreneurs who saw potential in politically mobilizing Armenians.

Coming to the United States as a teenager, Manoukian served in the air force and after that attended college at California State University, Northridge. Despite migrating in 1975 and serving in the US armed forces, he did not obtain citizenship until 1992. But his exposure to one Armenian organization in particular—the ANCA—provided Manoukian with the political experience and wherewithal to begin thinking about running his own political campaign.

FIGURE 13.   Portrait of Rafi Manoukian.

It was with the ANCA Western Region that Manoukian received his first exposure to municipal politics. Working with the ANCA, Manoukian acquired grassroots experience and learned about local politics in the United States. But, as he shared in our discussion, it was personal experiences that prompted him to pursue political office. When the opportunity arose to run for city council, Manoukian seized it. In making this decision, he did not act alone; in addition to members of the ANCA, Nazarian, and Krekorian, Manoukian worked with the political consultant Eric Hacopian. Although this was the first campaign Hacopian ran in Glendale, he would become a particularly important person for the political careers of several Los Angeles–based Armenians. From the 1980s on, all these actors had recognized the potential of the Armenian population in Glendale and pondered the most effective ways to mobilize it.

In addition, most of those working on Manoukian's campaign already had launched, or eventually would launch, their own political careers. One of those involved, Krekorian, told me what questions prompted him: "How can we put this growing Armenian population, which was now starting to come in at much greater numbers, how can we get them more engaged in public affairs and utilize the numbers of this community to pursue their interests?" While working on Jackie Goldberg's campaign for city council in 1993, Krekorian collaborated with the political strategist Hacopian, who was the field consultant on the same campaign. Finding a commonalty in their shared democratic activism and Armenian heritage, they formed a strong working relationship. Shortly thereafter, they teamed up with another Armenian democratic activist, Nazarian, who worked as congressman Brad Sherman's aide between 1997 and 1999. In 1998, Nazarian, Hacopian, and Krekorian worked together on Barry Gordon's democratic campaign for a congressional seat. Gordon lost the election by only three points. Nonetheless, the effectiveness of their grassroots initiatives created awareness of potential elsewhere. As Nazarian shared with me, "Election Day comes, [Gordon] gets 46 percent of the vote. [Jim] Rogan gets 49 percent of the vote, doesn't even break majority. . . . So the minute we saw that we thought, 'Wait a minute, there's an opportunity here. If we flip enough Armenians to vote Democrat, we can take on Rogan. So let's do a test run.'" And the opportunity to undertake a "test run" emerged shortly thereafter: in 1998, as Krekorian prepared for an assembly race, Glendale resident Manoukian, himself a longtime activist for the ANCA, expressed the desire to campaign for city council. Krekorian had also worked with several people from the ANCA before this, and, with Hacopian and Nazarian, they formed a team of volunteers and organized Manoukian's campaign. These ethnopolitical entrepreneurs, by then, brought with them experience and insight, and all wanted to use these tools to realize Armenians' political potential. The intention of their experiment in Glendale, as Nazarian emphasized to me, was "to test the voter registration drive, the voter absentee drive, the turnout effort, et cetera." But the result of this experiment surprised even those organizing it: they registered thousands of new voters and won the 1999 council election. And this election established a precedent for subsequent Glendale Armenian political campaigns.

While a very significant part of the campaign's success related to demographic concentration—according to census data, Armenians in Glendale constituted 34.1 percent of the overall population by 2000—other factors also played equally important roles in helping Manoukian win. For example, television stations began running twenty-four-hour Armenian programming at about the same time. As a result, Manoukian and others could regularly appear on Armenian television and explain not only the importance of voting but also how to do so. Local television programming and other ethnic media (such as social media) are crucial in newcomers' political mobilization (Bleich, Bloemraad, and de Graauw 2015; Haynes and Ramakrishnan 2015). As Wan-Ying Lin and Hayeon Song argue, ethnic media not only preserve immigrants' cultural identities, but they also facilitate their post-migration settlement "by providing local news and information they can use in the host society" (2006, 363). As communication technologies have developed (from newspapers to television programming to social media), their impact on immigrants' social and political engagement with the host society has grown accordingly. And, for Glendale Armenians, Manoukian's election made this impact apparent. Ethnic media provided a means through which ethnopolitical entrepreneurs could communicate their vision (and the means of achieving it) to the Armenian population. In an interview with the campaign's communications director, Ara Khachatourian, he articulated the following to me:

> Charter came into Glendale and bought out Marcus Cable [in 1998] and decided they would start a twenty-four-hour channel. In an effort to increase subscribers to their higher tier of programming, they opened up a channel on that. And we were instrumental in helping people migrate from basic cable to the second tier. And we were granted, and Horizon was granted, the channel. So we worked in conjunction with Charter. So that was a fortuitous time for these campaigns because what we had started with Rafi [Manoukian] was spearheading how to vote. So Rafi's commercials [had] him as the spokesperson on how to vote.

AAS data reinforce the importance of ethnic media: among those surveyed, approximately 40.6 percent claimed that they get news from television "daily," while an additional 16.4 percent indicated they do on "most days."[9] Thus, the timing with multimedia proved especially auspicious for ethnopolitical entrepreneurs to realize their objectives.

In addition, Manoukian and his team's specific grassroots campaign strategies also proved effective: The people involved in Manoukian's campaign canvassed tirelessly and increased voter turnout exponentially. The team targeted specific districts and demographic populations. As Nazarian explained to me at Raffi's Place, those working on Manoukian's campaign, without neglecting other districts, specifically targeted Glendale's southern districts, where the largest share of newcomers were concentrated. Furthermore, specific demographic populations among the Armenians proved more receptive than others. One member of the team, Areen Ibranossian, who, as a teenager, volunteered to do outreach and register new voters for Manoukian's campaign and, later, worked as Krekorian's chief of staff, shared his experiences with me:

> Women were far more receptive and willing to participate than men. . . . My "go-to" was the grandma. If you talk to the grandma, and she was home by herself, she would take you to all the other neighbors, say, "This is a good kid, do whatever he asks you to do, sign the papers." So if you could find a grandmother, you were in. And they understood—they got

the cohesive message. The men tended to be far more cynical across the board. . . . The women were really the ones who carried it. . . . When they would question you and say, "Why are you doing this?," and I would explain to them how I was inspired for our community to be helpful, that resonated more than for the older men, who were kind of just like, "Ah, they're all the same." They just had a resistance to it. I mean, some of them you could break down. But that I remember distinctly: my goal was older *tatiqs* [grandmothers].

Ibranossian and other volunteers found Armenian women, especially older Armenian women, the most receptive among those with whom they interacted while doing outreach in Glendale. While Armenian men from different regional backgrounds ("across the board") often proved reticent or "cynical," Armenian women not only appreciated what the volunteers were doing but also used their social influence to help ethnopolitical entrepreneurs spread awareness and register additional voters ("take you to all the other neighbors"). As Ibranossian noted to me, they saw beyond Armenians' internal differences ("they got the cohesive message")—something that has proved a major challenge for ethnopolitical entrepreneurs (see chapter 4). Armenian women and, in particular, Armenian grandmothers (or *tatiqs*), were centrally important in helping Manoukian and his team win the election.

In addition, Manoukian's team employed two other distinct techniques: absentee voting and ride-sharing. As another Glendale Armenian politician, Kassakhian, acknowledged in an interview: "Absentee ballot was a key part of the strategy. At that time . . . Clinton changed the welfare laws. [They were] changed in a way that [meant] you had to be a citizen to get benefits. So a lot of the Armenians who didn't care about being citizens had become citizens because of Clinton's change in the rules. But they were not registered. . . . So we went and tried to register as many voters as we could." The ethnopolitical entrepreneurs took advantage of national opportunities to actualize their goals creatively.[10] In terms of the ride-sharing program, Manoukian explained: "We basically told people, 'If you don't have a ride, we'll provide one on Election Day.' We had a number of people with cars hanging out with some sort of communication device. . . . They would call into our office for a ride, and we'd send someone to go pick them up. . . . That was a major factor." And the results surprised the strategists as much it did their opponents. By fundraising among and doing outreach to, largely, prospective Armenian voters in Glendale, Manoukian and his team demonstrated the potential of an Armenian voting bloc. In a personal discussion with me, the campaign's strategist, Hacopian, conceded: "In order to mobilize Armenians to vote, we formed a more elaborate campaign. Back in the day, there was a limited number of voters. They all knew the process. You didn't have to get them to vote. You could run campaigns for five or ten thousand dollars. Well, Armenians also donate to campaigns at much higher rates than other people. So, essentially, they raised the cost and how much you can do." This campaign proved a catalyzing moment for Armenian ethnopolitical entrepreneurs in Glendale. While Manoukian was the frontrunner, his campaign brought together people who had themselves launched or would launch successful political careers. These were some of the first actors to actualize a unified and mobilized Armenian population in Glendale. And their mobilization in Glendale had much broader implications: the sundown town of the 1960s, a conservative bastion of the 1970s, and the headquarters of the American Nazi Party through the early 1980s had become, rather suddenly, an important democratic hub of Armenian political prominence.

The electoral implications of Armenian voter support had become apparent by the early 2000s. In 2000, the *Economist* ran an article titled "From Monica to Armenia," in which the author acknowledges that Armenians and other liberal newcomers in the area would determine the congressional race between Jim Rogan (a Republican and a major proponent of Clinton's impeachment) and Adam Schiff (a Democrat and a major proponent of Armenian Genocide recognition).[11] However, by the early 2000s, in Glendale the focus had expanded from merely trying to gain the support of Armenian voters to securing office for Armenians themselves. And this new generation of elected officials also shifted many political associations with Armenian Americans. While political actors such as Zarian and former California governor George Deukmejian had previously established an association between Armenian Americans and the Republican Party, these Armenian activists started shifting this association, largely, to the Democratic Party.

Nonetheless, despite this ideological shift among elected officials, Los Angeles Armenians remain ideologically diverse. According to data from the AAS, for example, Los Angeles Armenians self-identify as "Democrat" at about a 42.8 percent rate. Furthermore, just over 41 percent of voters from AAS data voted for Hillary Clinton in 2016 (while 18.6% voted for Donald Trump).[12] Among different subgroups, there also exists a range of distinct views. For example, in response to the AAS question about same-sex marriage, US-born Los Angeles Armenians expressed support at a rate of 78.2 percent, while Iranian-born Armenians' rate of support was 48.1 percent.[13] Thus, Armenian ethnopolitical entrepreneurs mobilized intra-ethnically diverse voters across the political spectrum (or, in Brubaker's language, sought to "evoke them, summon them, call them into being" [2004, 10]). In fact, Rogan's bid was perceived as so dependent on Armenians that the congressman traveled to Armenia and lobbied for

an ultimately unsuccessful Republican-sponsored Genocide recognition reso-
lution in the House.[14]

Despite Armenians' ideological diversity, the work of a small cadre of ethnopolitical entrepreneurs—who seized on the opportunity that Armenians' demographic concentration in Glendale presented and the backlash Armenians
received from the established residents—led to a series of successful ethnic campaigns. These campaigns relied heavily on canvassing, absentee voting, ride-
sharing, organizational support, demographic targeting, financial donations,
and multimedia coverage. The campaigns brought a variety of different actors
together to work toward the achievement of the ethnopolitical entrepreneurs'
vision. They established a precedent, one that employed creative strategies to
unify Glendale's internally diverse Armenian population. In subsequent city
elections, Armenians became increasingly dominant. For example, Bob Yousefian and Manoukian served as mayors of Glendale—Yousefian in 2004–2005 and
Manoukian in 2002–2003 and 2005–2006. And, in 2005, Ara Najarian, Yousefian, and Manoukian took three out of the five available city council seats. In
2005, Kassakhian also replaced Doris Twedt as Glendale's city clerk.

Nonetheless, while a majority of Glendale's ethnopolitical entrepreneurs are
themselves first-generation immigrants, they represent only one end of a spectrum. Second-generation immigrants also operate as ethnopolitical entrepreneurs. They re-create the same modes of the first-generation immigrant
ethnopolitical entrepreneur—canvassing, absentee voting, ride-sharing, organizational support, internal financial support, multimedia coverage—but, simultaneously, introduce both new challenges and advantages.

Ardashes (Ardy) Kassakhian

My fieldwork overlapped with the Forty-Third District's State Assembly seat election in 2016, one in which Kassakhian, Glendale's then city clerk, ran. Kassakhian let me shadow him during this campaign, and, as a result, we ended up
spending a lot of time together. I accompanied Kassakhian to various speaking,
fundraising, community (Armenian and non-Armenian), and city events. We
also attended several political events involving other elected officials with whom
Kassakhian worked on his campaign. In addition, I volunteered in his campaign
office, where I interacted with his staff. At times, I would drive Kassakhian to
events or meetings. In between phone calls, Kassakhian would update me on
the day's campaign-related news. Over the course of several months, we spent
many hours chatting about Glendale's Armenians, his background, his career,
and the campaign itself. During the months leading up to the election, I also
met hundreds of people—city officials, businesspeople, lawyers, prospective

voters, and many others. These months of fieldwork with Kassakhian gave me a firsthand account of the workings of an ethnopolitical entrepreneur's campaign.

Kassakhian was born in Boston. His Armenian father was born in Jerusalem, and his Armenian mother, in Athens. The two met as students at Yerevan State University (YSU). His mother's family moved to Soviet Armenia in 1947, and his father moved there in the 1960s to pursue his higher education. On completing his degree at YSU, Kassakhian's father was enrolled in graduate school at Harvard University. After moving around a few times, the Kassakhians settled in Southern California in 1984 (and, via Hollywood, in Glendale in 1985). For university, Kassakhian attended UCLA, where he became involved with the Armenian Student Association. He ultimately became the student group's sitting president. In 1997, he spearheaded a student initiative to prevent the endowment of an Ottoman studies chair in the Department of History. Following the retirement of professor Stanford Shaw—who infamously denied the Armenian Genocide—the Turkish government offered funding in support of establishing such a chair. Kassakhian's success with this initiative made him quite visible among the Armenians of Los Angeles. People from the community associated Kassakhian with his successful student activism. Local Armenian leadership sought him out and helped him make several important connections. For example, through his contacts with Armenian organizations, such as the Armenian Assembly of America and the ANCA, he was introduced to congressman Frank Pallone (New Jersey), who, along with John Porter (Illinois), had founded the Congressional Armenian Caucus (CAC) in 1995.[15] At a meeting, Congressman Pallone offered Kassakhian an internship in Washington, DC. In DC, Kassakhian learned about US politics and ethnic lobbying. Moreover, he developed an appreciation for co-ethnic political representation. As he shared with me: "I could count on both hands and both feet the number of Armenians on the Hill in DC. And I saw what kinds of decisions were being made in DC. And I thought, 'This is pathetic.'" As an intern in the nation's capital, Kassakhian became knowledgeable about the internal workings of US government and the importance of political representation. As he relayed in a personal conversation: "We [Armenians] sit here wringing our hands back here in Glendale and our other ghettos, but we don't even show up on the field. If we don't show up, why do we complain about the outcome and score?" During his time as an intern and on several subsequent return visits to DC, Kassakhian became increasingly interested in co-ethnic mobilization and electoral politics. These experiences coincided with Manoukian's campaign, which launched in 1998. Once back in Los Angeles, Kassakhian volunteered to help undertake outreach on that campaign.

In 2004, Kassakhian began organizing his own campaign for city clerk, which had been recently vacated by Twedt. The 2005 city clerk election was heavily

FIGURE 14. Portrait of Ardashes (Ardy) Kassakhian.

contested, with nine candidates (four Armenian) running for the position. Kassakhian was the first to obtain the office by election since 1929—it was previously designated by city council. In launching his own campaign, Kassakhian worked with the same cadre that helped Manoukian get elected in 1999. Kassakhian implemented and expanded on the same strategies Manoukian had employed previously. And his campaign's success reflects the growing awareness and success of Armenian ethnopolitical entrepreneurs in Glendale.

However, as a second-generation Armenian, Kassakhian's experience was distinct from that of Manoukian. Manoukian had gained many insights from his grassroots outreach with the ANCA in Glendale, while Kassakhian's involvement with student organizations (especially the Armenian Student Association) gave him a distinct sort of grassroots experience. Kassakhian's time in DC also provided him with insights and ambitions that Manoukian did not aspire to achieve. And, because of his student activism at UCLA with youth organizations, Kassakhian targeted new prospective voters. He campaigned on platforms of mobilizing Glendale's Armenian youth, such as young adults and college students. His orientation toward Armenian incorporation among young adults helped increase Armenian visibility and influence in local electoral politics. He also worked closely with other Armenian elected officials, ethnic organizations, and ethnic media. Building on the strategies of Manoukian and his team, Kassakhian widened Armenian ethnopolitical entrepreneurs' demographic range by including generations of Armenians who had spent most of their lives in the United States but continued to identify as Armenian. Kassakhian therefore reflects a distinct sort of elected official: the second-generation ethnopolitical entrepreneur.

·Beyond outreach strategies, second-generation ethnopolitical entrepreneurs' differences also relate to self-perception. Manoukian spoke about feeling foreign (referring to himself as an "FOB") and about the extended delay in obtaining US citizenship. In contrast, Kassakhian spent two years of his youth in Armenia. His experiences as an American living in Armenia contrast strikingly with Manoukian's as an Armenian living in the United States. As Kassakhian shared in one of our conversations:

> I went to school in Hayastan [Armenia] for two years. First and second grade I went to school in Yerevan. . . . I remember being upset when my parents dragged me to Yerevan. I remember at the airport asking my mom, "Do they have Chicken McNuggets in Hayastan?" And being livid when there weren't any. I remember a kid in Yerevan breaking my Darth Vader action figure, like she tore off the head of it. I mean, they don't have superglue in Hayastan! They only had one flavor of ice cream in Hayastan—it was white! It wasn't even vanilla! But even those things that are comical, it resonates.

Unlike Manoukian, Kassakhian takes his Americanness for granted. Their divergent backgrounds and experiences of the United States highlight the scope of diverse ethnopolitical entrepreneurs. While they commonly rely on ethnicity to mobilize diverse prospective voters, their motivations, backgrounds, and orientations differ. Based on various factors, ethnopolitical entrepreneurs also possess a range of distinct ideological positions (see chapter 5). In addition, unlike Kassakhian, who articulated a sense of otherness, the second-generation ethnopolitical entrepreneur may identify more in his capacity to unite populations. In contrast to Manoukian, as a second-generation ethnopolitical entrepreneur, Kassakhian understands his role with a strong sense of belonging both as an Armenian and as a US representative.

At the same time, Kassakhian has faced some challenges that Manoukian has not. For example, Kassakhian's spouse is not Armenian. In addition, he speaks Armenian with something of an American accent. As a result, first-generation immigrant Armenians may at times question his "authenticity." However, as a US-born Armenian, he also has advantages that Manoukian may not have. For example, Kassakhian's political socialization and familiarity within US institutions enable him to "transcend" the ethnopolitical entrepreneur role and run for higher office. Like the political beginnings of Judy Chu of Monterey Park, Kassakhian's may depend on mobilizing co-ethnic support; however, he has since run for higher office among majority nonethnic constituents outside of Glendale. For second-generation ethnopolitical entrepreneurs, they can use ethnoburbs as sites for political grooming before launching campaigns beyond the local cities in which they live and work. But this springboard effect often applies less to first-generation ethnopolitical entrepreneurs. For example, Manoukian, like Lily Lee Chen of Monterey Park, has not campaigned beyond Glendale. For immigrant ethnopolitical entrepreneurs, their campaigns can sometimes limit them to local elections, where co-ethnics represent a majority of their voters.

Despite these differences, Manoukian and Kassakhian approached their campaigns similarly. As Manoukian complained about the short shrift Armenians received from local politicians and community members, Kassakhian had similar things to say. In addition, despite their divergent backgrounds and orientations, both understood their obligations to other Armenians in similar language. In a personal discussion, Kassakhian told me:

> My dad came to the States because he got into Harvard University. So it's not like my family came here as refugees. We didn't come here barefoot, you know, tired and huddled masses, yearning to breathe free. We were here because my dad and my mom were supersmart, hardworking people. So there was a sense, like, "Damn it, we deserve to be here! And we're going to contribute to this country that attracts the best and the brightest. . . ." There was a period of adjustment and discrimination, not just against Armenians from non-Armenians here in the US, but also by Armenians to Armenians. There were these people, like, "Who are these people making us look bad, these . . . these *rabiz*, these FOBs."[16] And I realized, at that moment, that I had an obligation as someone born here, raised here, who spoke the language, who understood many aspects of the culture—it was incumbent upon me to be an advocate for these people. I could be that bridge. I had to be a spokesperson. They could not speak for themselves.

In his campaign for city clerk, Kassakhian relied heavily on outreach, absentee voting, ride-sharing, organizational support, internal financial support, and multimedia coverage. These strategies have proved effective in terms of Glendale's internally diverse yet highly mobilized immigrant-majority population. And this effectiveness, in part, has inculcated a sense of civic engagement among many Armenians in Glendale and Los Angeles more generally. According to data culled from the AAS, for example, over 28.4 percent of Armenians surveyed indicated that it was "very important" that those for whom they vote be Armenian, and 41.14 percent said this is "somewhat important."[17]

But Kassakhian's experiences also articulate an interesting duality in the motivations of ethnopolitical entrepreneurs: while they opportunistically employ (or, as Brubaker asserts, "summon") ethnicity to gain positions of political leadership, many often manifest a genuine concern for members of their co-ethnic populations from which they and their families come. While the first- and second-generation entrepreneurs may have distinct scopes, they share this duality. This duality proves quite beneficial when running for political office in ethnoburbs; however, when ethnopolitical entrepreneurs aspire to hold "higher" office, this duality can introduce some challenges.

In the 2016 election, Kassakhian had set himself a difficult task. He had already secured and held office in Glendale for over a decade. But he aspired to obtain higher political office. In order to accomplish this, he needed to gain the support of non-Armenians. Armenians in the San Fernando Valley continued to play an important role; however, Armenian voter support alone would not ensure his electoral success in the Forty-Third State Assembly District election—a district that includes Burbank, Glendale, La Crescenta–Montrose, La Cañada Flintridge, and other neighborhoods in Los Angeles County. Kassakhian ultimately lost his bid for the State District Assembly to Laura Friedman by a relatively wide margin—64.5 percent to 35.5 percent. Most of his voters were, in fact, Armenian. He failed to generate widespread support outside of the Armenian base. His campaign's results reinforce the oversized role of demographic concentration in ethnopolitical entrepreneurs' success, and they also reflect a potential challenge confronting those who wish to run for office on the state or national level: once associated with a specific ethnic population, ethnopolitical entrepreneurs run the risk of becoming labeled an "ethnic candidate," which can limit their ambitions to obtain higher office. While some do overcome this potential barrier, such as Congresswoman Chu from Monterey Park, Kassakhian's case manifests a precarious duality of the ethnopolitical entrepreneur—that is, driving a career by mobilizing co-ethnic voters and yet aspiring to hold political office beyond the ethnoburb.

Nonetheless, in Glendale, despite their generational differences, Manoukian, Kassakhian, and several other ethnopolitical entrepreneurs (such as Nazarian, Krekorian, and Hacopian) inverted traditional paradigms and introduced new modes by which immigrant political incorporation is taking place. Their outreach efforts increased Armenian immigrant voter registration and encouraged political participation among diverse newcomers as well as second-generation young adults. Because their target population was, largely, co-ethnic constituents, their campaigns often took place in the Armenian language and through ethnic media sources—which made proficiency in the English language an unnecessary part of newcomers' political incorporation. Ethnopolitical entrepreneurs' campaigns are, in this sense, an education in contextual knowledge and US political socialization. In fact, Manoukian's and Kassakhian's campaigns, which were motivated by the need for local co-ethnic representation, promoted greater local, civic awareness among newcomers as compared to second- or third-generation co-ethnic residents. Also, by referring to homeland and history, they rooted immigrants' transnational ties in the local and cultivated intra-ethnic cohesion (Appadurai 1996; Levitt and Jaworsky 2007; Waldinger 2012). In other words, ethnopolitical entrepreneurs "translate" how everyone within the community is affected by US legislation and policy. As another Armenian ethnopolitical entrepreneur from Iran, Vrej Agajanian, who gained office in 2017, in part, with the assistance of his Armenian-language television program, told me, "My program appeals to every Armenian because the subject matter is concentrated on political and social issues of the United States. . . . So everyone who is living here wants to listen because they will benefit. My point is, regardless of where you came from, everyone is living here, you have to know the rules and regulations here." And these outreach efforts have proved effective: according to data from the AAS, 52.2 percent of respondents state that they are "very interested" in politics and public affairs, while an additional 36.9 are "somewhat interested."[18]

This brief overview of Manoukian's and Kassakhian's elections reflects the importance of individual ethnopolitical entrepreneurs in the processes of political incorporation in contemporary US suburbs. Several preexisting factors converged to actualize the visions of these entrepreneurs—a strong sense of ethnic identity (albeit regionally diverse), the existence of opportunity structures, backlash from the established community, a naturalized population eligible to vote, and co-ethnic financial, organizational, and multimedia support. Despite the intra-ethnic diversity of the Armenian population (coming from Armenia, Iran, Iraq, Lebanon, Syria, the United States, and elsewhere), ethnopolitical entrepreneurs helped establish pathways through which Armenian newcomers and other co-ethnics could access and participate in their local political institutions. As an immigrant himself, Manoukian ran a campaign that resonated with the majority Armenian newcomer population in Glendale. As a second-generation immigrant, Kassakhian followed many of the same strategies but also expanded the demographic focus to include younger Armenian voters. Manoukian and Kassakhian represent an important evolution in US ethnic politics (particularly in specific urban ecologies, such as ethnoburbs). These suburban ethnopolitical entrepreneurs merge the political entrepreneur, whom John Mollenkopf identifies as an actor who seeks to establish "new governmental bases for exercising new powers" and is "looking for ways to use government authority or government revenues" (1983, 4–5), and the ethnicity entrepreneur, whom Philip Kasinitz describes as an actor who makes a "living by bridging the gap between the polity and the [ethnic] community" and "capitalize[s] on both the state's interest in supporting ethnic organizations and the needs of local politicians to make ties" to their co-ethnic populations (1992, 163–164).

Like other political entrepreneurs, ethnopolitical entrepreneurs within US ethnoburbs look for ways to use governmental authority or revenue; however, these political actors come from suburbs' ethnic populations. As such, they make their livings by bridging the institutional gap between the polity and their own ethnic populations. While the scholarship has traditionally understood political entrepreneurs and ethnicity entrepreneurs as distinct, the evolution of US suburbs has led to their convergence. This convergence is key in understanding the evolution of contemporary US politics. Ethnopolitical entrepreneurs rely on the co-ethnic constituents on behalf of whom they make sustained claims and reconfigure city authority. By doing so, these actors have transformed how and when many newcomers become politically incorporated. The presence of ethnopolitical entrepreneurs removes barriers to participation in US political institutions. These barriers typically include proficiency in the English language or familiarity with US political processes. In the case of Manoukian, himself a first-generation immigrant, he and his team ran a campaign targeting and relying on other immigrants. As such, ethnopolitical entrepreneurs, supported via local ethnic organizations and media, reflect a new phase in the evolution of US ethnic politics. They play an increasingly integral role in the mobilization of immigrants throughout the United States.

Nonetheless, ethnopolitical entrepreneurs cannot take demographic concentration or reactive ethnicity for granted. This chapter has outlined the conditions, actors, and strategies that gave rise to Glendale's political evolution. By taking advantage of significant demographic shifts, ethnopolitical entrepreneurs—not only those seeking office but also leaders from local Armenian organizations and media—devised creative strategies to mobilize and register prospective Glendale Armenian voters. However, like the residents of so many other multiethnic suburbs, the Armenians of Glendale are an intra-ethnically diverse and fractured population. They come from various countries of origin and bring distinct social remittances. How, then, did these actors construct a voting bloc out of a predominantly first-generation immigrant population? The next chapter explores how Manoukian, Kassakhian, and other Armenian ethnopolitical entrepreneurs in Glendale overcome internal fractures and "create constituents."

CREATING CONSTITUENTS

Constructivist Political Incorporation

Situated on over fifteen acres—or approximately four blocks—of Glendale's main thoroughfare, Brand Boulevard, the Americana at Brand is a high-end shopping mall and residential complex. It is also one of the most recognizable sites in the city. It hosts concerts, has a trolley car and a "dancing" water fountain, and, during the holiday shopping season, becomes a veritable winter wonderland (complete with a towering Christmas tree and artificial snow falling from the "sky"). Because it has become so popular, it may be hard to believe that, only ten years before I began my fieldwork, many Glendale residents resisted the shopping mall. They associated the developer, Rick Caruso and Caruso Affiliated, with another of Los Angeles's high-profile, traffic-generating shopping malls, the Grove. Sleepy, "boring" Glendale, whose economy was flagging in the early 2000s, residents believed, could not attract the sort of clientele Caruso had hoped would come flocking to the prospective mall.

Nonetheless, Caruso tenaciously pursued the project for nearly four years. He had to fight pitched legal battles with General Growth Properties, the owner of the other major mall in Glendale, the Glendale Galleria. To help overcome the challenges he confronted, Caruso sought community support in the form of a referendum (which consisted of three measures). And, to gain the support of the residents, he sought assistance from city officials, many of whom, by then, were Armenian.[1] Several Armenian ethnopolitical entrepreneurs agreed to work with Caruso. For the referendum, he brought on board Adrin Nazarian to act as the campaign manager and Eric Hacopian to work as a consultant. With the support of Armenian ethnopolitical entrepreneurs and, ultimately, Armenian voters, Caruso was able to realize his ambition for a high-end shopping mall in Glendale.[2] The Americana has now become one of Glendale's most popular (and lucrative) draws.

Nazarian explained to me why he and Hacopian became involved with the referendum vote and why, he felt, they were successful:

> There were something like twenty-some consultants working for Caruso. For Eric and me, this was not a onetime deal. This is a community that we care about, that we politically helped develop. . . . There was also a personal responsibility that Eric and I had to the community, to Glendale, to a lot of the elected [officials], whom we had already been helping to get elected, formulating policy, or moving the city forward. And also getting rid of the old barriers of the city. Because, you know, it was a very restrictive city, where a certain group controlled it and did not want anybody else to come in and have a say. And that's why it was very difficult for Armenians to get elected. As we changed that, we also wanted to help advance Glendale. And a lot of the residents, who were of that mindset, who had fled the Iranian and Lebanese revolutions for better and safer harbors, who had fled Soviet Bolshevism and lack of opportunity and killing of creativity and creative thinking, I think a lot of these things spoke to them. Why not advance the city!

The Americana is one of many examples that manifest Armenian ethnopolitical entrepreneurs' contributions to Glendale, even when those contributions may not prove immediately evident. Taking advantage of demographic concentration and backlash, Armenian ethnopolitical entrepreneurs played important roles in politically mobilizing and incorporating internally diverse Armenians. This mobilization, in turn, led to significant changes in the local political culture. And, as Nazarian explained to me, these changes have extended beyond Glendale's political institutions; in fact, they signified a larger socioeconomic evolution and reconfiguration of the suburb.

Still, because Armenians share the same ethnicity, it may be tempting to assume that the work of ethnopolitical entrepreneurs is quite easy; one may think that they merely invoke ethnicity and a co-ethnic voting bloc instantly forms. Other considerations compound this tempting oversimplification. For example, research consistently shows that race and ethnicity remain extremely important in determining voters' decisions (Wolfinger 1965; Collet 2005; Hajnal and Trounstine 2014). For this reason, it may seem somewhat intuitive that Armenians vote for other Armenians in electoral contests. Nonetheless, my fieldwork in Glendale made clear that mobilizing co-ethnics on the basis of shared ethnicity is not a simple task. Rather, I daily witnessed the challenges ethnopolitical entrepreneurs confront in creating voting blocs out of fractured co-ethnic populations.

FIGURE 15.   The Americana at Brand mall and residential complex in Glendale, California.

I met Anna in the Americana's Barnes and Noble's café, where we reminisced about Yerevan. We met toward the beginning of my fieldwork; I had only recently come back to the United States after spending an academic year teaching at the American University of Armenia. Anna, who had moved to Los Angeles from Armenia in 1997 at the age of twenty-six, was particularly enthused that I could communicate in Eastern Armenian. She and I chatted about current issues in Armenia. We had chatted for over an hour before it occurred to me that I should begin the interview. The conversation maintained an upbeat and positive tempo. However, when we spoke about Armenians' intra-ethnic diversity in Glendale, the tone shifted. Leaning closer to me, she whispered: "I don't like Armenians from *those* countries because they are way too adapted to Muslim countries. You know, when you look at their face, you never know what's going on behind [it]. In Hayastancis [Armenians from Armenia], I can see them, but in the others, it's different." Anna had strong opinions about what differentiates Armenians from distinct regional backgrounds. She implied that Armenians from "Muslim countries" manifest dishonesty, while Armenians from Armenia tend to be more straightforward. Anna articulated a common sentiment among Armenians from Armenia, particularly those who had moved to the United States as adults. And, in turn, Armenians from "Muslim countries" had quite a lot to say about Armenians from Armenia, as well.

During my fieldwork, I met with Shushan on several occasions. She and I would typically chat at a popular deli near the Americana. At the beginning of the Iranian Revolution in 1979, she moved to the United States at the age of thirty-three. Shushan came from the upper echelons of Iranian society. Like so many other Armenian newcomers who encountered different streams of Armenians for the first time, Shushan also struggled making sense of the different subgroups of Armenians in Glendale. After nearly thirty years of living in the United States, she still struggled with the different Armenians she encountered:

> We cannot digest them [Armenians from Armenia]. Is communism the reason, or, really, is that our nation and we are not? But I'm starting to analyze it, and I'm saying we are not [like that]. I'm saying we, Iranian Armenians, are real Armenians. We were brought to Iran from Armenia, and we started creating and we kept our morals and everything very high. These people, and actually Lebanese Armenians, they came from genocide, so they lost their identities somehow. But the ones inside, as my daughter says, they are leftover Turks and Russians. So I don't think they know what they are. . . . Parskahays [Armenians from Iran] are flexible because Iranians are flexible. This is very much Iranian influence. Parskahays are softer, more polite, and, how do I say, *hyuraser* [hospitable].

Shushan, usually quite composed, became noticeably flustered reflecting on the perceived differences among Armenians in Glendale and elsewhere in Greater Los Angeles. She acknowledged that, as an Iranian Armenian, she could not relate to Armenians from different backgrounds (particularly those from post-Soviet countries). For Shushan, Armenians who were exposed to communism and genocide had "lost" their identities, while Iranian Armenians had "kept" ethnic values and standards. Instead of focusing on common ancestry issues, she stressed the internal differences of Armenians based on their diverse backgrounds. Ironically, despite her conviction that Iranian Armenians were the "real Armenians," she also highlighted the influence of Iranian customs.

Anna and Shushan make clear some important internal fractures among Armenians in Glendale and elsewhere in Greater Los Angeles. Particularly among those from the first generation, country of origin plays an important role in determining not only how many Armenians think about themselves but also how they think of other Armenians. Perceived differences based on country of origin generate fractures and disagreements among the multilocal Armenians. These fractures often influence Armenians' decisions about where to live, how to socialize, or even whom to marry. As such, country of origin plays an important role in socially organizing many Armenians in Greater Los Angeles and, to an extent, in many other places throughout the diaspora. Still, regional origin is only one of many fault lines that generate schisms among Armenians. These fractures also relate to generation, educational attainment, and socioeconomic status. And these divisive fault lines exist among Armenians from the same country of origin, too.

I met Rubina at her husband's spacious office in downtown Glendale, where she told me about her journey to the United States.[3] Born in Tabriz but raised in Tehran, Rubina left Iran and came to the United States at the age of twenty-five in 1963. Initially, she worked in the Bay Area, but, after two years, she returned to Iran, where she, her husband, and their children remained for nearly twelve years. In 1977, she and her family returned to California for a brief visit. On this trip, some friends who had settled in Glendale encouraged Rubina and her husband to diversify their financial portfolio by purchasing a home in one of the city's hillside neighborhoods. Before returning to Iran, they took their friends' advice and bought a home on one of Glendale's more affluent streets. The following year, in December 1978, they returned to Glendale to spend the holidays in their new home. But escalating tensions (eventuating in the 1979 revolution) prompted them to remain in California.

Rubina recounted her early impressions of the Armenians she encountered from the Soviet Union and other Iranian Armenians from different socioeconomic backgrounds:

> The Persian Armenians, the Iranian Armenians, had kept their old, Armenian traditions. They were more religious, connected, attached to the church, and [they] dream[ed] of having their own land, someday, somehow, [and] visiting the homelands. These things didn't exist for the Armenians coming from [Soviet Armenia]. But, on the other hand, those coming from Soviet Armenia were—at least they would consider themselves—high-cultured. They were thinking that because they were all professors. . . . We used to make fun of them [for] that. When they introduced themselves, there [was] a long, long list of titles, like doctor professor researcher, I don't know, stuff like that. We were more modest. And there [was] something a little different. They were coming from Soviet culture, and they were all well educated. Among Iranian Armenians, most of them, I can say more than 60 percent of them, were coming from the rural areas after the revolution. So, when they opened their mouths, you [could] see they [were] speaking . . . dialects. I respect all the Armenian dialects. But when they opened their mouths, it was kind of with Persian words mixed with it.

Rubina reiterated many of Shushan's opinions about what distinguishes Iranian Armenians and "Soviet" Armenians. Both Shushan and Rubina stressed how Iranian Armenians preserve "Armenian culture" (or, for Shushan, "morals"). They also emphasized mannerisms, which they believed separated the two populations (characterizing Iranian Armenians as "softer, more polite" and "more modest," respectively). Rubina, however, also self-differentiated from other Iranian Armenians with whom she had come into contact. While Rubina's earlier migration drew from some of Iran's most elite circles, subsequent US legislation diversified the growing Iranian Armenian population coming to Los Angeles (see chapter 1). In our conversation, Rubina acknowledged the challenges she confronted communicating with the increasingly diverse Iranian Armenians, too. These reflections embody not only the collision of several historical Armenian diasporic nodes converging on one another for the first time but also the collision of different socioeconomic immigrants from the same countries of origin.

All of these internal fractures, which Anna, Shushan, and Rubina articulated to me, highlight the challenges ethnopolitical entrepreneurs must overcome in creating a sense of a single, unified group. Even within a single co-ethnic population, members do not organize organically or effortlessly based merely on shared ethnicity; in fact, as the impressions of Anna, Shushan, and Rubina make clear, quite the opposite phenomenon often manifests itself. In other words, shared ethnicity alone does not create a voting bloc. Rather, suburban immigrant political incorporation results from the work of ethnopolitical entrepreneurs trying to create cohesion among highly fragmented populations.

While undertaking fieldwork in Glendale, I gained firsthand insight into how ethnopolitical entrepreneurs navigate these challenges in their efforts to create a unified voting bloc. As a volunteer in Ardy Kassakhian's campaign office, I frequently interacted with his staff both in the office and on the campaign trail. They often shared stories with me about confronting and overcoming perceived intra-ethnic differences. For example, Sevana, who managed most of the other volunteers—delegating tasks, making telephone calls, organizing meetings, and managing personalities—shared stories of her various encounters, most pleasant, but some hostile. Although still quite young herself, she had already acquired a rich cache of experiences working in local suburban politics. In several instances, those with whom she interacted had confronted her based on her regional identity (she is a second-generation Iranian Armenian). Sevana recounted one of these exchanges:

> This one woman said, "I watch all these television programs where they are talking about politics. Why is that Parskahay [Iranian Armenian] woman call[ing] in and ask[ing] these questions about when do we vote, how do we vote?" And she goes off on this tangent about [how] Armenian women in Iran never had to work, [and] therefore they aren't educated and don't know how to vote or how to do anything. Therefore,

we should only canvass with Parskahays because they are dumb. . . . I said to her, "What difference does it make? At the end of the day, we've all been through a struggle—whatever country we come from. We've all survived. And now we're here as one community. If you can't think of us as one community, it's your fault!"

Sevana's story reflects two important realities for ethnopolitical entrepreneurs: (1) the resistance they encounter based on co-ethnics' diverse backgrounds and (2) the work they must do to overcome this internal fragmentation to create a voting bloc. Backlash has generated solidarity (or reactive ethnicity) among the diverse Armenians of Glendale; however, the perceived differences persist and, in some cases, preclude ethnopolitical entrepreneurs' efforts to mobilize and incorporate prospective constituents. Thus, in ethnoburbs, ethnopolitical entrepreneurs need not only spread the word and encourage voter participation; they must also devise creative strategies in constructing a unified voting bloc among such internally diverse co-ethnics (regionally, socioeconomically, and ideologically).

Chapter 3 explored what an ethnopolitical entrepreneur is; this chapter assesses how they politically incorporate newcomers and other co-ethnics. Ethnopolitical entrepreneurs rely heavily on ethnic membership to mobilize prospective co-ethnic constituents. But these co-ethnic constituents (and many of the other ethnopolitical entrepreneurs with whom they compete) understand ethnic membership in quite distinct, often contentious ways. Ethnopolitical entrepreneurs' specific approaches to constructivist ethnic politics (or, in Brubaker's [2004] framing, invocations of ethnicity) determine, in large part, their electoral successes or failures. In developing the constructivist scholarship, this chapter argues that, when applied to the work of ethnopolitical entrepreneurs in dynamic US ethnoburbs, constructivist ethnic politics acts not only as a gauge through which to measure changing ethnic demography and electoral results; it is also a socialization process through which many immigrants in suburbs become politically incorporated.

Suburban Immigrant Political Incorporation
Constructivist Theories of Ethnic Politics

Kanchan Chandra's *Constructivist Theories of Ethnic Politics* (2012) sheds light on studies of political incorporation in multiethnic suburbs. Although the model this volume presents pertains to changing ethnic demography and electoral politics, a constructivist approach to ethnic politics elucidates the incorporation processes through which ethnopolitical entrepreneurs create unified voting blocs.

Constructivist perspectives have become pervasive in the humanities and social sciences. Constructivism refers to the position that many things we perceive as "natural" result from human intervention or creation. In discussions about ethnic identities, constructivists typically argue against the "primordialist" notion that individuals or groups have a single, fixed ethnic identity (Geertz 1973; McKay 1982). Rather, constructivists believe that ethnic identities, which can change by human intervention or construction, are multiple (Suny 1999; Posner 2017).

In *Constructivist Theories of Ethnic Politics*, Chandra does *not* claim that ethnic identities are created "out of thin air" or that they are always fluid: "To say that ethnic identities are constructed is only to say that they can change, not that they always do. . . . Constructivist scholarship does not propose that such fluidity always exists or exists to the same degree. But it reminds us that fixity cannot be taken to be an intrinsic feature of ethnic identities but must be explained" (2012, 150–151). Similarly, in the context of ethnoburbs, ethnopolitical entrepreneurs do not create ethnic identities. In Glendale, Armenians have come to Los Angeles with a very strong sense of ethnic identity. And it is on this strong sense of ethnic identity that ethnopolitical entrepreneurs most centrally depend. However, Armenians' diverse histories in dispersion (see chapter 1) and diverse regional backgrounds have given rise to a broad range of interpretations of what it means to possess an Armenian ethnic identity. As such, a constructivist lens helps clarify how ethnopolitical entrepreneurs overcome internal cleavages and create voting blocs out of internally fragmented co-ethnic populations.

In a co-authored chapter from the same volume, Chandra and Cilanne Boulet argue that "Politicians fashion ethnic identity categories to propose to voters. Voters activate one of the ethnic identities from the set presented to them by politicians, resulting in an initial activated ethnic demography" (2012, 233).[4] They introduce a way of conceptualizing the broad range of possible activated ethnic demographies at a given time. Building on Chandra and Boulet's model, David D. Laitin and A. Maurits van der Veen argue that political entrepreneurs who identify as members of a specific ethnic identity win elections when they distribute political benefits (or "pork") to prospective voters (2012). Their model confirms James D. Fearon's (1999) theory that the politics of pork proves more beneficial when it is based on features that individuals cannot choose or change, such as ethnic membership. While "political benefits" typically relate to material items like jobs or subsidies, Laitin and van der Veen (2012, 357) note that the elective affinity between ethnicity and pork occurs even in the absence of the latter—that is, they argue that as long as membership in a particular population (or category)

yields some sort of benefit or reward (including a symbolic or status-based benefit), the affinity between ethnicity and voter support persists.

This finding reinforces the research highlighting the centrality of race and ethnicity in the position-taking behavior of many voters (Hajnal and Trounstine
2014). For Armenians in Greater Los Angeles, AAS data reinforce these findings:
among those surveyed, approximately 69.5 percent indicated either "very important" or "somewhat important" in response to the question "How important is it
for you that a candidate is Armenian?" In contrast, 42.8 percent self-identified as
"Democrat," while 17.8 percent self-identified as "Republican" (an additional
23.7% self-identified as "Independent").[5] These data suggest that, for Los Angeles
Armenian voters, ethnicity is significantly more influential than political party or
ideology. Nonetheless, while Armenian ethnopolitical entrepreneurs succeed by
invoking or summoning ethnicity (Brubaker 2004), they confront different interpretations of what it means to be Armenian among prospective voters. In addition,
Glendale's Armenian ethnopolitical entrepreneurs often compete against other
Armenian ethnopolitical entrepreneurs, who are also running on the basis of
shared ethnicity. They put forward competing sets of attributes of an Armenian
ethnic identity repertoire. As such, shared ethnicity alone does not win elections;
instead, political candidates must calibrate (and continually recalibrate) according
to the prospective constituents they seek to incorporate politically.

Barbara Ballis Lal argues, "Ethnic identity entrepreneurs representing sub-
ordinate/minority groups acquire a very extensive power by virtue of their office and professional credentials which enables them to construct and enforce
their specific conceptions of what ethnic identity is and the cultural requirements
this essentialized identity entails" (1997, 396). In contemporary suburban ethnic politics, ethnopolitical entrepreneurs cannot rely on professional credentials
to impose essentialized identities on to co-ethnic constituents. Instead, diverse
candidates participate in dynamic interactions with co-ethnic constituents, in
which different attributes of ethnicity are continually recalibrated.

Building on the constructivist model of van der Veen and Laitin (2012), the
remainder of this chapter unpacks the strategies ethnopolitical entrepreneurs
use to secure an optimal winning coalition (or voting base) among co-ethnic
constituents. The ways in which they invoke ethnicity have electoral implications. And this is especially true when multiple Armenian political candidates
run against one another in the same election. In these dynamic contests, ethnopolitical entrepreneurs put forward different interpretations of what it means to
be Armenian. By mobilizing support based on competing repertoires of Armenian ethnic identity, ethnopolitical entrepreneurs in Glendale accomplish two
tasks at once—namely, they construct unified voting blocs and, in the process,

politically incorporate immigrants into the city's political institutions. These processes involve not only the political candidates themselves but also those with whom they work, such as people from ethnic organizations, ethnic media, and candidates' teams (strategists, canvassers, fundraisers, and others).

The Processes of Constructivist Ethnic Politics

Drawing from Chandra and Boulet's larger model, van der Veen and Laitin (2012, 279–285) include the following processes in evaluating how ethnic identities change over time: (1) attribute replacement, (2) change in salience, and (3) attribute recombination.[6] The first process involves a minority population acquiring attributes of the majority population (Moscow Armenians, for example, "passing" as Russian).[7] The second process involves circumstantial differences bringing about increased salience of specific attributes. In the case of Armenians, a significant contest of attribute salience has resulted from the multipolar migration of Armenians and resettlement into a single site in Glendale (chapter 1). The third process involves the creation of new categories through the grouping of a specific set of attributes on one or more dimensions. This process involves populations taking on new categories over time or in response to specific events—for example, after the fall of the Soviet Union, the category of "Soviet Armenian" became "Armenian." While the analysis disaggregates these processes, all three take place simultaneously and influence electoral politics.

Awareness of these changes to ethnic demography proves important in how prospective ethnopolitical entrepreneurs organize campaigns. On the basis of the information they have about co-ethnic voters, ethnic candidates decide specifically what sets of attributes across dimensions they will activate in their respective campaigns. For this reason, successful ethnopolitical entrepreneurs (like other elected officials) must continually revisit and recalibrate the specific attributes they manifest and promote.

ATTRIBUTE REPLACEMENT

Attribute replacement occurs when a minority population invests in attributes of the majority population. By acquiring these majority population attributes, ethnic populations are able to "pass" (van der Veen and Laitin 2012, 280). But, by acquiring too many majority attributes themselves, ethnopolitical entrepreneur candidates risk losing co-ethnic voters. While Armenians may negatively view the loss of certain Armenian attributes, they are less likely to condemn the acquisition of certain American attributes. As a result, candidates maintain a delicate balance between appearing sufficiently American to Americans and sufficiently

Armenian to Armenians. As one city council member, Ara Najarian, shared in a personal interview:

> In my campaign, it was very important to me, and not just for electoral value but for societal value, for me to forcefully contradict that. So I talked about my Armenian dad, who fought on Okinawa in the United States Marine Corps. And I showed my Cub Scout experience, to grab the racists by the lapels and say, "My name ends in 'ian' and I am every bit just as American as you, and if you don't like it, you don't understand what America is all about." So that was actually a big part of what we tried to do in the campaign.

By incorporating certain traditions associated with the mainstream United States (service in the US Marine Corps, membership in the Cub Scouts), Najarian deliberately publicized American attributes to emphasize his concomitant American and Armenian loyalties. He also promoted other non-descent-based attributes, which distinguished him from other Armenian candidates. For example, Najarian was the only Armenian elected official in Glendale who, at the time of my fieldwork, was from the Republican Party.[8] Accordingly, despite depending on Armenian voter support, his political beliefs did not always cater to many Armenian newcomers (see chapter 5). In our conversation, he spoke extensively about the relationships he had formed with several non-Armenians and how necessary they were to win "higher" political seats than those on the local municipal level (city council, city clerk, etc.). Without "replacing" at least some Armenian attributes with American attributes, ethnopolitical entrepreneurs face challenges obtaining higher seats in electoral politics. However, by "passing," candidates can acquire votes among nonethnic constituents. Thus, acquiring, activating, and publicizing majority attributes can lead to increased support.

But these attributes need to be believable; therefore, the entrepreneur stands to benefit by embodying the attributes projected. Najarian, who, during my fieldwork, was one of the only elected officials of Armenian descent in Glendale to receive support from both Armenians and non-Armenians, shared the following:

> I was very Anglo growing up. . . . So I was kind of like your all-American kid growing up with a weird name. You know, captain of the football team, swim team, Little League. . . . [But] I'm a true Armenian American. I think I have strong ties to Armenians, and I think I can relate to Hayastancis. But I've got strong American roots, where I can relate to the old white Republicans. So I do play that. But that's just me. Forget the political—I still have those two spheres of life.

To be sure, the ethnopolitical entrepreneurs who are born in the United States and yet grow up in traditional Armenian households find they can handily replace attributes. Their ability to "pass" as either American or Armenian gives them an advantage over more recently arrived entrepreneurs as well as second- or third-generation Armenians. But they also understand the potential precariousness of replacing too many attributes and relying too heavily on non-Armenian voters. In speaking of Armenian organizations' support of his campaigns, Najarian noted this delicate balance: "By definition, the more Anglo support I get, the less relevant their support becomes. I mean, their support is still important, but it's not the only way to do it." By replacing too many attributes—and getting "more Anglo support"—Najarian ran the risk of losing some support among Armenians and Armenian organizations in Glendale.

Second- or third-generation Armenians quite often need to "validate" their Armenianness in exchange for votes. Because these political actors possess so many majority population attributes and so few ethnic population attributes, they acquire and activate commonsensical attributes among all the internally diverse Armenians. Paul Krekorian, for example, whose family has lived in the United States for multiple generations, spoke of the challenges encountered when dealing with Armenian media. In an interview with Krekorian and his chief of staff, the latter described to me how ethnicity fragmented one campaign:

> [An agent in the media] was very overt about him [Krekorian] not being 100 percent Armenian. That was not even a question. And the language part was also an issue. And he continued this beyond the election race. It boiled down to attacks based on policy positions. There was a ban on gay marriage on the ballot . . . so [agents] spun it that [the candidate] wants to teach homosexuality to kindergarteners. It was stuff you can't even imagine. So [agents] would use these irrational, obscure policy positions to hammer him, and say, "This is why he's bad for us. This is why you need to vote for [his opponent]."

Attribute replacement can cut both ways in terms of influencing electoral results. In the example given, some actors involved with media attacked Krekorian for not possessing a sufficient number of attributes identifiable as "Armenian."

CHANGE IN SALIENCE

For many ethnopolitical entrepreneur candidates, constructing a sense of cohesion means selecting and projecting an optimal set of basic attributes.[9] Instead of imposing a new set of attributes, the main thrust of their campaigns often involves activating attributes that form a consensus among the largest number of people who self-identify as Armenian. As van der Veen and Laitin argue, "Every population has some number of commonsensical dimensions—but from this commonsensical set, some dimensions may become activated to serve as the basis of activated categories in some societies, while others may not" (2012, 281). For many of those who have worked on campaigns, finding common ground means activating something as basic as a common Armenian surname. This "stripping down" of attributes and increasing the salience of specific attributes creates more cohesion among an internally diverse population. Areen Ibranossian, who has worked extensively in canvassing efforts, shared his experience:

> You definitely have to tailor your message to your audience. So, as an Armenian from Iran, I had a much easier time with people from Iran, based on dialect, based on culture, there was a lot more familiarity. So I could breeze through that quicker. There was a lot more trust between me and them. They would look at me, and say, "He's one of us," and feel a lot more comfortable. With Armenians from Armenia, or from Lebanon, or from other Arabic countries, there was a bit of a language barrier because of the Western dialects. And somewhat of a cultural difference. . . . But, ultimately, the main message was, "We need someone in our community to represent us." And once you got past the trust issues and the dialect issues, and you stripped it down to that message of "Look, there's no other person with an 'ian' name on that council . . . ," they understood that. . . . And so that was the main tool. . . . Once you got down to that, people were on board.

Ibranossian acknowledged that he had to look past the differences he felt between himself and those with whom he spoke. Because he is himself an Iranian Armenian, he made a conscious effort to avoid issues, which lacked salience among other Armenian subgroups. The process of changing the salience of specific attributes helps explain the success of the ethnopolitical entrepreneurs and those with whom they work. But Ibranossian's experiences also confirm Laitin and van der Veen's findings that ethnic membership, even in the absence of material incentives, acts as a political benefit and generates support among diverse coethnic voters ("'We need someone in our community to represent us'"). This sort of symbolic capital proves particularly effective when only one Armenian candidate participates in an election.

In addition, the country of Armenia has become a salient attribute of Armenian identity. Prior to Armenia's independence from the Soviet Union in 1991, many diasporic Armenians did not consider Armenia a central dimension of their ethnic identities. However, since the country's independence, the attribute salience of Armenia has heightened considerably. In my fieldwork interviews, the emotional or symbolic attachment to Armenia recurred. This is likely true especially in Los Angeles and Glendale, as migration has overlapped with the country's independence, political realignment (Armenia's Velvet Revolution in 2018), and ongoing war with Azerbaijan in Artsakh/Nagorno-Karabakh (1988–1994, 2020). As such, among Glendale's internally diverse population, Armenia and Artsakh/Nagorno-Karabakh have emerged as salient attributes that unite Armenians from various places. And this salience has strong electoral implications. For example, a Los Angeles–based Armenian newspaper's general editor stressed the centrality of the national cause:

> [For instance,] if I'm talking about Electric Yerevan [the mass protests in Armenia's capital in 2015 against rising electricity costs], I'm talking about the importance of the aspirations for those residing in Armenia, but also making sure that people sitting here know why it's significant for that [event] to prevail. Because it's a national agenda that we're pursuing. And our mission has always been to advance that national agenda. Otherwise, my existence as a diasporan is stupid. I'm just someone of Armenian origin living in Los Angeles. . . . So the way we speak to everyone is that everything is based on this national ideal.

For this Armenian media personality, the attribute of national allegiance had especially powerful salience. This change in salience has helped unify an otherwise internally fragmented population. While Armenians come to Glendale from a diverse range of geopolitical origins, the emerging salience of the attributes of Armenia and Artsakh/Nagorno-Karabakh expands readership and influences a growing electoral constituency. The same newspaper also runs political ads and hosts ethnopolitical entrepreneurs for interviews. Once the set of attributes is operationalized, it has political incorporative potential.

But efforts to change the salience of specific attributes can generate its own sort of backlash (and political disincorporation). In my interviews and fieldwork, one divisive theme that recurred related to how leaders speak about "traditional Armenian" values (or attributes). These "traditional" or "secondary" attributes were typically related to gender, sexuality, masculinity, and domesticity. Chandra distinguishes "basic" and "secondary" attributes: "I define the set of 'basic' attributes that characterize individuals as that set of attributes which we take as commonsensically given, even though they can in principle be decomposed further. 'Secondary' attributes, by contrast, are transparent constructs of basic attributes which, even though they function as the raw materials for categories at a higher level of analysis, can be disaggregated into their basic components" (2012, 106–107). During their campaigns, Armenian candidates have been attacked by opponents for failing to embody secondary attributes, perhaps reminiscent of values

espoused by specific generational cohorts. Given the fluidity of Armenian suburban identity, these contentious attacks can become rather embittered over specific attributes. Nayiri Nahabedian, an Armenian ethnopolitical entrepreneur
from Lebanon, understands these dynamics very well.

Growing up, Nahabedian and her family moved several times; they left Lebanon
for Boston when Nahabedian was in the sixth grade but returned when she was in
the eighth grade. They then returned to Boston, where she and her family remained
until her senior year of high school. When she was a senior, they relocated to Glendale. Her parents felt an affinity to Southern California, for, according to Nahabedian, it more closely resembled Lebanon than did Massachusetts. Having spent
a considerable amount of time in the more deeply rooted Armenian community
of Boston (Watertown), Nahabedian found the Glendale Armenian experience
unique: "Armenians were seen as a positive thing [in Boston], and we were rare,
you know. And we weren't rare or positive in Glendale." After inuring herself to
this bit of "culture" shock, she graduated from Glendale High School and then attended Glendale Community College for two years before transferring to UCLA.

Later, while pursuing a master of social work at UCLA, Nahabedian met one
of governor Pete Wilson's staff at a National Association of Social Workers legislative day event; this staff person happened to be an Armenian woman.[10] This
encounter inspired Nahabedian to pursue policy issues in her personal career.
But Nahabedian wanted to work in policy reform (or "behind the scenes," as she
told me); she was less interested in holding political office. Nonetheless, she became friends with other Armenian ethnopolitical entrepreneurs—in particular,
Eric Hacopian, Adrin Nazarian, and Paul Krekorian—through an Armenian
young professionals group, the Armenian General Benevolent Union Young Professionals. Nahabedian cultivated these ties, even though, at the time, she still
did not aspire to hold political office. Hacopian encouraged Nahabedian to participate in various political actors' campaigns, such as fundraising, phone bank-
ing, and data collection. Thus, in the late 1990s and early 2000s, she acquired
considerable grassroots experience. During this time, Nahabedian became involved in the campaigns of Adam Schiff, Scott Wildman, Krekorian, and others.
She also worked closely with the Armenian National Committee of America
(ANCA) and Armenian media to promote Armenian initiatives and candidates.
Throughout this period, she remained committed to policy reform and grassroots initiatives, but, as before, she resisted running for political office.

In 2005, however, Nahabedian wanted to support a newly formed Glendale
commission—the Commission on the Status of Women. From among the many
applicants, Glendale's city council (on which Rafi Manoukian held a seat) appointed Nahabedian to this commission. At the same time, she decided to run for

FIGURE 16.   Portrait of Nayiri Nahabedian.

Glendale's board of education. In 2007, she successfully secured a seat and, since then, has remained a board member of the Glendale Unified School District.

In 2010, Nahabedian ran for the Forty-Third District's assembly seat. She ran against another Armenian, Chahe Keuroghelian, and a non-Armenian, Mike Gato. In the campaign, Keuroghelian used ethnic media to attack Nahabedian because she was divorced and childless. He attempted to activate a series of attributes associated with what he claimed were "traditional Armenian" identity markers. The attributes of unmarried (divorced) and childless were stressed to disqualify (or restrict) Nahabedian's categorical Armenian ethnicity. She articulated these dynamics to me:

> Try running without being married or not having kids! Oh! . . . They like their boys more than they like their girls. And there was hostility toward me. If you have me and you have him, the two Armenians, there was hostility. And there was another Hayastanci woman who would be on

TV and just say crazy things like I left my kids in an orphanage in Armenia. Or, I didn't color my hair back then, so callers would call in and say
something like, "Give her ten bucks so she can color her hair." And there
was an underlying curiosity as to whether I was gay or lesbian.

On this and other campaigns, Nahabedian encountered hostility from other Armenians based on her gender and appearance. Because she was an unmarried
woman, some Armenians also openly interrogated her sexuality. The salience of
attributes she stressed, as a woman ethnopolitical entrepreneur—her level of education, independence, and professional success—contended with the salience of
the attributes her co-ethnic opponent stressed, based on his beliefs that Armenian
women should be married and have children. Her opponent's effort to restrict this
change reflects the contentiousness of processes involved in identity reconfiguration. While successful in several local elections, the effort to change the operative
repertoire split Armenians. In the 2010 Forty-Third District election, the divided
Armenian population failed to rally a strong Armenian voter turnout and secure
the nomination. As a result, both Armenian candidates were soundly defeated.[11]

ATTRIBUTE RECOMBINATION

As ethnopolitical entrepreneurs activate specific attributes of an ethnic identity
repertoire in order to influence electoral results and facilitate immigrant political incorporation, they can also combine a new set of attributes to mobilize co-
ethnic constituents. They often rely on commonsensical (or "basic") attributes
recognizable to most individuals, but string together or combine them with "secondary" attributes to reconfigure ethnic identity dimensions. In the process, they
must work with or compete against others who are themselves activating categories of membership. In addition to ethnic political candidates, members of ethnic
organizations or media also participate in attribute recombination. While research has demonstrated that ethnic organizations do not inhibit political incorporation (Portes, Escobar, and Arana 2008), my fieldwork suggests that they, in
fact, accelerate it. What Timothy L. Smith wrote of ethnic organizations in the
1970s applies to Glendale Armenians today: "Ethnic organizations coalesced out
of both economic and psychic need and found meanings for personal and communal life in the cultural symbols and the religious ideas that their leaders believed were marks of a shared inheritance and, hence, of a common peoplehood.
Both the structure and culture of these emerging ethno-religious groups helped
participants compete more advantageously with members of other groups" (1978,
1168; quoted in Bakalian and Bozorgmehr 2009, 98). Complementing the work of
co-ethnic political candidates in ethnoburbs, ethnic organizational actors recombine and synthesize diverse basic and secondary attributes to attract inter-

nally diverse newcomers. By recombining attributes, Armenian organizational leaders (like political candidates) remain "representative" of the internally diverse co-ethnic population—or, at least, of an optimal winning coalition.

In terms of promoting Armenian-related causes and political candidates, the ANCA is a particularly influential organization in California and, more generally, the United States (Gregg 2002). As a grassroots political organization, its goals and priorities often dovetail with those of various Armenian political candidates. In fact, Manoukian, the ethnopolitical entrepreneur who helped run the first successful Armenian voter-based campaign in 1999, had worked for this organization for several years before launching his own political career (see chapter 3). Functioning in ways similar to political candidates, the ANCA strives to affect local, state, and national legislation. They also must adapt to changes (or recalibrate attributes) over time. In 2012, the ANCA launched an initiative, HyeVotes, for the primary purpose of registering Armenians to vote during campaign periods in which the ANCA believes Armenians have a stake. While the ANCA did this before 2012, HyeVotes has enabled the organization to focus more energy on voter registration and political participation. According to Nora Hovsepian, the chair of the ANCA Western Region, HyeVotes has registered over twenty-five thousand new Armenian voters (from a personal interview with Hovsepian). During my fieldwork, Armenian political candidates consistently admitted that they no longer dedicated as much energy to outreach among Armenians, as that had become the domain of the ANCA's subsidiary, HyeVotes. Over time, Armenian political organizations and entrepreneurs have formed an uneven and, at times, vaguely symbiotic relationship. For this symbiosis to actualize the stated goals, both types of ethnopolitical entrepreneur—that is, political candidates and ethnic organizations—must activate a similar set of attribute values for the ethnic identity repertoire of "Armenian."

As Armenians entered Los Angeles in greater numbers after several international upheavals in Iran, Iraq, Lebanon, and the former Soviet Union (see chapter 1), the ANCA has also changed the salience of specific activated attributes. Hovsepian of the ANCA articulated to me the early identity repertoire: "The American Armenian community was not very politicized at that time [pre-1970s]; it was for self-preservation, maintaining the identity, language, et cetera. There wasn't a lot of political activism." Working with the ANCA for multiple decades, Hovsepian has witnessed the evolution of the organization's strategies based on the evolving dynamics among the Armenians of Greater Los Angeles (including Glendale). In the early 1970s, outreach involved commonsensical attributes—such as maintaining Armenian language proficiency. But new waves of Armenians forced organizations to add and recombine attribute values, including political activism, to the existing operative repertoire. Hovsepian summed up this evolution:

We have this amalgam of different elements in our community, and this has shaped how our organization has functioned. So with the ANCA, originally, it was almost exclusively Genocide recognition, but, as the community [in Los Angeles] started to evolve, we started to evolve beyond Genocide recognition. We started seeking solution and reparation. And when Armenia became independent in 1991, it needed support from the diaspora. . . . One of our organizational priorities is also to help and support the development and safety of Armenia. And that's through lobbying of foreign aid and just Armenianness about Armenia. And then when Artsakh [Nagorno-Karabakh], when that war happened from 1991 to 1994, again, the same thing—there was this uprising in nationalism to join the fight, not literally, but with support. So that's our third priority—seeking the independence and security of Artsakh. And the fourth priority has been the community mobilization, community development, community organizing. So that falls into the local realm.

Hovsepian explained to me how, in Los Angeles, Armenian ethnopolitical entrepreneurs add or recombine attributes in strategic ways that prove maximally conducive to electoral success and political incorporation, which, in turn, affects the amount of influence the ANCA has with both Armenian and non-Armenian elected officials. Through these constructivist strategies, they reconfigure ethnic identity repertoires, create voting blocs, and help "their" candidates win elections. In Glendale, these processes have meant continually recalibrating an evolving and fluid collective ethnic identity. Over the course of several decades, ANCA members and Armenian elected officials have added and recombined attributes that relate to Armenian genocide recognition, the Republic of Armenia, and Artsakh/Nagorno-Karabakh. These recalibrations have played important roles in constructing "groupness" (Brubaker 2002) or voting blocs among the internally diverse Armenian population and incorporating them into local political institutions. Furthermore, by recalibrating based on changes to ethnic demography and appealing to the evolving Armenian population, electorally successful ethnopolitical entrepreneurs, in turn, create new policies and influence municipal institutions on behalf of their co-ethnic populations.

It is worthwhile to note, too, the other side of ethnopolitical entrepreneurs' constructivist strategies—namely, what they leave out of their campaigns. Since they attempt to engage an optimal winning coalition among internally diverse Armenians, they selectively choose from various ethnicity-related attributes (or widely accepted, "basic" attributes). At the same time, they typically avoid divisive policy or ideological positions. Nonetheless, like the co-ethnic constituents on whom they rely, ethnopolitical entrepreneurs inhabit a broad ideological spectrum. By mobilizing on the basis of ethnicity (or specific Armenian-related causes), they can sometimes seek and receive support from voters whose policy agendas may not align with their own. I return to this potentiality in chapter 5, but, at the moment, it is worth keeping in mind the role of de-emphasizing or avoiding altogether certain attributes in these processes of immigrant political incorporation.

A New Generation of Voters

When we met, Marine had recently changed jobs. She had been one of very few Armenian school principals in Glendale. But, after receiving an offer to become the director of curriculum and instruction for a school district in Los Angeles, she seized the opportunity.

Marine was born in Iran. Her family decided to immigrate to Armenia during the 1979 revolution. At sixteen years of age, she moved with her family to California. By the time she came to the United States, she had spent her life almost evenly split between Iran and Soviet Armenia. When I asked her if she identified as an Iranian Armenian, an Armenian from Armenia, an Armenian American, or something else, she said: "People make [differences] visible. Personally, I don't see any difference—Armenian is Armenian. We have so many things we do—it doesn't matter where we come from. Whether we came from Ethiopia or Kuwait, we do exactly the same things. We have similar passions. We have similar mentalities. But the way we treat each other, we make differences seem more prominent." Unlike Anna, Shushan, Rubina, and many other first-generation Armenians with whom I spoke during my fieldwork, Marine and her peers tend to see past internal distinctions. Instead, she highlights the artificiality of the categories and essentializes a new, pan-Armenian identity, one in which everyone shares "similar passions" and "mentalities." The change in ethnic demography—from country of origin to pan-ethnic identity—reflects the transformative processes among multi-origin immigrants as they evolve into a new diaspora.

But this orientation also reflects the ethnic socialization (or "ethnicization") processes taking place in contemporary US ethnoburbs. Ewa Morawska describes ethnicization as a by-product of "the lengthening sojourn of transatlantic migrants, growing intermarriage, the purchase of homes, the learning of (some) English, and the bearing of children in the new country, [which] caused immigrants to develop local, American attachments and interests and to assume (not unproblematic) ethnicized identities as Hungarian Americans, Italian Americans, Lithuanian Americans, and Polish Americans" (2001, 187). The framing of ethnicization also explains the fluid and dynamic understandings of ethnic identity in contemporary US urban and suburban spaces. In addition, it includes the construction of new ethnic identities while in the United States. Armenian ethnopolitical entrepreneurs capitalize on the fluidity of changing ethnic demography or identity among their prospective constituents. While several first-generation immigrants participate in boundary-making activities, many later-generation immigrants strive to eliminate those boundaries. For example, another Iranian Armenian, who migrated as a fourteen-year-old in 1986, articulated this perception quite succinctly: "I just say I'm Armenian. I was born in Iran, but it's not a part of my identity." Unlike immigrants who had spent a larger part of their lives in their countries of origin, those who came during childhood or were born in the United States rarely stressed internal differences as important. Glendale's ethnopolitical entrepreneurs, who run campaigns on the basis of shared ethnicity, are not responsible for generational ethnicization, but, by stringing together attributes resonant among all Armenians, their efforts and visibility facilitate the process.

Younger first and second-generation Glendale Armenians often spoke of feeling connected to US society and its institutions. Living in an ethnoburb, where they participate directly in the city's politics, many younger immigrants (or 1.5-generation) and second-generation Armenians confessed that they embrace American influence. One respondent from Lebanon, who moved to the United States at the age of fifteen in 1986, shared his experiences with me: "I feel a lot more Americanized now, and I don't think of it as a bad thing. . . . When I was in Lebanon, we looked at Arabic as a [different] culture, so we'd rather speak Armenian. But at least here we don't look at American society in the same way. We've kind of embraced it because of the opportunities it gave us. I didn't forget my [Armenian] identity, but I'm a lot more Americanized because of the culture. And I like it!" While older generations stress country of origin among Armenians, 1.5-generation and second-generation immigrants forge a pan-ethnic identity, one rooted in the fusion between American and Armenian. In many ways, the second generation is repeating the same processes of their parents by replacing country of origin with the United States as an important category of membership. Like the respondent from Iran who conceded the influence of Iran on her Armenian identity, 1.5-generation and later-generation Los Angeles Armenians deconstruct their parents' boundaries and create new ones that blend American and pan-Armenian identity markers. Future ethnopolitical entrepreneurs, undoubtedly, will continue factoring these dynamics when running campaigns in Glendale.

A constructivist model thus captures the fluidity and complexity of processes of political incorporation within many of the United States' multiethnic suburbs. As this chapter has argued, constructivist models can illuminate not only how ethnic demography or identity changes over time but also how immigrant political incorporation in US suburbs takes place. While Glendale Armenians consist of a single ethnic population from multiple origins, the same model can explain more heterogeneous demographies, such as Black Americans, Asian Americans, Pacific Islanders, or Latinos. Among these diverse populations, different ethnopolitical entrepreneurs emerge to construct and represent prospective constituents. However, they must distinguish themselves from other ethnopolitical entrepreneurs. This urge creates a competition for "authenticity." The attributes they string together have direct electoral implications. By activating the "right" combination of attributes, ethnopolitical entrepreneur candidates incorporate immigrants into US political institutions, win political office, and, eventually, remake the municipal institutions.

By effectively employing constructivist ethnic political incorporation, Glendale's ethnopolitical entrepreneurs have overcome perceived internal differences and stratifications. And, in the process, Glendale's Armenians achieved a nearly unprecedented level of electoral incorporation in less than a single generation. But political incorporation does not inherently engender feelings of inclusion. And, in terms of newcomers' feelings of inclusion or empowerment, several other aspects of a suburb's administration, such as its police, schools, and bureaucracies also play important roles in the experiences and feelings of newcomers. Chapter 5 shifts the focus of this story to some of the shortcomings that can occur as a result of or in connection with the emergence of ethnopolitical entrepreneurs in US ethnoburbs.

5

IS POLITICAL INCORPORATION ENOUGH?

Racial and Ethnic Suburban Politics

Tamar invited me to her elegant home in one of northern Glendale's well-to-do neighborhoods.[1] Over coffee, she told me how she had ended up in Glendale. In 1963, Tamar moved from Iran to Washington, DC to join her husband, Ruben, who was enrolled at Howard University. Tamar planned on pursuing a graduate degree; however, after her husband completed his studies, he took a job in Tehran. Consequently, by 1975, Tamar and her family had returned to Iran, where the economy, still under the shah, was booming. Back in Tehran, Tamar enrolled her daughter in an American school. Tamar herself began working as a researcher at a center associated with the University of Tehran. Although her move back to Iran initially proved seamless, after a few years, sensing the country's political instability, Tamar and her daughter returned to the United States in January 1979—this time, to Connecticut. After enrolling her daughter in a boarding school, Tamar boarded a flight back to Iran. During the flight, however, the plane made a detour and landed in Athens, Greece. In Athens, the pilot announced that the passengers had to disembark, as the airport in Tehran had closed on account of Ruhollah Khomeini's return. Stranded in Greece for three weeks, Tamar eventually found a flight back to Iran via Paris. She and Ruben collected their things and fled the country promptly thereafter.

Searching for a new home, they chose Glendale because of its growing Armenian population. Although Tamar had lived in the United States for nearly thirteen years, she had not, in DC, experienced firsthand prejudice based on her ethnicity or immigrant background. However, in Glendale, she has at times

122

found herself a target of discrimination. She recounted to me one encounter in a local supermarket:

> Maybe it was five or six years ago. I was still working. Here I'm coming with my shopping cart. Now I don't remember what was my groceries. Maybe it was too much. You see, Americans, they have these negative feelings about Armenians. I don't remember, really. The part that really bothered me—it was a young guy and a girl, maybe husband, wife, boyfriend, I don't know. It was a young couple in front of me. Here I am [at the checkout counter] putting my stuff in the line, I'm in line, and they are before, and I'm putting it here. And the guy turns back and tells me, "Here, in the US, we say excuse me." Oh my God. It was like boiling water. I got so upset, I could not even answer this guy. And then, I don't know how the conversation ended, but I said I'd been in this country for thirty years. And the guy turned back and said, "Your accent doesn't show that." I was so upset. I didn't even look at how much was my bill.

By working hard for several decades, Tamar and Ruben have achieved a high quality of life. In addition, they live in Glendale, where Armenians constitute a plurality of the overall population and occupy most elected positions. Nonetheless, unprovoked hostility, like what Tamar experienced in the supermarket, continues to make even the most well-established suburban immigrants feel as though they somehow do not belong. Encounters like the one Tamar recounted remind us that, even in places like Glendale, where Armenians fought and overcame several barriers from the 1980s to the early 2000s (see chapter 2), racial and ethnic minorities can still be made to feel like outsiders.[2]

When talking to Armenians in Glendale, I found that a strong sense of political or social inclusion did not always exist despite co-ethnics' high level of electoral success. While many acknowledged the importance of voting co-ethnics into office, they also confessed that these political accomplishments had symbolic rather than practical significance. Because Glendale's Armenian ethnopolitical entrepreneurs had reallocated so many resources on behalf of their co-ethnic constituents, it surprised me that so many voters said that their political incorporation did not necessarily correlate with a sense of inclusion or belonging.

This chapter anticipates and qualifies the potential assumption that high levels of immigrant political incorporation and co-ethnic electoral success may result in some sort of multiethnic suburban utopia. In fact, immigrant political incorporation—even at the level the Armenians of Glendale have achieved it—does not necessarily result in newcomer voters feeling a sense of belonging. As Tamar's experience in the grocery story reflects, members of politically dominant ethnic populations can easily become targets of ethnic or racial discrimination in their suburban communities.

While scholars have confirmed that experiences of xenophobia and discrimination—such as that described by Tamar—influence immigrants' sense of inclusion (Kitchen, Williams, and Gallina 2015), this chapter adds to this research by looking at some other, less explored areas to explain why, even in ethnoburbs, political and electoral incorporation "is not enough" (Browning, Marshall, and Tabb 1990; Burns 2006). This chapter unpacks three challenges that ethnopolitical entrepreneurs either do not solve or may, in fact, introduce. First, the chapter investigates Armenians' representation in the city's municipal workforce. As the scholarship on bureaucratic incorporation has demonstrated, newcomers' perceptions of inclusion into the polity often depend on the municipal workforce's ability to engage with immigrants. A disconnect can therefore arise where significant disparities exist between the municipal workforce and the city's demographic composition. Given the gradual nature of municipal career employment, US cities can have both high levels of immigrant political electoral success and relatively low levels of bureaucratic representation, particularly at senior-level positions. By analyzing Glendale's municipal workforce composition, this chapter considers the implications of Armenians' relative absence from many key positions in the city's bureaucratic workforce.

Second, the chapter examines another reason ethnopolitical entrepreneurs do not always bring their voters a sense of political belonging or inclusion in the polity—namely, symbolic capital. As noted in chapter 4, ethnic membership and the symbolic or status-based significance of co-ethnic representation are key political benefits ethnopolitical entrepreneurs offer prospective voters in their campaigns. Still, while ethnopolitical entrepreneurs' successes do lead to significant and practical reallocations, some ethnic political actors also take advantage of the symbolic capital newcomers associate with co-ethnic representation. Because ethnopolitical entrepreneurs mobilize newcomers on the basis of shared ethnicity (instead of political ideology), they sometimes promote issues that can work against the very populations that elect them. This potentiality highlights both a certain degree of opportunism among some of those whom voters elect to office and institutional limitations to affect change even among the most electorally successful immigrant populations.

Third, the chapter explores how the emergence of some ethnopolitical entrepreneurs may result in the political exclusion of other immigrant populations. As a multiethnic ethnoburb, Glendale is home to a diverse population. Apart from Armenians, Filipinos, Mexicans, Koreans, and many others live in Glendale. According to 2010 census data, Glendale's Asian and Latino residents constituted 16.4 percent and 17.4 percent, respectively, of the city's overall population.

While Glendale's Armenian ethnopolitical entrepreneurs have achieved electoral successes by mobilizing other Armenians, this success has had some unintended consequences for non-Armenian immigrant populations. Although Armenian elected officials may not have consciously sought to limit other newcomers' electoral incorporation within Glendale, their successes have meant ethnopolitical entrepreneurs from other ethnic and racial minorities face serious obstacles. This chapter therefore not only investigates Armenians' small (yet growing) presence in Glendale's bureaucratic workforce, but it also analyzes the relative absence of other immigrants among the city's elected officials.

Suburban Bureaucratic Incorporation

In February 2018, Yasmin Beers became Glendale's first female city manager. Born in Iran to an Iranian father and an Armenian mother, she and her family migrated to the United States during the Iranian Revolution in 1979. After living in Hollywood for eight years, they moved to Glendale, where Beers attended high school. In 1987, she began working for the City of Glendale. At the time, she was only seventeen years old. She worked as a library page at the Grandview Branch Library, where she earned $3.75 per hour. Throughout college, Beers worked in different capacities at the library and, after graduating, took a salaried position there. As a city employee at the library, she worked her way up the administrative ladder over twelve years, and when a deputy city manager position opened at the city's town hall, she applied. Selected from ninety applicants, Beers was appointed to the position in 2000. As the deputy city manager, she expanded her range of responsibilities by taking on budget oversight and preparation, capital improvement oversight, employee development, community outreach, and many other tasks. Ten years later, she was appointed assistant city manager, and her responsibilities expanded even further. In this role, she worked an additional eight years. When Glendale's city manager, Scott Ochua, vacated the office, Beers acted as interim city manager for four months, beginning in November 2017, and became the city manager in February 2018.[3]

When I met Beers, she had only recently moved into her new, spacious office in Glendale's city hall. Beers and I spoke at length about her long career working in various capacities for the City of Glendale. As a municipal career official, she understood her role as distinct from that of the elected officials whom I had shadowed and interviewed in Glendale:

> Where we are today is completely different than where we were eighteen years ago when I came into this office. We just published our

demographics report. . . . It's amazing to see the changes in the organization. But it takes time. Now that we have folks from the Armenian
community, the Korean community, et cetera, it's slightly more reflective, not reflective, but slightly more reflective of the community. Then
you're going to see folks getting promoted into the ranks. But that's going
to take time, because a whole bunch of these folks are new. It's going to
take for them to grow in the organization.

Distinct from the rapidity with which the city's elected officials obtain office,
Beers achieved her senior leadership position after more than thirty years of employment with the city. Over the course of a long career, Beers climbed the proverbial ranks of the city's administrative staff. Her career in the council-manager
government of the City of Glendale reflects the gradual processes by which municipal bureaucrats and city managers achieve senior leadership positions. As
Beers told me, a city's bureaucracy (and, in this case, management) grows slowly
as new employees join the workforce and gradually rise to positions of leadership. In Glendale, when I collected data for this book, the gradual nature of these
processes resulted in a sort of demographic imbalance: the managerial and bureaucratic workforce did not always reflect the demography. Despite Armenians'
overrepresentation among its elected officials, they were conspicuously underrepresented in the city's fire department, police force, school leadership, and city
management—although, as Beers stressed, this was changing.

In addition to elected officials, a suburb's many unelected officials also significantly influence newcomers' incorporation. These officials—from the police
force to school principals—play important roles in the personal experiences and
perceptions of immigrants. Despite a relative absence in political incorporation
scholarship, there does exist a growing scholarly model—often framed as *bureaucratic incorporation*—that unpacks the everyday experiences among newcomers when they interact with unelected city officials. In this literature, scholars
analyze the ways immigrants, particularly the undocumented, face barriers in
engaging with electoral and legislative politics. This scholarship has demonstrated that bureaucratic officials often respond to the needs of those whom the
law does not recognize.

Lorrie A. Frasure and Michael Jones-Correa (2010) identify the emergence of
different bureaucracies (service oriented and discipline oriented) that result from
demographic shifts and suburban transformation. Furthermore, Paul G. Lewis
and S. Karthick Ramakrishnan (2007) unpack the important role of law enforce-
ment personnel (and other civil servants) in facilitating immigrants' incorporation in developing policies and practices separate from elected officials. In addition,
Helen B. Marrow (2009) analyzes how external governmental policies structure

municipal bureaucrats' responses and interactions with many newcomers. As she argues, "Government policies can therefore influence incorporation processes by exerting both direct 'control' over bureaucrats' behaviors and indirect 'influence' (Meier and O'Toole 2006) over bureaucrats' conceptions of their professional roles" (Marrow 2009, 759). And, from a slightly distinct vantage, Rocío Calvo, Joanna M. Jablonska-Bayro, and Mary C. Waters (2017) demonstrate that interactions with medical health representatives influence immigrants' perceptions of belonging in the United States.

While this scholarship has expanded the existing research's focus to include the personal experiences or feelings of immigrants in response to their interactions with a city's bureaucratic workforce, it still hinges on some untested assumptions about the importance of strong electoral representation and political incorporation (manifested through voter registration). Even when the scholarship acknowledges the importance of co-ethnic political leadership, it tends to assume that policies, ultimately, influence newcomers' feelings of inclusion or exclusion. As Irene Bloemraad argues: "Locally, social networks, community organizations, and ethnic leadership play critical roles in helping newcomers. This local infrastructure is in turn shaped by government policies. Migrants acquire resources and support for political participation through the actions—or inactions—of government, and government actions shape immigrants' very impressions and understandings of citizenship" (2006, 9). Glendale Armenians' distinctly successful electoral incorporation allows us to investigate whether political incorporation and feelings of belonging correlate. In a single generation, immigrants in an ethnoburb can significantly influence the political institutions of their communities—as they have in Glendale—but do these political influences translate into feelings of inclusion in the polity?

Among Glendale's elected officials and its municipal workforce, Armenians' demographic representation occurs on both ends of a spectrum. When I collected data in the city, Armenians were noticeably underrepresented among Glendale's municipal bureaucrats and civil servants, particularly in positions of senior leadership. Since the late 1990s, the city has collected data on the demographic distribution of its workforce; it publishes this data as a report every other year (with some inconsistency).[4] In Glendale's workforce demographic reports, "Armenian" is its own racial category—separate from "white." On the basis of city data, the total number of Armenians employed by the city nearly doubled between 2003 and 2016, from 9.9 percent to 18.3 percent (City of Glendale 2018, 1-1). This growth is particularly salient in specific areas. For example, the longitudinal data reflect significant increases in terms of Armenian municipal employment in the Department of Community Services and Parks. Between 2003 and 2016, Armenian employment in this department nearly doubled, from

TABLE 6. Glendale's demographic workforce data for Armenians, 2003–2016

	2003	2004	2005	2006	2007	2008	2009	2010	2011	2012	2013	2014	2015	2016
Total workforce (salaried and hourly) (%)	9.9	11.1	11.6	12.7	13.0	13.9	14.8	15.7	16.2	15.9	17.1	17.3	18.3	18.3
Department of Community Services and Parks (%)	16.4	17.8	19.2	21.3	20.8	23.2	27.8	29.7	30.1	31.3	31.8	31.0	31.1	29.6
Fire department (%)	0.9	2.1	2.0	2.6	3.0	4.5	4.7	5.5	5.5	5.5	5.9	5.3	5.4	7.1
Police department (%)	5.1	7.0	6.5	5.4	6.5	6.3	6.2	6.3	6.6	7.7	8.5	9.4	9.5	10.1

Source: City of Glendale, *Workforce Demographics* (2018), 1-1, 8-8, 8-9, 8-15.

16.4 percent to 29.6 percent (8-8). However, in other important departments, Armenian demographic representation remained largely underrepresented. For example, while employment in the fire department increased from 0.9 percent to 7.1 percent between 2003 and 2016 (8-9), Armenians remained largely underrepresented as compared to the city's overall demographics. Similarly, Armenian employment in the police department between 2003 and 2016 increased from 5.1 percent to 10.1 percent (8-15), but this increase, again, was not commensurate with the city's overall demographic trends.

This disparity was also true of the city's management. As of 2018, a nonelected Armenian managed only one of the fourteen departments, the Public Works Department. Armenians managed two other departments, those of the city clerk and the city treasurer, but both are elected positions. Among school principals (Glendale has over thirty public schools), four were Armenian, while four out of five elected members of the Glendale Unified School District Board were Armenian.[5] Among Glendale Community College's fifteen collegiate divisions, not a single Armenian held a chair position.[6] Among the seventeen (noninterim) members of the college's administrative cabinet (including superintendent, executive vice president, and associate vice president, among others), again, not a single person was of Armenian ancestry.[7] In contrast, three (out of five) elected members on the college's board were Armenian.[8] In terms of the college's demographic composition, Armenian for-credit students represented 33.3 percent, while noncredit Armenian students made up about 40.7 percent, respectively, of the overall student body during the 2018–2019 academic year.[9] In contrast to elected officials, Armenians were underrepresented in executive and civil service positions throughout the city.

These demographic disparities do not reflect exclusion per se. Rather, since the majority of Glendale Armenians are first-generation immigrants, the disparities reflect the gradual processes through which municipal actors enter the workforce and ascend to managerial positions.[10] As such, the numbers presented here do not reflect a fixed reality; rather, they change over time. Nonetheless, they vividly make clear the difference between political or electoral and bureaucratic incorporation. Unlike elected officials, who can obtain leadership roles through a single campaign, senior municipal bureaucrats obtain management positions over the course of long careers with the city.

Because scholarship on immigrant political incorporation often ends at the ballot box, it does not account for the everyday realities of the very populations it purports to assess—that is, the immigrants themselves. The scholarship has done much to advance voter demographics (Putnam 2000; Bevelander and Pendakur 2009; Voicu and Comşa 2014) as well as successful strategies of political entrepreneurs (Hochschild and Mollenkopf 2009a; Hochschild et al. 2013). But

TABLE 7. Total demographic data for age ranges of Glendale's workforce (Armenians and whites), 2016

	21–25	26–30	31–35	36–40	41–45	46–50	51–55	56–60	61+	TOTAL
Total salaried city workforce (Armenian) (%)	0.9	1.9	3.0	2.7	2.8	1.3	0.7	0.8	0.8	14.9
Total salaried city workforce (white) (%)	0.7	2.8	4.4	4.9	6.4	7.3	6.2	4.9	2.5	40.2

Source: City of Glendale, *Workforce Demographics* (2018), 13-1.

far less sociological and political scientific research has investigated immigrants' everyday experiences of political incorporation (Bloemraad 2006; Lewis and Ramakrishnan 2007; Calvo, Jablonska-Bayro, and Waters 2017). As a result, the scholarship that explores the personal experiences of immigrant political incorporation leaves unquestioned many of its primary assumptions.

In Glendale, Armenians often told me that their political incorporation did not lend itself to feelings of individual or collective inclusion. This may relate to people's perceptions of the ethnopolitical entrepreneurs themselves; some Glendale Armenians think certain co-ethnic elected officials are too assimilated. Or perhaps many immigrant voters simply are not au fait with the benefits of having co-ethnic elected officials within their suburb. Whatever the reason, they continue voting for Armenian ethnopolitical entrepreneur candidates at high rates. As Matt Barreto and Sergio Garcia's (2011) regression analyses reflect, Armenians vote for Armenian candidates at one of the highest rates in the country.

In Glendale, the finding that the political incorporation of newcomers does not necessarily result in feelings of belonging or inclusion for many suggests that scholars may inflate the significance of political incorporation in positively influencing the perceptions of immigrants.

Still, unless something unforeseeable alters US immigration policies, the existing data suggest that younger professionals in many ethnoburbs will, over time, gradually fill more positions in the municipal workforce. Armenians in Glendale and those classified as "white" represent inverse age demographics: in the workforce report (reporting from 2016, but published in 2018), the three most sizable age groupings, for Armenians, were the youngest, twenty and under, twenty-one to twenty-five, twenty-six to thirty, and thirty-one to thirty-five (54.4% of all Armenians employed); except for those over sixty years and older among whites, the largest age groupings were the oldest, forty-one to forty-five, forty-six to fifty, fifty-one to fifty-five, and fifty-six to sixty (53.4% of all whites employed) (City of Glendale 2018, 13-1). These numerical disparities also reflect gradual, generational shifts taking place in the city's workforce. A high-ranking (non-Armenian) municipal actor with over two decades of hiring experience in the city made a very similar claim: "Most of the Armenians that we employ are second generation. Their parents were likely born elsewhere—whether it's Lebanon, Soviet Armenia, Iran, somewhere in Europe, or elsewhere. So that's kind of what I've seen of the individuals I've hired." As this happens, the older generation may begin to feel more integrated into mainstream Glendale. However, 1.5- and second-generation Armenians, as many officials told me, are far more "Americanized" than their parents. Thus, a paradoxical concomitance arises: Glendale's individual immigrants may begin to perceive themselves as increasingly integrated (and empowered) as the second generation becomes more American and enters the city workforce at higher rates. These municipal employees will ascend the ranks and assume roles of executives, directors, division chairs, presidents, and managers.

Similarly, as Glendale's Armenians become more incorporated into the bureaucratic workforce, voters may begin selecting candidates because of their merit rather than their shared ethnicity. Another high-ranking, nonelected (also non-Armenian) official confessed in an interview: "The Armenian community specifically is looking for more diversity in the [city] organization, for the city of Glendale to be a microcosm of the community it represents. So, at the end of the day, they're asking for people to be able to respond to their needs who may understand their needs better than someone who may not be Armenian, or whatever the case may be." If ethnicity begins losing some of its value among increasingly "Americanized" Glendale Armenians, perhaps those for whom they do ultimately vote will run campaigns based on larger community issues rather than on linked fates and shared ethnicity.

As a result, immigrant political incorporation may have as much to do with voting as with the gradual and inevitable processes of multigenerational ethnic integration into municipal workforces. These findings, therefore, complicate traditional understandings by contending that political and electoral incorporation may not, in fact, prove the ultimate phase in ethnic and racial populations' becoming members of the polities in which they live. For some populations, this disconnect will lessen gradually over time, whereas for others, racist hierarchies will continue to marginalize even those with long histories in the country. In the United States, these racist hierarchies persistently continue to marginalize populations and offer them disparate resources (Gerstle 2001; Fox 2012). Thus, immigrant political incorporation may empower newcomers, but it does not guarantee (or, in some cases, even affect) feelings of inclusion or belonging within a polity. In this way, political incorporation may be the beginning rather than the end of "bringing outsiders in" (Hochschild and Mollenkopf 2009a).

Ethnopolitical Entrepreneurs' Symbolic Capital

I visited Nvard in her classroom at Thomas Jefferson Elementary School. We met during the school day because I wanted to observe firsthand Nvard's Armenian/ English dual-language immersion class. Many students at Thomas Jefferson Elementary School spend 50 percent of the school day receiving instruction in a foreign language. Language options include Korean, Japanese, Spanish, and (Eastern) Armenian, among others.[11] Some Glendale middle schools, such as Eleanor J. Toll Middle School and Woodrow Wilson Middle School, offer students the opportunity to continue in their dual-language immersion programs beyond elementary school. In 2006, the Glendale Unified School District Board enacted the legislation to allocate funding for these programs. Before visiting Thomas Jefferson Elementary School, I met with members of the board, and they told me about their efforts to ensure that many public schools in Glendale made available the fifty-fifty Armenian/English immersion programs. These programs facilitate both integration and linguistic preservation among the children of Armenians in Glendale. And these programs are very popular. When I spoke to the principal of Thomas Jefferson, Armineh (who is an Armenian from Iran), she explained that the waiting list to enroll in Armenian immersion courses grew every year.

Nvard generously allowed me to observe and participate in her Armenian-language class. The morning of my visit, she taught her students basic science; she spoke only in Armenian, and the students read from their Armenian-language textbooks. While relatively fluent in (Eastern) Armenian, I soon realized my technical vocabulary had some limitations.[12] On a couple of occasions, I had to ask my "classmates" to explain the novel vocabulary from their textbooks.

During the students' lunch period, Nvard and I chatted about her journey to Glendale's public school system. In response to the earthquake in Gyumri, Armenia (1988), and the escalating conflict in the first Artsakh/Nagorno-Karabakh war (1988–1994), Nvard's parents decided to relocate to the United States in 1989. At age sixteen, Nvard settled with her family in Hollywood. After graduating from the University of Southern California in 1996, she and her family moved to Glendale. In 2005, she completed a master's in education and began teaching at an elementary school. When we met, Nvard had been teaching in the dual-language immersion program at Thomas Jefferson since 2013. Because her employment results, in large part, from the work of Glendale's ethnopolitical entrepreneurs, I was especially curious to gain her perspective.

Her response, however, surprised me: "My personal career was never driven by that [Armenian political representation]. . . . I pay more attention to national politics. I didn't own a house in Glendale. I think the people who own property tend to follow those issues much more closely, because it actually affects them. . . . But it [local politics] never really affected me as a renter." Even though Glendale's Armenian officials' reallocations directly affect Nvard's work and life, she confessed feeling unaffected by the co-ethnic elected officials. Rather than focus on her work in the school or the electoral accomplishments of Armenians in Glendale, she confirmed what researchers have noted regarding homeownership and feelings of inclusion among immigrants (Kitchen, Williams, and Gallina 2015). Despite the visibility of elected officials, their work and contributions often remain less evident to the populations they serve. This disconnect recurs even among those whose lives are directly affected by the work of co-ethnic political entrepreneurs.[13]

While Glendale's Armenians consistently told me that Armenian representation had little to no effect in their everyday lives, many of the same people stressed the symbolic importance of Armenian candidates running for and holding public office (see chapter 4). And practically all of those whom I interviewed conceded that they typically vote for co-ethnic candidates. This concession points to another potential limitation: by politically mobilizing and incorporating co-ethnics, ethnopolitical entrepreneurs may ensure that their voters (and they themselves) receive symbolic capital; however, this sort of capital may not always translate into feelings of belonging. By deriving symbolic capital for those on whom they rely to win office, ethnopolitical entrepreneurs may limit their capacities to provide them optimal practical (or functional) benefits.

The disconnect between the symbolic and the functional highlights a persistent pattern that is not unique to the Armenians of Glendale, where voters select candidates based on ethnicity or race rather than the candidates' political ideologies or values (Hajnal and Lee 2011; Hajnal and Trounstine 2014). But this selection criterion also makes possible the potential opportunism of ethnopolitical entrepreneurs, who may seek to gain political office by exploiting voters' desire for symbolic capital. While, in the case of Glendale's Armenians, these shortcomings do not undermine the important legislation ethnopolitical entrepreneurs have enacted on behalf of Armenian voters, it does make clear the potential limitations of running campaigns based on shared ethnicity. This conflict of interests—ethnic loyalty and practical needs—also explains, in part, the lack of feeling a sense of belonging that can result among Glendale's Armenian voters.

Many Glendale Armenian voters whom I interviewed acknowledged the limitations of voting for candidates to acquire symbolic capital, but very few allowed these limitations to affect their selections. Several even criticized the ethnopolitical entrepreneurs they had elected. An Armenian from Armenia, who migrated at the age of thirty-six (in 1996), asserted: "Even though we have so many Armenians in the city council et cetera, they are trying to be as unbiased as possible. In fact, they are trying so fervently that they sometimes act against Armenians. Sometimes when I read Glendale news, I feel that we are always discriminated [against]. It's not my prejudice—it's definite. We go through higher scrutiny than any other ethnic group." But, when asked why she continues to vote for Armenians in local elections, she emphasized the symbolic motivation behind her voting behavior: "I definitely [vote] more in municipal elections, because I want the mayoral seat to be taken by Armenians, to be honest." Another voter, an Armenian from Iran, who migrated in 1979 (at age thirty-three), expressed a similar sentiment: "If they are worthy people, probably they could help, and it's good. But, unfortunately, the majority, for me, they are not. . . . If you're going to ask for us to vote, but not talk about Armenians because you're so scared, why are we putting you in that office?" An Armenian from Armenia, who migrated at the age of thirty-six (in 2010), succinctly voiced his experience of ethnopolitical entrepreneurs' limitations: "They are Americans. First of all, they are Americans. They think like Americans. And, in my opinion, they're afraid that someone will tell them that they are racist. So, they aren't really Armenian politicians." An Iranian Armenian, who migrated in 1994 (at age sixteen), made a similar point even more forcefully: "I've seen nothing that I can say has affected me. Keep in mind, just because they are Armenian doesn't mean they can push Armenian agendas." Nonetheless, all these respondents confessed that they consistently voted exclusively for co-ethnic candidates. Thus, even among those who criticized Armenian elected officials, they also conceded the lure of symbolic capital in the form of co-ethnic representation. This highlights the extent to which ethnopolitical entrepreneurs rely on ethnicity to gain office, and voters, in turn, derive symbolic capital from co-ethnic representation. But acquiring symbolic capital does not automatically generate feelings of belonging in the polity; furthermore, choosing candidates based largely on ethnicity does not necessarily guarantee ethnopolitical entrepreneurs' full commitment to voters' interests.

In fact, voting to acquire symbolic capital may even lead voters to undermine their own interests. This manifests itself on a variety of issues that affect the voters. In Glendale, one example of how voters can vote against their own interests relates to housing. While Armenians are socioeconomically diverse, less affluent newcomers make up a higher proportion of Glendale's Armenian population. As elsewhere in California, Glendale's rising housing costs and the scarcity of affordable options have made the city financially untenable for many immigrants as well as nonimmigrants (Quigley and Raphael 2005). Many have had to relocate to less expensive neighborhoods. In addition, Glendale's appeal among prospective residents has led to an influx of new luxury developments. These new developments cater, largely, to high-income earners. While some Armenian ethnopolitical entrepreneurs have made responding to these housing issues a priority, others have strongly opposed any housing regulations. For example, two of the ten candidates who ran in Glendale's 2017 city council election, Zareh Sinanyan and Ara Najarian, articulated quite distinct views on the topic of housing regulations. During his campaign, Sinanyan, who had previously served as a city council member and mayor, publicly criticized Glendale's housing regulations (or the lack thereof); he called them discriminatory toward Armenians and other immigrant populations. Instead, he promoted rent control and more affordable housing.[14] In contrast, Najarian, who had previously served in several positions in Glendale—mayor, city council member, chair of the Glendale Housing Authority, and chair of the Glendale Transportation and Parking Commission—strongly resisted rent control and other regulations. He argued that rent control would depreciate Glendale's housing market. From a policy perspective, Najarian's approach to housing was more popular among many nonimmigrant Glendale residents, whereas Sinanyan's housing approach had more appeal among newcomers.

Despite their very different views on this and other issues, both Sinanyan and Najarian relied heavily on co-ethnic voters.[15] And, in 2017, Sinanyan and Najarian won reelection, receiving 9,504 and 9,962 votes, respectively.[16] Because Glendale's plurality voting system allows people to select up to three candidates, Sinanyan and Najarian most likely relied on many of the same Armenian voters to win re-election. While Armenians in Glendale—particularly those among its large, first-generation immigrant population—have vociferously sought more housing regulations as well as rent control, this policy priority did not prevent many from voting for Najarian, who quite openly opposed such measures. This highlights a potential drawback of ethnopolitical entrepreneurs: they "create" voting blocs out of a sense of linked fate and shared ethnicity, and, in turn, their co-ethnic voters derive symbolic value in electing them (regardless of their political agendas); as a result, voters may elect officials whose political agendas directly conflict with their own interests. Thus, while Armenians in Glendale (as elsewhere) may derive symbolic capital from electing co-ethnic officials, this does not guarantee that those who profit from this symbolic capital will necessarily serve their practical needs.

To a certain extent, the different policy positions of Glendale's ethnopolitical entrepreneurs simply reinforce the internal diversity of the Armenian population itself. Regarding the issue of affordable housing, many Glendale Armenians, particularly among the second- and third-generation, support Najarian. He also understood this internal division and to whom he was seeking to align himself. He told me the following:

> They want affordable housing, certain degrees of rent control. They want lower electric rates, lower water rates. They want more parking in their neighborhoods. And those are legitimate issues. Then you start

to get into the Armenian mentality from those really not from the United States. This is like the first-generation or newly immigrated: "Why can't you place me in that affordable housing unit? We know you can do it. Why can't you get my son a job in the city? We know you can do it. Why can't you have my illegal home addition approved? We know you can do it.

Najarian's rationale reiterates a phenomenon that James Zarsadiaz (2022) unpacks in his study of Asian immigrants in East San Gabriel Valley—namely, that Asian homeowners often allied with white homeowners to maintain the class privilege and lifestyle ("country living model") of their conservative, Anglocentric suburbs. In *Resisting Change in Suburbia: Asian Immigrants and Frontier Nostalgia in L.A.*, Zarsadiaz argues: "Interestingly, many Asian homeowners publicly or passively supported calls to restrict 'Asian-ness' because it did not fit with the country living model and that restrictions purportedly served the greater good" (19). In Glendale, socioeconomic, cultural, and generational diversity means Armenians want different things for different reasons. As chapter 4 explains, some streams of Glendale Armenians feel threatened by other Armenian subgroups. And, as Zarsadiaz argues about Asians in East San Gabriel Valley, they may even align with non-Armenians to defend their own personal values or those they associate with Glendale.

Nevertheless, the exclusive focus on ethnicity—both for ethnopolitical entrepreneurs and for the immigrants they politically mobilize and incorporate—can sometimes have the very opposite effect of inclusion. The constructivist model outlined in chapter 4 highlights the processes by which ethnopolitical entrepreneurs selectively invoke ethnicity to create voting blocs and incorporate newcomers. This typically involves adding or (re)combining attributes; however, in practice, it also means leaving out several important attributes related to political ideology. By excluding specific policy prerogatives from their uses of ethnicity and relying on the symbolic capital voters derive from co-ethnic representation, some ethnopolitical entrepreneurs bring outsiders in by, paradoxically, promoting policies that can prevent or delay their integration.

During my fieldwork, I experienced firsthand a genuine commitment and dedication to Armenians among the ethnopolitical entrepreneurs I interviewed and shadowed. But what that commitment meant or for which Armenians that commitment applied depended on each individual ethnopolitical entrepreneur and his or her personal ambitions and beliefs. As such, constructing constituents based on ethnicity not only leads to the political incorporation of newcomers; it also creates symbolic capital, which some ethnopolitical entrepreneurs yield to implement changes that affect different parts of an ethnic population in

FIGURE 17. The Brand Apartments in central Glendale, California.

different ways. Because of the focus on ethnicity and the symbolic capital it generates, co-ethnic constituents run the risk of voting against their own interests. These conflicting interests, for some, explain why successful electoral and political incorporation does not always correlate with an individual or collective sense of belonging among immigrant populations.

Skewed Incorporation

By taking advantage of demographic concentration and creating unified co-ethnic voting blocs, ethnopolitical entrepreneurs not only can generate votes from those whose interests they may not always serve; they also can risk displacing or excluding other populations within the same multiethnic suburb. Willow Lung-Amam articulates inherent tensions that arise between new and established populations in suburban place making: "As new groups come in and lay their ideas upon the landscape, they subtly challenge or subvert those of former groups. Their news signs and symbols assert a kind of moral authority that is often viewed as a threat by established residents, be they White, Black, poor, or middle class" (2017, 9). To be sure, many ethnoburbs (including Glendale) reinforce Lung-Amam's important insight about the threat new populations pose to already established residents. However, new populations not only challenge and subvert established residents; they also challenge and preempt opportunities for other new populations.

In Glendale (as in other ethnoburbs), the emergence of one politically domi-nant ethnic population often means the political exclusion of others. By creat-ing a voting bloc based on ethnicity (and not on political ideology), ethnopolitical entrepreneurs run the risk of creating domains of power, which are exclusion-ary with regard to other prospective ethnic and racial political candidates. Thus, in addition to asymmetrical demographic representation in the civic workforce, symbolic power domains can also result in the political exclusion of other pro-spective newcomers (and ethnopolitical entrepreneurs).

Editha (Edith) M. Fuentes was born and raised in the Philippines' capital, Ma-nila. In 1975, not long after graduating from the University of Santo Tomas, Fuentes moved to Connecticut. After a brief stay in Connecticut, she moved to Florida, where she began working for the City of Coral Gables. Fuentes began her career in a lower-level administrative position as a zoning clerk. Like Yas-min Beers in Glendale, Fuentes worked her way up the city workforce over the next eighteen years—ultimately becoming the city's zoning department direc-tor. After serving in this position for nearly three years, Fuentes took a job with the City of Miami as the building, zoning, and unsafe structures director. She remained in this role until the early 1990s.

In 1993, Fuentes moved to Glendale, where she continued her career as the city's planning and zoning administrator. She worked in this capacity for nearly twenty years. After retiring in 2012, Fuentes decided to run for Glendale City Council. Like Rafi Manoukian and his team back in the late 1990s, Fuentes rec-ognized potential in Glendale's untapped Asian populations—particularly its Filipino voters—and therefore sought to politically incorporate these residents. However, while Fuentes was campaigning in late 2012 and early 2013, her mother passed away. As a result, she returned to the Philippines in the middle of her campaign. While she still garnered quite a few votes, this tragic event took Fuen-tes's attention away from the campaign. She ended up in sixth place after Ara Najarian, Laura Friedman, Zareh Sinanyan, Chahe Keuroghelian, and Sam L. Engel Jr.[17] She attempted to run again in the city's 2015 election. She and her team approached this campaign more aggressively in terms of their outreach efforts. While she did get more votes in her second campaign, she did not receive enough votes to gain office. She finished fourth behind Paula Devine, Vartan Gharpe-tian, and Erik Yesayan.[18]

Fuentes possesses an impressive professional resume and educational back-ground. Beyond nearly forty years of experience in city leadership roles, she also has graduate degrees from Florida International University and the University

of Southern California. During her second campaign, she even received the political endorsement of the former international boxing star and, at the time of
this writing, Filipino congressman Manny Pacquiao. Despite her extensive professional work experience, educational training, and celebrity endorsements,
Fuentes still could not secure a seat on Glendale's city council. Several Glendale
Armenians against whom she ran often had far less (or no) professional experience and yet still received more votes.

When I asked Fuentes why she believed she had not been elected, she acknowledged that some race- or ethnicity-based voting tendencies among Glendale
residents forestalled her efforts: "It's like me running against the tide. Here's this
small Filipino American female that's trying to get inside, between the two hard
rocks—the Caucasians and the Armenians. . . . They go to vote with blinders, like
I'm only going to vote for an 'ian' last name or a 'yan' last name. I'm only going
to vote for a Caucasian last name, you know? Or an American last name. So that's
where we are." In our conversation, Fuentes consistently stressed her fondness
for her Armenian colleagues and neighbors in Glendale. She spoke warmly of
the professional and personal relationships she had formed with Armenians in
Glendale. Even in her campaigns, she worked closely with Glendale Armenians
as well as members of the city's Latino and Asian populations. Furthermore, Armenian ethnopolitical entrepreneurs sought her out to remain active in Glendale after her unsuccessful campaigns: in 2020, Ardy Kassakhian nominated
Fuentes to serve as Glendale's planning commissioner. Glendale's city council
unanimously approved the appointment.[19] Nonetheless, her inability to win a
city council seat highlights a problem that can arise with ethnopolitical entrepreneurs' ethnicity-based campaigns in ethnoburbs: prospective ethnic political leaders who are not a part of the demographically largest and most politically
mobilized racial or ethnic populations may find themselves in nearly unelectable
positions ("between two hard rocks"). Rather than displacing the previously established white members, Glendale Armenians' mobilization has led to the political consolidation of white voters—or, as Marisa Abrajano and Zoltan Hajnal
(2015) argue, "white backlash"—as well as the electoral exclusion of other ethnic populations.[20] As Fuentes's experiences attest, ethnopolitical entrepreneurs'
voters often determine their electors through the limited prism of ethnicity or
race rather than based on the candidates' views or qualifications ("They go to
vote with blinders"). Hajnal and Jessica Trounstine have argued a similar point
about urban politics more generally:

> The growth of the minority community has not, as some had hoped,
> paved the way for an interminority coalition that is challenging white
> control. Instead, blacks, Latinos, and Asian-Americans appear to be

regularly competing for the often meager political and economic prizes that are available in the local political arena. Blacks and Latinos, the two groups that are often seen as having common economic and racial interests and as being potential coalition partners, seldom support the same candidates. (2014, 74)

While Hajnal and Trounstine's findings reflect voting tendencies in large cities, such as Los Angeles, New York, Chicago, Houston, and Detroit, the same limitation holds for ethnoburbs as well. However, in the context of ethnoburbs, voting along ethnic or racial lines may prove even more skewed: rather than competing for "meager political and economic prizes," in ethnoburbs, a "winner takes all" scenario may prove even more likely to emerge. Constructing and incorporating ethnic voting blocs among one ethnic population can narrow the range of voters' choices as well as place insurmountable electoral challenges on those from demographically smaller ethnic or racial minorities.

As Fuentes's campaigns manifest, the triumphant narrative of immigrants emerging and replacing prejudicial, white institutional actors belies the reality and embeds another narrative—namely, the relative political exclusion of other immigrant populations within the same ethnoburb. While Glendale Armenians' political saturation has meant significant gains for the Armenian population, it has also meant less representation among other newcomers. Given their demographic

FIGURE 18. Edith Fuentes and Manny Pacquiao.

sizes relative to that of the Armenians, these populations do not have equal access to local institutions and resources. As a result, the emergence of new dominant immigrant populations may also come at the political expense of other newcomers. This political exclusion of other immigrant populations highlights another challenge for ethnopolitical entrepreneurs.

Some of the challenges confronting ethnopolitical entrepreneurs' prospective voters relate to demographics, symbolic capital, and skewed incorporation. These challenges do not undermine the important role ethnopolitical entrepreneurs play in facilitating the political incorporation of many newcomers within contemporary US ethnoburbs. However, these are challenges that confront a future generation of ethnopolitical entrepreneurs. Chapter 6 revisits some of these challenges and explores ways that future ethnopolitical entrepreneurs can mitigate them.

THE ARMENIAN AMERICAN MUSEUM
Building the Future Suburb

In the years leading up to the centenary of the Armenian Genocide (2015), members of several Armenian organizations, such as the Armenian National Committee of America (ANCA), the Armenian Cultural Foundation, the Armenian General Benevolent Union (Western District), and the Armenian Genocide Centennial Committee, began discussing a commemorative landmark in Glendale.[1] They eventually founded the Armenian American Museum and Cultural Center of California, which comprises ten Armenian organizations. In 2014, members of this organization's board of trustees opened discussions with Glendale city officials regarding a location for a possible museum. In 2016, Armenian elected officials in Glendale—in particular, then mayor Zareh Sinanyan—proposed a central location for the museum at a site the city had allocated for a parking structure. At the same time, the museum's board of trustees worked with other representatives on the state level to gain momentum and financial backing for the project. For example, California State Assembly member Adrin Nazarian made sure the museum was included in the state budget. His support led to the allocation of $1 million for the proposed Armenian American Museum. Then, in 2017, senator Anthony Portantino, who represents Southern California's Armenian-concentrated Twenty-Fifth Senate District, helped secure an additional $3 million for the museum project. Armenian organizations and individual donors also contributed millions of dollars. These and other forms of support led, in 2018, to the Armenian-majority city council approving a ground lease, which established the site of the future museum in the city's Arts and Entertainment District in Glendale's Central Park.

Since I completed data collection for this book in 2018, the Armenian American Museum project has developed in many important ways. In 2019, the museum board appointed Shant Sahakian the executive director of the Armenian American Museum. Sahakian, who also has served as an elected official on the Glendale Unified School District Board of Education since 2017, leads community outreach efforts for the museum. In addition to working with ethnopolitical entrepreneurs in Glendale, museum board members have gained additional financial support from political representatives on the county, state, and even federal levels.[2] For example, the museum board has successfully raised funds from Fifth District supervisor Kathryn Barger, who allocated $1 million from the county.[3] Senator Portantino secured an additional $5 million in 2019 and yet another $1.8 million in 2021.[4] And, on the federal level, congressman Adam Schiff helped secure $950,000 of federal funding in 2022.[5]

The museum's financial support from different governmental bodies not only reflects the advantages of a politically mobilized (and incorporated) Armenian population in Glendale; it also reflects an evolution in terms of Armenians' role in the city. While in the mid-1990s Armenian banquet hall owners had to fight vociferously against ordinances directly targeting Armenian businesses, by the early 2020s the Armenian American Museum project had come to embody the extent to which Armenians have become influential members of the city. The Armenian American Museum's executive chairman, Berdj Karapetian, who ran unsuccessfully for city council in 1989 (see chapter 3), concisely summed up this evolution to me:

> [It is] because of the years and decades of goodwill that the Armenian community of California has produced. It didn't happen because one day we're here, so now we go and ask. It's a generation. [It is] the next Armenian Americans here in California developing, cultivating relationships, developing a good reputation, and making people realize that we are an integral part of California and have made our contribution to our state. It is a dividend of what we are receiving out of those years of investment.

The Armenian American Museum will not be merely a building where Armenians from many backgrounds can learn about their history in the United States; rather, it will embody a new generation of multiethnic US suburban residents whose contributions cultivate and enrich their cities throughout the country. The museum exemplifies the local implications of ethnopolitical entrepreneurs' invocation of ethnicity to incorporate immigrants and influence political institutions.

The story of Glendale's Armenians reflects both a local and national evolution. In the past several decades, immigrants from all corners of the world have

FIGURE 19. Rendering of the Armenian American Museum (Colorado Street entrance). Designed by Alajajian.Marcoosi Architects Inc. the museum will "promote understanding and appreciation of America's ethnic and cultural diversity by sharing the Armenian American experience." Land allocation and funding initiatives for the museum were, in part, spearheaded by Glendale's ethnopolitical entrepreneurs. Sources: Armenian American Museum (https://www.armenianamericanmuseum.org); Alajajian.Marcoosi Architects Inc.

converged on the same sites and influenced their local institutions, businesses, and aesthetics. From various origins, these immigrants bring with them diverse cuisines, music, ideas, and so much more. In turn, they commit to creating new lives for themselves in new spaces. The distinctly self-governing nature of US suburbs, shifts in demographics (particularly regarding immigrants from the 1970s onward), intergroup antagonism, reactive ethnicity, and the consequent emergence of ethnopolitical entrepreneurs have led to a transformation of the political landscape in the United States. While, in this book, the immigrants call themselves Armenians and refer to Glendale as their home, this story could as easily describe those calling themselves Chinese, Filipino, Korean, Mexican, or Vietnamese in various other ethnoburbs throughout California and, increasingly, the United States. To be sure, a book about any of them would have a distinct narrative trajectory, but the underlying story about political enfranchisement through grassroots initiatives and place making in contemporary US suburbs would reflect similar realities. All these places and populations reflect the structural evolution immigrants are catalyzing as a result of their interactions with suburban political institutions.

The 2020 presidential election shed light on the immense implications of these demographic and political shifts. As Donald Trump pursued any means he could to overturn an election he had lost, many Americans learned far more about political procedures than they ever anticipated (or probably even wanted to know).[6] In the closely watched and highly fraught postelection period, the public also learned more about national voting tendencies. Many people became aware of how immigrants have reconfigured urban, suburban, and exurban ecologies and that segregated Black-white racial binaries no longer exclusively apply in many of these spaces. Americans also learned that immigrants constitute over half of the suburban population in large metropolitan areas, and, in some of these places, newcomers make up far higher portions of the overall population.

In trying to stay current on the election commotion, I often came across journalists' (and some academics') hypotheses on this "abrupt" shift in the suburbs. For example, a FiveThirtyEight article tried to make sense of this unexpected turn of events:

> Suburban and exurban counties turned away from Trump and toward Democrat Joe Biden in states across the country, including in key battleground states like Pennsylvania and Georgia. In part, this may be because the suburbs are simply far more diverse than they used to be. But suburbs have also become increasingly well-educated—and that may actually better explain why so many suburbs and exurbs are turning blue than just increased diversity on its own.[7]

Attributing the change in suburbs to increasingly diverse and educated populations makes sense. And, in a way, it is correct: in the past several decades, the United States' suburban residents have become more diverse and educated. However, at the same time, this explanation is limited: in the past several decades, the United States in general has become more diverse and educated (De Brey et al. 2021). Furthermore, because of the country's selective immigration policies, immigrants often have higher educational attainment than native-born Americans (Chakravorty, Kapur, and Singh 2016).

But the United States' suburbs did not abruptly shift in the last several years. Rather, they have evolved over several decades. In 1972, C. E. Perkins, then city manager, warned the Glendale Rotary Club to prepare itself, for the city could no longer remain isolated in an increasingly diverse country (Arroyo 2006, 82). What Southern California suburban leadership has been acutely aware of since the 1970s has now become a more mainstream reality. But this "reality," of course, is quite complex. Ethnic and racial minorities within the United States' evolving suburbs do not merely self-mobilize and form spontaneous voting blocs. The highly educated demographic pluralities that form do not necessarily translate into "flipped" voting districts and states. Instead, these communities undergo constant permutations and realignments. The salient attributes that mobilize some population segments today may not resonate later. As in urban centers following the Great Migration (Browning, Marshall, and Tabb 1984; Tolnay 2003), the creative strategies of ambitious political entrepreneurs create the means to institutionalize shifting demographics and dynamic circumstances. However, while those urban political entrepreneurs might have been distinct outsiders throughout much of the twentieth century, ethnic political entrepreneurs have become important actors—and not merely those who run for office, but also those involved with ethnic organizations and multimedia—in mobilizing internally diverse suburban residents and converting them into unified voting blocs. Increasingly, these voting blocs are becoming the bedrock on which a new chapter in US political history is developing.

Before the 2020 election, it might have been easy to associate the political evolution of US suburbs with California alone. And, indeed, many existing ethnoburbs are in multiethnic California (Li 2009; Zhou, Tseng, and Kim 2008; Lung-Amam 2017; Fittante 2018). However, the 2020 election news cycle focused on the suburbs of traditionally Republican stronghold states, such as those in Georgia and Arizona. On account of immigration policies favoring high-skilled newcomers, this phenomenon will continue to expand throughout the United States. Pending a sudden shift in immigration policies, links between immigrant politics and suburban communities will only grow in future local and national elections. What this book describes may therefore soon become the norm rather than the exception. While this phenomenon might have begun taking shape in California in the 1970s, it is accelerating and spreading in several other states—Georgia, Michigan, Nevada, North Carolina, Virginia, and many others. The late twentieth-century awakening of the sleepy sundown towns of California may soon become the narrative for the rest of the United States. We have the opportunity, then, to learn from and build on the experiences of ethnopolitical entrepreneurs in various ethnoburbs.

In many ways, the diffusion of the political phenomenon this book describes will engender positive, innovative changes. Newcomers not only integrate into US society; they enhance and influence its institutions. These newcomers value their cultural heritages, but they demand a voice in their new communities. In return, they share their customs, beliefs, traditions, businesses, cuisines, and more. Those who convert this diversity into local and national political outreach institutionalize these contributions. They become the leaders of city councils, school boards, and, increasingly, local administrations. While it takes on a more globalized aspect today, this process is a familiar one. Italian, German, Jewish, and many other immigrants went through similar processes in urban centers throughout the United States. Their multistranded contributions deeply influenced how newcomers mobilized in the nineteenth and twentieth centuries. Among others, ethnopolitical entrepreneurs are facilitating how they mobilize today. It is this collective political reconfiguration that gives the United States its distinctive stamp. And this imprint will only grow, as actors become politically incorporated into US institutions and policies.

But these changes can also prove conflictual—the growing pains of an evolving demography. These new iterations continue to embed socioeconomic inequalities and prejudices. They also continue to amplify inequitable distribution of income and racist practices in the United States. Some immigrant, ethnic, and racial populations in contemporary suburbs still receive more access to higher-quality education, better medical care, and safer communities than others do (Lung-Amam 2020). Many immigrants too often face the brunt of racial profiling, police brutality, and social injustice (Gordon 2019). As urban centers across the United States have gradually sought to mitigate these injustices—albeit with uneven success—the burden extends to ethnopolitical entrepreneurs and city administrators to ameliorate disparities within their communities (Alba et al. 2014; Clerge 2019). Because many immigrants experience these social iniquities first-hand, the ethnopolitical entrepreneurs whom they elect may prove the actors best suited to create policies that empower the marginalized and disenfranchised segments of the populations they serve. In Glendale, elected ethnopolitical entrepreneurs have provided affordable housing, social services, dual-language immersion programs, and many other public services that empower newcomers and provide them the means to overcome several postmigration challenges.

Nonetheless, even in Glendale, where first-generation immigrants have attained such a high level of political and electoral incorporation, ethnopolitical entrepreneurs confront many obstacles. The disconnect many Glendale Armenian voters perceive often reflects the fact that the election of ethnopolitical entrepreneurs leads to the accumulation of symbolic capital for many voters but that this symbolic capital may not improve the practical conditions of newcomers—and, in some cases, those whom they elect may even work against their interests. As cities' bureaucratic workforces and management begin to resemble the communities more closely, this sense of disconnect among voters may change. Nonetheless, Glendale Armenians remind us that political and electoral incorporation may not, in fact, signify the ultimate immigrant achievement. Rather, the electoral success of some ethnic and racial populations may reflect the opportunism of some ethnopolitical entrepreneurs or the limitations of voting on the basis of ethnicity alone. Furthermore, successful immigrant incorporation in ethnoburbs also introduces another potential cyclicity—namely, that of political exclusion. While the mobilization of one "group" may threaten the displacement of previously established residents, it can also translate into the political exclusion of others (or the political consolidation of white voters). To overcome these potential pitfalls, ethnopolitical entrepreneurs will have to learn how to incorporate local political candidates from other populations and persuade their co-ethnic constituents to vote for them based on their potential to contribute to the community at large rather than merely on shared ethnicity. While this ambition may prove less tenable among majority first-generation voters, the populations are changing. And, as co-ethnic voters become more integrated into their respective multiethnic, multiracial suburbs, the potentiality of adding non-ethnic attributes to the identity dimensions they activate may prove more realizable in the future.

Despite the important challenges ethnopolitical entrepreneurs either cause or confront, ethnoburbs have tremendous potential to facilitate racial and ethnic integration as well as newcomer political incorporation (Lichter, Parisi, and Taquino 2015). And the sort of political incorporation they pursue is facilitating not merely postmigration transition among immigrants but also the evolution of political institutions. US suburbs are fast becoming spaces in which heterogeneous actors contribute their diversity and, as a result, create inclusive institutional reforms and reallocations (Lung Amam 2017). While intergroup antagonisms may persist, diverse residents come into contact in schools, at supermarkets, in town hall meetings, and at public parks. Clashes inevitably occur, but problems are also resolved, as new generations socialize within increasingly racially, ethnically, and culturally diverse spaces. From these encounters, political participation increases (Wong et al. 2011). Among those participating, some even aspire to become elected officials so that they, too, can contribute to the diversity and richness of their suburban communities. Multiethnic suburbs foster political participation, a process necessary to continue upending antiquated beliefs, practices, and policies (Jones-Correa 2008). As ethnopolitical entrepreneurs provide the institutional reforms necessary to push back against residual prejudices, newcomers can voice their concerns and promote their specific needs without fear of suppression.

On April 4, 2017, eleven candidates won in Glendale's city elections. These elected officials served as the city clerk and the treasurer and on the city council, the Glendale Unified School District Board, and the Glendale Community College Board of Trustees. Of the newly appointed officials, ten were Armenian.[8]

In a public statement, an ANCA spokesperson celebrated "their" candidates' successes, stating:

> The ANCA–Glendale Board congratulates all winning candidates, their victories are a true reflection of our community's collective voice. Although, this election posed many challenges, I am proud to say that with the support of our community our endorsed candidates came out

victorious. We are excited to work with our elected officials to actualize our policy priorities, such as the development of affordable housing in South Glendale, support for small business, job creation, safety, and the construction of the Armenian American Museum. We are confident that our elected officials will work hard to ensure a brighter future for our city, our schools and college.[9]

In the days that followed, several Armenian ethnic news media ran articles expressing their praise of Glendale's Armenian officials and the people who voted them into office. Indeed, this level of Armenian representation was unprecedented in Glendale's history. Only in 1999, with Rafi Manoukian's campaign, had Armenian voters in Glendale begun electing co-ethnics.[10] Armenians were not relying on non-Armenian political actors who promised to represent them in exchange for their votes. Rather, this historical "middleman minority" (Bonacich 1973), in essence, had removed the middleman (politically) and, in a very short period of time, become a formidable majority among elected officials. In fact, only a few decades prior to Manoukian's election, Glendale had been a bastion of conservatism and a headquarters of the American Nazi Party as well as the Ku Klux Klan. Archival editorials provide many instances that bear witness to the backlash Armenians and other ethnic and racial minorities encountered in what, through the 1960s, had been a sundown town. While less overt forms of racism and antagonism continue to color Armenians' experiences in Glendale, they have done much to overcome many of the barriers set up to deter them. And, instead of a marginalized and overlooked population, Glendale's Armenians have come to represent, both literally and figuratively, many aspects of the city.

Rapid demographic changes have created new voting potentialities in the United States' increasingly multiethnic suburbs. But these demographic changes do not power institutional transformation alone. As Willow Lung-Amam has argued, "Diversity that is hung on street banners, celebrated in parades, and marketed in economic development brochures is shallow and fragile. It does not bestow on communities a badge of tolerance or inclusivity" (2017, 179). As political entrepreneurs invented new strategies and built coalitions to mobilize disempowered ethnic and racial minorities in the United States' large urban centers throughout the second half of the twentieth century, relatively novel political actors—or ethnopolitical entrepreneurs—have emerged to construct voting blocs among multiple generations of co-ethnics. These constructions prove dynamic, and ethnopolitical entrepreneurs constantly reconfigure the attributes of membership in order to stay up-to-date with the population's evolving ethnic identity as well as the country's evolving political and social ethos. In constructing voting blocs, ethnopolitical entrepreneurs, in some cases, are obtaining office and influencing the political institutions of their local communities. And, increasingly, the consequences of suburban immigrant political incorporation have much larger implications. As the 2020 US presidential election demonstrated, these changes are beginning to percolate to the national level.

In Glendale, the foundational changes wrought by actors such as Eric Hacopian, Adrin Nazarian, and Rafi Manoukian in the late 1990s have become more commonplace. It is true that the exact level of Armenian representation in Glendale varies each election cycle. In addition, redistricting may cause some shifts in terms of the percentage of overall Armenian representatives. Nonetheless, Armenians' political influence in Glendale will likely persist even as the city's population continues to change. This influence may take on new dimensions, as first-generation immigrants become more integrated into the United States. They will increasingly become leaders not only among elected officials but also among city management. Moreover, a new generation of ethnopolitical entrepreneurs, who plot their own trajectories in terms of creating more inclusive and innovative policies, will likely emerge.

Between the 1970s and the 1990s, Armenians entered Glendale as foreign, unwanted newcomers. Residents spoke out against and openly criticized them. Elected officials enacted ordinances to restrict their influence in the city. These discriminatory attacks, however, led to the formation of reactive ethnicity among the internally fractured Armenians of Glendale. Capitalizing on reactive ethnicity with creative, constructivist strategies, ethnopolitical entrepreneurs politically mobilized co-ethnics and created a voting bloc through which they could win elections and fight back against backlash. In so doing, ethnopolitical entrepreneurs helped established Armenians' political prominence in Glendale. Several of Glendale's "old guard" continue to voice their frustrations about the changes newcomers bring to the city; however, these debates increasingly take place in town hall meetings, in an environment of open and inclusive debate. Ethnopolitical entrepreneurs do not create harmonious, multiethnic utopias, but they do facilitate greater dialogue among disparate actors in processes of community building and place making.

While Armenians had achieved a demographic threshold to influence Glendale's policymakers before 1999, the collective efforts of ethnopolitical entrepreneurs mobilized the internally diverse Armenian population and made them the city's most politically influential group. In addition, by working with developers and other businesses, Glendale's ethnopolitical entrepreneurs have helped transform Glendale from a sleepy, "boring" suburb into an economically thriving center. Angelenos regularly visit Glendale's commercial malls, such as the Galleria and the Americana, and its multiethnic restaurants and shops. While Armenians' dense concentration, by itself, does speak to this shift, the scholarship has highlighted that political power does not relate to the number of residents in a particular polity; instead, political power stems from the number of people who engage the political institutions (Wong et al. 2011). This book has sought to shed light on the political actors who help create the opportunity for participation among newcomers in many US suburbs. Given the distinctly planned nature of suburbia in the United States, ethnopolitical entrepreneurs ensure that those plans incorporate the desires, ambitions, and visions of its multiethnic, multiracial, multicultural inhabitants—and, often, in their native languages. Therefore, the presence of ethnopolitical entrepreneurs ensures that the suburban ethos reflects a larger swath of the population and its needs.

Glendale, Monterey Park, Fremont, and several other ethnoburbs, particularly in California, may still be outliers, but they offer templates that many other US suburban political aspirants can adopt as their communities also transition. These communities offer models of overcoming (or using) antagonisms and cultivating newcomers' contributions to their suburbs' aesthetic, commercial, cultural, and political domains. They also reflect the benefits of this receptivity: Glendale's economy and housing market have grown exponentially in the past two decades. In addition, Glendale consistently ranks among California's safest and most desirable cities.[11] While the influx of newcomers from diverse backgrounds may at first have overwhelmed many of Glendale's previously established residents (and caused some to relocate), those who remained have witnessed the efflorescence of their suburb and its economy. As proves true throughout coastal California, the housing market in Glendale is increasingly prohibitive. But several of Glendale's ethnopolitical entrepreneurs have also helped create social services and subsidized housing, particularly for newcomers. By engineering policies for different expressions in schools, places of worship, and markets, suburbs are no longer an escape but an entry point into US society. While suburban elected officials at one point could only offer newcomers potential spaces in which to conform, many now invite them to adapt and redefine these spaces and their institutions. In these dynamic communities, ethnopolitical entrepreneurs offer immigrants and other minorities the means to claim spaces as their own and contribute to them in meaningful ways.

Because ethnopolitical entrepreneurs emerge where demographic changes create new voting opportunities, suburban transformation will unfold unevenly across the United States. In less racially diverse states, segregation based on background, race, and income will continue to occur unless the leadership seizes the opportunities now to make the necessary changes. Learning from the many benefits redounding to those communities that have embraced (or been made to embrace) inclusive policies and multiethnic participation, these community leaders should introduce legislative reform to anticipate and facilitate their own community transformations. Rather than allowing privileged populations to flee or hoard diminishing spaces, suburban political leaders should begin to diversify their communities, even before the collective voices of residents have been mobilized. The twentieth century of urban centers and the early twenty-first century of many Californian suburbs attest to the gradual yet inevitable transformation of these spaces. Political leadership across the country should begin preparing the groundwork for more open and equitable participation among diverse residents. By anticipating these changes and leveling the proverbial playing field, elected officials can improve their public schools, generate more vibrant housing and commercial sectors, and create safe, family-oriented neighborhoods.

This book is about a relatively privileged population. Despite their multilocal and diverse socioeconomic backgrounds, Armenians are "white ethnics." They do not confront the same oppressive racial hierarchies that exclude and marginalize so many immigrants from Africa, Central America, South America, and elsewhere. In addition, their strong social and professional networks have given many Armenians advantages in terms of attaining higher education and high-income employment (Fittante 2018). Like many immigrants from East Asia, Armenians have been able to navigate the United States' social inequalities and avoid "segmented assimilation" (Portes and Zhou 1993; Zhou 1997; Zhou and Xiong 2005). However, Armenians are also an intra-ethnically diverse population. While Iranian Armenians who immigrated in the 1970s and 1980s often came with wealth, most post-Soviet Armenians who came during the 1990s and early 2000s did not have the same resources. While many early Iranian Armenians settled in large, luxurious homes in Glendale's hills, many of its post-Soviet Armenians settled in southern Glendale's more densely concentrated districts or elsewhere. Glendale's ethnopolitical entrepreneurs have thus run campaigns that speak to the entire Armenian population on the basis of shared ethnicity. As a result, a great deal of the legislation they have passed targets the improvement of those with fewer resources (who make up a large share of their voting bloc). Immigrant political incorporation in contemporary ethnoburbs therefore represents processes that could tend—perhaps a bit idealistically— toward the elimination of sociopolitical disparities. Future ethnopolitical entrepreneurs will, I hope, share my idealism.

EPILOGUE

In 2015, I began collecting data at Glendale's Central Library. I went to the library to scour its archives and microfilm collections for an answer to the question that originally motivated my research—that is, why did so many Armenians end up in Glendale? But the library was under construction; some parts of it were still open, but many others had already closed. Every morning, I tiptoed down dusty and papered corridors to the basement rooms, where the archives were stored. Eventually, even the research department at the library closed. Luckily, by then, I had collected the data necessary to answer the question.

For the rest of my fieldwork in Glendale, I daily passed the temporarily closed library on my way to interviews and meetings or merely on walks around Glendale. In 2017, toward the end of the second half of my fieldwork, the renovated library reopened. This new library, with its sleek interior makeover, has an auditorium, a children's room, digital workshops, a "reading spa," workshop rooms, 3-D printers, and a "makerspace." The library contains a few other unique features as well, including a meditation room—ReflectSpace—a space for visitors to contemplate human atrocities. In addition, the library provides a special collection of books about the Armenian Genocide. In an interview given to the press, Shant Sahakian, a Glendale Unified School District Board member and the executive director of the Armenian American Museum, linked Armenia and Glendale: "I had the privilege of guest lecturing at Tumo Center in Yerevan and visiting Tumo Stepanakert in 2016 and immediately thought about the value of free learning centers and what type of positive impact they can have back in Glendale."[1] As Sahakian articulated regarding his experience of Glendale's renovated library, Armenians' collective and global experiences have converged on a single site.

During the reopening, one could also walk across the green space surrounding the library and visit a temporary art installation. Designed by Ara Oshagan and Levon Parian, the photographic exhibit commemorated the Armenian Genocide with large, evocative portraits. The visual artist Ramela Grigorian Abbamontian said of the exhibit: "These portraits, like the survivors themselves, function as testimonies of the Genocide and the subsequent lives in the Diaspora. In other words, these works are images of resistance. The survivors' direct, confrontational gazes are no longer those of terrified young children fearfully looking into their perpetrators' eyes begging for their lives, but rather, they are the defiant eyes boldly looking out and claiming a place—a voice—in history."[2] Abbamontian's assessment of the library's exhibit speaks also to Glendale's ethnopolitical entrepreneurs and to the Armenian population more generally. Members of Glendale's city council allocated resources ($15 million) to the library's renovation. In the renovation process, many (Armenian and non-Armenian) community members actively participated. These community members contributed their unique ideas and creativity. In so doing, they have created a beautiful, modern space for everyone in

FIGURE 20.   A portion of *iWitness: Armenian Genocide 1915*, a photographic and sculptural exhibition on display near the Glendale Central Library (2017).

Glendale as well as its many visitors. One does not need to be Armenian to enjoy the library, but for those who are, they can enter the public space and immediately connect their historical and global experiences to those in their new suburban home. By mobilizing co-ethnic constituents, ethnopolitical entrepreneurs in Glendale have translated the demographic concentration of Armenian newcomers into public services and political institutions that they actively participate in reconstructing and reimagining. The transformation of Glendale's public library is a microcosm of Glendale, which, in turn, is a microcosm of the gradual, sweeping transformation of the United States. As Abbamontian pointed out regarding the library's exhibit, the United States' immigrants are no longer terrified outsiders begging for acceptance; they now demand a place and a voice in the development and contribution of their communities and, ultimately, the country.

Notes

INTRODUCTION

1. At the time of my fieldwork, this stretch of the street was still Maryland Avenue. In 2018, Glendale's city council, which consisted of four Armenians and one non-Armenian, renamed it Artsakh Avenue in honor of the Armenian community of Glendale. Artsakh (or Nagorno-Karabakh) is a breakaway state between Armenia and Azerbaijan. Armenia and Azerbaijan have fought two wars over this territory (1988–1994 and 2020, respectively).

2. For a discussion of the circumstances giving rise to this transition, see Benjamin Carter Hett's *The Death of Democracy: Hitler's Rise to Power and the Downfall of the Weimar Republic* (2018).

3. See Peter Dreier, "A California Suburb Reckons with Its Nazi Past—and Present-Day Controversy Follows," *Salon*, August 19, 2017, https://www.salon.com/2017/08/19/a-california-suburb-reckons-with-its-nazi-past-and-present-day-controversy-follows/.

4. The 2011 American Community Survey estimates 214,628 Armenians lived in Los Angeles County at the time its data were collected. When I collected data for this book, roughly 40 percent of Los Angeles Armenians lived in Glendale.

5. For a list of current appointments, see City of Glendale, "Boards and Commissions," https://www.glendaleca.gov/government/departments/city-clerk/boards-and-commissions (accessed February 10, 2022).

6. Anna Purna Kambhampaty, "Asian American and Pacific Islanders' Record Turnout Helped Flip Georgia Blue; Now They Could Shape the Future of the Senate," *Time*, December 20, 2020, https://time.com/5922707/aapi-voters-georgia-senate-runoffs/.

7. In this racially diverse county, Black and Latino voters also played extremely important roles. For example, see US Census Bureau, "Quick Facts: Gwinnett County, Georgia; Georgia," https://www.census.gov/quickfacts/fact/table/gwinnettcountygeorgia,GA/PST045219 (accessed February 10, 2022).

8. As S. Karthick Ramakrishnan reported, "Voter turnout, which we measure as the voting rate among adult citizens, jumped 49.3% among Asian Americans in 2014 to 59.5% in 2020. . . . The only group with higher gains in voter turnout was Pacific Islanders, whose voting rates among adult citizens increased from 41.2% in 2016 to 55.7% in 2020—a 14-point gain in absolute terms, and a one-third increase in proportional terms over the 2016 baseline." S. Karthick Ramakrishnan, "In 2020, AAPIs Saw the Highest Increases in Voter Turnout," AAPI Data, May 18, 2021, http://aapidata.com/blog/2020-record-turnout/.

9. Quoted in Dartunorro Clark, "Georgia's Diversifying Suburbs Could Be Boon for Democrats in the Senate Runoffs," *NBC News*, January 4, 2021, https://www.nbcnews.com/politics/politics-news/georgia-s-diversifying-suburbs-could-be-boon-democrats-senate-runoffs-n1252293. The NGP, founded by Stacey Abrams, is a nonpartisan organization that works to register Georgia voters, particularly younger voters and racial and ethnic minorities.

10. Despite what took place in the 2020 and 2021 elections, this new chapter in US political history does not necessarily signify a wholesale partisan shift in the country's politics—from right to left on the political spectrum. Suburban immigrant political incorporation does not inherently give rise to a new generation of Democratic (or Republican) voters. This interpretation would oversimplify a more complex reality. Indeed, ethnopolitical

entrepreneurs themselves as well as their co-ethnic constituents inhabit both ends of this spectrum (see chapter 5). Rather, the new chapter refers to a new epicenter in where and how political mobilization takes place in many sites across the United States.

11. While new to politics in the United States, many Armenian diaspora communities brought considerable political experience from diverse host societies. For example, in Lebanon, the "confessional" system reserves seats for Armenians in Parliament; Armenians are also often members of the ministerial cabinet. Similarly, in Iran, Armenians are guaranteed two representatives to the Majlis in each election (Isfahan and Tehran). Thus, many Armenians did bring with them a culture of "contentious politics" (Tilly and Tarrow 2015), but, post-migration, these experiences more often "translated" into active roles in community organizations rather than positions as elected officials.

12. See Becky M. Nicolaides and Andrew Wiese, "Suburban Disequilibrium," *New York Times*, April 6, 2013, https://opinionator.blogs.nytimes.com/2013/04/06/suburban-disequilibrium/.

13. Suburbs are distinct from exurbs, which refer to rural counties that have been incorporated into metropolitan areas—that is, typically occurring outside of suburban spaces (Taylor 2011; Golding and Winkler 2020).

14. In *Ulysses*, James Joyce articulates this sense of duality: "We'll put force against force. . . . We have our greater Ireland beyond the sea. They were driven out of house and home in the black [18]47. . . . Ay, they drove out the peasants in hordes. Twenty thousand of them died in the coffinships. But those that came to the land of the free remember the land of bondage" (1986, 270).

15. Although less frequently used, *Americanization* is another term that occurs in the social scientific scholarship. It occurs less often because it relates only to immigrants' post-settlement experiences in the United States and, in addition, is a bit more ambiguous. Roger Waldinger argues that this ambiguity results, in part, from how Americans construct nationhood: "Only in the U.S. does one find so deep a conflict between the fundamentally liberal principles to which the American people have been committed right from the beginning and a contradictory, no less deeply held view that restricts legal or functional membership in the people on the basis of origin and kind" (2007, 138). In analyzing Americanization, scholars often evaluate first-generation (or foreign-born) immigrants' coping strategies as they transition from country of origin to the United States (Hill 1919; Barrett 1992; Van Nuys 2002; Biavaschi, Giulietti, and Siddique 2017). Traditionally, Americanization related to coercive strategies, which resulted in the assimilation of immigrants into the US "mainstream." More recent studies, however, have broadened this scholarship and unpacked newcomers' coping strategies and evolving emotional orientations to assimilationist pressures (de la Garza, Falcon, and Garcia 1996; Branton 2007; Abrajano 2010; Yang and de la Garza 2016; Biavaschi, Giulietti, and Siddique 2017; Fittante and Wilcox-Archuleta 2020).

16. The percentage of Armenians holding office varies based on the result of elections. For a list of the current demographic composition of elected officials in Glendale, see City of Glendale, City Hall, https://www.glendaleca.gov/government/city-hall/contact-city-officials (Glendale's city council, city clerk, city treasurer, and appointed officials) (accessed March 28, 2023); Glendale Unified School District, Board of Education, https://www.gusd.net/domain/6 (accessed March 28, 2023); and Glendale Community College Board of Trustees, https://www.glendale.edu/about-gcc/board-of-trustees/board-members (accessed March 28, 2023).

17. Because of cost limitations, I could not perform a random probability-based sample and instead relied on insertional knowledge of the Armenians of Los Angeles to distribute the survey as widely as possible. Despite the intensive data-gathering process, the data are not from a probability-based sample and, as a result, it is difficult to make claims or generalizations about the entire population with the survey's data alone.

1. THE ARMENIAN DIASPORA

1. The Kardashian family refers to the lawyer and businessman Robert Kardashian and his children, such as Kim Kardashian, who are prominent in the entertainment and social media fields.

2. From a different point of view, Khachig Tölölyan argues: "Curiously, the earlier, 1931 edition of this reference work [*Encyclopedia of the Social Sciences*] has an excellent entry on diasporas, authored by Simon Dubnow, who writes primarily on the Jewish diaspora as the paradigmatic case. But he also stipulates that the Greek colony-cities of Antiquity might be called diasporas, and adds that the Armenians, whose dispersion began in the mid-eleventh century, are also a 'typical' diaspora. Indeed, up until the late sixties, on the rare occasions when western scholars thought of diasporas, they took the Jewish diaspora to be the paradigm case and the Armenian and Greek dispersions to be the two other noteworthy examples of it" (1996, 9).

3. Khachig Tölölyan, "Diaspora: It's Hard to Say," *AIM: Armenian International Magazine*, February 28, 2001, 2, https://www.academia.edu/33490115/The_Armenian_Diaspora_Its_Hard_to_Say_in_AIM.

4. Some sources argue that the date of adoption was 314 CE (Bournoutian 1994).

5. This number includes only those titles for which there are known dates or places of publication, or both. For a list of these books and others, see the reference manual *Hay girk'ĕ 1512–1800 t'vakannerin: Hay hnatip grk'i matenagitut'yun* (Voskanian, Korkotian, and Savalian 1988).

6. Even as late as 1913, Yerevan's total population was thirty-four thousand—an indeterminate but significant number of which were of Tatar/Turkic/Azeri ethnic origin (*Statesman's Year-Book* 1921).

7. The Eastern vernacular was based on the Armenian of the Araratian plain. Both Western and Eastern intellectuals sought to find the "true" Armenian among the common people, but the Eastern side created a new language based on several dialects and the Western used a neutral dialect of the Ottoman capital—modified from 1852 on by the rapidly expanding Armenophone newspapers—as a lingua franca that eventually displaced the urban dialects.

8. The particular territories were those lost during the Russo-Turkish War of 1877–1878.

9. Three years earlier, the Allies penned the Treaty of Sèvres, which mandated the creation of an Armenian homeland (the so-called Wilsonian Armenia). This territory would have included much of historic Armenia as well as eastern Anatolia. However, shortly thereafter, further negotiations with the new Turkish Republic led to the creation of the Treaty of Lausanne and left Armenia, instead, with the much smaller territory, which today covers the Republic of Armenia.

10. From the mid-twentieth century onward, Armenian communities would also emerge in Oceania.

11. This section reproduces content from Daniel Fittante, "But Why Glendale? A History of Armenian Immigration to Southern California," *California History* 94, no. 3 (2017): 2–19.

12. Ferrer's poem is featured in a volume of historical tracts by Peter Force (1886, 3:31–35).

13. For further details on the local prejudices leveled at Armenians, see LaPiere 1930; Mirak 1983. For how these prejudices affected the second generation, see Bulbulian 2000.

14. Prior to 1965, the Egyptian Revolution (1952) had also depopulated a prominent Middle Eastern Armenian community and brought many Armenians to the United States. Armenian communities continue to exist in some places in the Middle East, such as Beirut and Tehran, but in much smaller numbers.

15. The Jackson-Vanik Amendment responded to Soviet legislation that sought to decrease Jewish emigration. It made trade relations with the United States dependent on a country's (in this case, Soviet bloc countries') freedom of emigration (Martin 2021). After the Iranian Revolution, the US government classified Iranian Armenians as a "persecuted religious minority" under the Lautenberg Amendment and, again, under the Specter Amendment. The latter amendment lowered the evidentiary threshold by which Armenians (as well as other religious minorities, such as the Baha'i, Jewish, Mandaean, and Zoroastrian communities) could "qualify" as "persecuted" and thus more easily move to the United States. With the increasing economic and geopolitical difficulties besetting Iran, many Iranian Armenians have opted to take advantage of these policies. Compensating for the absence of a US embassy in Iran, the Hebrew Immigrant Aid Society has facilitated the migration of many thousands of socioeconomically diverse Iranian Armenians from Iran to Southern California via Austria, where the organization is based (Fee 2021).

16. History and Social Justice, "Glendale," http://sundown.afro.illinois.edu/sundowntownsshow.php?id=1107 (accessed 2017).

17. *Glendale Evening News*, January 8, 1919.

18. *Glendale Evening News*, January 20, 1919.

19. Some other early Armenian settlers included the Pampians (or Pampaians)—Haigazoon, Vahan, and Hasmig. The *City of Glendale, South Glendale Historic Context Statement* indicates that "the 1920 Census identifies Glendale families with the surnames Ablahadian, Arklin, Bogohossian, Geradian, Hadian, Ignatius, Magariam, O'Gassim (Ogassin), and Sahgian" (City of Glendale, South Glendale Historic Context, Historic Resources Group 2014, 21).

20. *Glendale Evening News*, July 22, 1922. In Van, Armenians launched a defense against the Ottomans during the Hamidian massacres in 1896. The same community would also defend itself against the Ottomans during the genocide in 1915. This latter initiative is known as the Defense or Siege of Van.

21. *Glendale News-Press*, August 28, 1976.

22. *Glendale News-Press*, April 24, 1985.

23. Pasadena also experienced a comparatively small surge of Armenian newcomers, particularly from Lebanon.

24. "Schools Seek Funds to Aid Armenians," *Daily News* (Los Angeles), March 20, 1988; "Armenian Emigration Threatens Funds," *Glendale News-Press*, April 1, 1988; "Supervisors OK Funds for Armenian Groups," *Los Angeles Times*, November 11, 1989.

25. In 1995, USA Waste purchased Western Waste for $525 million. See Margaret Ramirez, "Western Waste to Be Bought by USA Waste; Mergers: The Deal to Purchase the Torrance Company for $525 Million Is Part of an Industry Trend toward Consolidation," *Los Angeles Times*, December 20, 1995, https://www.latimes.com/archives/la-xpm-1995-12-20-fi-15993-story.html.

26. See Gregory Rodriguez, "Glendale's 'Racist Shadow' Shrinks as City Transforms Itself," *Los Angeles Times*, June 16, 1996, http://articles.latimes.com/1996-06-16/opinion/op-15622_1_city-officials.

2. THE ARMENIANS OF GLENDALE

Parts of this chapter appear in the journal article by Daniel Fittante, "The Armenians of Glendale: An Ethnoburb in Los Angeles's San Fernando Valley," *City & Community* 17, no. 4 (2018): 1231–1247.

1. Patric Kuh, "The Kuh Review: Carousel; Going for a Spin at the Glendale Restaurant, Where the Scene Rivals the Armenian Classics," *Los Angeles Magazine*, December 2, 2014, https://www.lamag.com/digestblog/kuh-review-carousel/.

2. Given Armenians' classification as "white" (or "white ethnic"), it may be a bit problematic to refer to this phenomenon as "white flight." Nevertheless, the same demographic displacement of the previously established residents did occur.

3. US Census Bureau, "Quick Facts: Glendale City, California," https://www.census .gov/quickfacts/fact/table/glendalecitycalifornia/IPE12022 (accessed March 28, 2023).

4. Katherine Schaeffer, "10 Facts about Today's College Graduates," April 12, 2022, Pew Research Center, https://www.pewresearch.org/fact-tank/2022/04/12/10-facts-about -todays-college-graduates/.

5. US Census Bureau, 2010 IPUMS ACS.

6. For a listing of current board members, see City of Glendale, "Boards and Commissions," https://www.glendaleca.gov/government/departments/city-clerk/boards-and -commissions (accessed February 10, 2022).

7. Many Armenians who moved to Glendale in the 1970s carry with them painful stories about discrimination, and racial profiling against Armenians persists to this day. However, among those raised in Glendale, they reported feeling included and treated equally. According to Armenian Angeleno Survey (AAS) data, only 16.1 percent of respondents believe the police treat Armenians unfairly (see AAS question #36 in the online appendix available at https://ecommons.cornell.edu/handle/1813/113257). As Herbert J. Gans (1979) asserts of other "ethnic white" communities, ethnicity has become largely symbolic.

8. While Lung-Amam's (2017) chapter "That 'Monster House' Is My Home" investigates white residents' responses to the "mansionization" of multigenerational Asian homes in Fremont, many of the chapter's descriptions closely resemble what has taken place for the Armenians in Glendale.

9. As Francis D. K. Ching, Mark M. Jarzombek, and Vikramaditya Prakash note, "Though Byzantine architecture introduced the dome as an important potential element in Christian architecture, the Byzantine dome was not visible externally. Armenian architecture, by way of contrast, pushed the dome up over the mass of the building. . . . The silhouette achieved would have a profound impact on future church design" (2017, 284).

10. I did not identify any archival evidence connecting the city's decision to place St. Mary's on the protected list with Armenians' acquisition of the church; however, there is sufficient circumstantial evidence to at least leave some questions unanswered.

11. See Steve Ryfle, "Glendale Studies Ways to Ease Preservation Law; Development: Officials Weigh Changes That Would Make It Easier for Owners of Historic Buildings to Modify Their Properties," *Los Angeles Times*, July 25, 1995, https://www.latimes.com /archives/la-xpm-1995-07-25-me-27709-story.html.

12. See Steve Ryfle, "Cultures Clash over Glendale Church Building; History: Large Armenian Congregation Wants Its Historic Structure, Built by Christian Scientists in 1926, off Protected List; Preservationists Oppose the Move," *Los Angeles Times*, April 18, 1995, https://www.latimes.com/archives/la-xpm-1995-04-18-me-56083-story.html.

13. Glendale Historical Society, "Who We Are," https://glendalehistorical.org/who-we -are (accessed February 10, 2022).

14. Ryfle, "Clash over Glendale Church Building."

15. Josh Kleinbaum, "Banquet Hall Zoning Code under Review," *Glendale News-Press*, February 12, 2004, https://www.latimes.com/socal/glendale-news-press/news/tn-gnp -xpm-2004-02-12-export12416-story.html.

16. David Pierson, "Passions Flame over Kebabs," *Los Angeles Times*, November 4, 2006, https://www.latimes.com/archives/la-xpm-2006-nov-04-me-kebab4-story.html.

3. GLENDALE'S ETHNOPOLITICAL ENTREPRENEURS

1. Portions of this chapter appear in Daniel Fittante, "Glendale's Ethnopolitical Entrepreneurs: Suburban Immigrant Political Incorporation," *Ethnopolitics*, published online, February 13, 2020, https://doi.org/10.1080/17449057.2020.1725284.

2. See Willow Lung-Amam, "Why Trump's Suburban Strategy Failed: Did Black and Brown Cities Deliver Democrats the Election? Yes—and So Did Black and Brown Suburbs," Bloomberg CityLab, November 12, 2020, https://www.bloomberg.com/news/articles/2020-11-12/the-role-of-black-and-brown-suburbs-in-biden-s-win.

3. See Santiago O'Donnell, "Voters Opt for the Familiar in Balloting for Council," *Los Angeles Times*, April 6, 1989, https://www.latimes.com/archives/la-xpm-1989-04-06-gl-1587-story.html; and Santiago O'Donnell, "Coalition Bid Fails in Glendale Balloting," *Los Angeles Times*, April 13, 1989, https://www.latimes.com/archives/la-xpm-1989-04-13-gl-1605-story.html.

4. For the history of the restaurant and its Iranian Armenian owners, see Jenn Harris, "The Story behind Raffi's Place, and Some of the Best Koobideh Kebabs in Glendale," *Los Angeles Times*, March 21, 2018, https://www.latimes.com/food/dailydish/la-fo-re-raffis-place-20180321-story.html.

5. The Forty-Sixth State Assembly District covers central and southeastern San Fernando Valley—in Los Angeles County, Hollywood Hills, Lake Balboa, North Hills, North Hollywood, Panorama City, Sherman Oaks, Studio City, Toluca Lake, Valley Glen, Valley Village, Van Nuys, and Universal City.

6. See Jean Harris, "The Story behind Raffi's Place, and Some of the Best Koobideh Kebabs in Glendale," *Los Angeles Times*, March 21, 2018, https://www.latimes.com/food/dailydish/la-fo-re-raffis-place-20180321-story.html.

7. Office of Governor Gavin Newsom, "Governor Newsom Proclaims Day of Remembrance of the Armenian Genocide 2022," April 22, 2022: https://www.gov.ca.gov/2022/04/22/governor-newsom-proclaims-day-of-remembrance-of-the-armenian-genocide-2022/. The wording of the bill commemorates California residents whose family histories have been affected by genocides: "The Legislature finds and declares that Genocide Remembrance Day would be a day for all to reflect on past and present genocides, but especially those that have felt the impact of these atrocities and groups that have found refuge in California, including, but not limited to, the Holocaust, Holodomor, and the Genocides of the Armenian, Assyrian, Greek, Cambodian, and Rwandan communities. Genocide Remembrance Day would be observed annually on April 24, also known as Armenian Genocide Remembrance Day, during the week the state of California traditionally recognizes Genocide Awareness Week." "AB 1801; State Holidays: Genocide Remembrance Day," Open States, https://openstates.org/ca/bills/20212022/AB1801/ (accessed March 28, 2023).

8. See AAS question #23 in the online appendix available at https://ecommons.cornell.edu/handle/1813/113257.

9. See AAS question #18 in the online appendix available at https://ecommons.cornell.edu/handle/1813/113257.

10. The approach to absentee voting has changed. Before 2005, the absentee votes would be mailed to the campaign office, and people from the campaign office would then submit them to the city clerk's office. They would submit thousands of absentee voting forms at a time. In 2005, Glendale passed a law in which absentee votes had to be sent directly to the clerk's office. This change, however, has not caused a substantial change in voter turnout.

11. The Monica of the title was Monica Lewinsky.

12. See AAS questions #29 and #31 in the online appendix available at https://ecommons.cornell.edu/handle/1813/113257.

13. See AAS question #46 in the online appendix available at https://ecommons.cornell .edu/handle/1813/113257.

14. For a detailed description of this aberrant act, see Eric Schmitt, "The 2000 Campaign: The House Races; Republican's Unusual Gift: A Vote on the House Floor," *New York Times*, October 7, 2000.

15. According to the official webpage of the Armenian Assembly of America, the CAC "works to strengthen the ties between the U.S. and Armenia and keeps members of Congress engaged on Armenia-related issues. The Caucus advocates for increased trade and assistance to Armenia, self-determination for Artsakh, and supporting U.S. recognition of the Armenian Genocide," works to strengthen the ties between the United States and Armenia, and keeps members of Congress engaged on Armenia-related issues. The Caucus advocates for increased trade and assistance to Armenia, self-determination for Artsakh, and supporting US recognition of the Armenian Genocide (accessed March 28, 2023).

16. *Rabiz* refers to popular Armenian music and culture. However, like the English expression "fresh off the boat," or FOB, the term is often used as a pejorative to connote a backwardness of culture, a lack of civic virtue, or materialism, particularly among Armenians from post-Soviet Armenia. For extensive discussions of this phenomenon, see the scholarship of Rik Adriaans (2017, 2018), Levon Abrahamian (2006), and Susanne Fehlings (2016).

17. See AAS question #32 in the online appendix available at https://ecommons.cornell .edu/handle/1813/113257.

18. See AAS question #21 in the online appendix available at https://ecommons.cornell .edu/handle/1813/113257.

4. CREATING CONSTITUENTS

1. Adrin Nazarian mentioned to me that non-Armenian elected officials in Glendale had begun working with Armenian media personalities to persuade Armenian voters to oppose the project.

2. It should be noted that not all Armenian media supported Caruso. For example, see Josh Kleinbaum, "Americana Comes Back to Frommer," *Glendale News-Press*, June 18, 2004, https://www.latimes.com/socal/glendale-news-press/news/tn-gnp-xpm-2004-06 -18-export9534-story.html.

3. Some parts of this chapter appear in the journal article by Daniel Fittante, "Constructivist Theories of Political Incorporation," *Ethnicities*, 19, no. 5 (2019): 809–829.

4. Chandra (2012, 229) defines "activated ethnic demography" as the set and size of a population's activated ethnic identity categories. Furthermore, she claims that attribute and category are relational (rather than intrinsic)—that is, something that is a category may be distinct from something that is an attribute in relation to a category. As she argues: "Are 'blue eyes' an attribute or a category? Blue eyes can be attributes in relation to a category in one domain of analysis (e.g., White) but categories in relation to attributes in other domains of analysis (grey eyes, light blue eyes, deep blue eyes, greenish blue eyes). And 'White' in turn, while it may be a category in relation to the attribute of being blue-eyed, is itself an attribute in relation to a category in a different domain of analysis (e.g., WASP—White Anglo Saxon Protestant)" (106).

5. Also, according to AAS data, 9.9 percent of those surveyed indicated no preference about whether candidates were Armenian ("Don't care") and 5.9 percent did not know ("Don't know").

6. I have slightly adapted these processes to fit changing ethnic demography and immigrant political incorporation in US ethnoburbs.

7. See also Laitin's *Identity in Formation: The Russian-Speaking Populations in the Near Abroad* (1998).

8. In addition, Najarian is married to a Latin American reporter, Palmira Perez.

9. This internal diversity extends beyond country of origin and generation. For example, Iranian Armenians or Soviet Armenians who grew up in prerevolutionary Iran or Soviet Armenia bring with them a distinct set of social remittances, as do those who were socialized in a postrevolutionary Iran or Armenia.

10. Before Wilson, from 1982 to 1986, the governor was George Deukmejian, an Armenian American.

11. See Ballotpedia, s.v. "Nayiri Nahabedian," https://ballotpedia.org/Nayiri_Nahabedian (accessed February 10, 2022).

5. IS POLITICAL INCORPORATION ENOUGH?

1. Portions of this chapter appear in the journal article by Daniel Fittante, "Perceptual Disconnect: An Ethnographic Account of Immigrant Political Incorporation," *International Migration* 58, no. 2 (2020): 3–14.

2. Another example of this sentiment is found in an editorial cartoon from the *Glendale News-Press*, October 4, 2019. In the cartoon, "Longing Yesterday," the artist Bert Ring depicts white Glendale residents responding to the city council's 2018 decision to change the name of a downtown street—from Maryland Avenue to Artsakh Avenue—to honor the community's Armenian population. For a response to this editorial cartoon, see "Glendale AYF Angered about News-Press Editorial Cartoon," *Asbarez*, October 5, 2019, https://asbarez.com/glendale-ayf-angered-about-news-press-editorial-cartoon/.

3. Beers resigned the position in August 2020.

4. For the most recent report, see City of Glendale, *Workforce Demographics, 2003 through 2016* (2018).

5. For a list of the members of the current board, see Glendale Unified School District, Board of Education, https://www.gusd.net/domain/6 (accessed March 28, 2023).

6. For current listings, see Glendale Community College, "Academic Division Chairs," https://www.glendale.edu/academics/academic-divisions/academic-divisions-chairs (accessed March 15, 2019).

7. For current listings, see Glendale Community College, "Administration," https://www.glendale.edu/about-gcc/administration (accessed March 15, 2019).

8. See Glendale Community College, "Current Board Members," https://www.glendale.edu/about-gcc/board-of-trustees/board-members (accessed March 15, 2019).

9. For current statistics, see Glendale Community College, "College Profile—Student Demographics," https://www.glendale.edu/about-gcc/gcc-overview/institutional-effectiveness/research/campus-profile/campus-profile-access-student-demographics (accessed March 15, 2019).

10. In the case of the fire and police departments, the statistical disparities may also result from the amount of time that is necessary for immigrants to acquire institutional, linguistic, and social familiarity.

11. Students may also take French, German, Spanish, or Italian; however, these immersion programs allocate only one hour of non-English instruction per school day.

12. The City of Glendale's dual-language immersion programs as well as its city literature all occur in Eastern Armenian, the standardized form spoken in the Republic of Armenia.

13. This disparity is not synonymous with indifference, however. The same respondents who do not acknowledge any visible or palpable effects of co-ethnic elected officials also speak about the importance of such officials' existence. Most of those I

interviewed said they consistently voted for Armenian candidates and wanted to see more Armenian representation. Some even had volunteered on these candidates' campaigns.

14. See Lila Seidman, "Glendale Landlords May Soon Have to Limit Annual Rent Increases to 7% or Pay Tenant Relocation Fees," *Glendale News-Press*, February 7, 2019, https://www.latimes.com/socal/glendale-news-press/news/tn-gnp-me-glendale-right-to-lease-20190206-story.html.

15. Barreto and Garcia (2011) undertook regression analyses of immigrant voting in Glendale. They analyzed twenty-two Glendale elections (for seats on the city council, school board, and community college board) between 2003 and 2011. From their sampling, they found "strong evidence of group cohesion in favor of Armenian candidates and far lower levels of support from non-Armenian Whites" (1). According to their report, "Armenians in Glendale show some of the strongest group voting patterns in the state" (6). Barreto and Garcia found that, quite often, up to 80 percent of voter support for Armenian candidates typically comes from co-ethnics. In fact, Barreto and Garcia's regression analyses demonstrate that Glendale experiences among the highest incidents of ethnically or racially polarized voting in the country.

16. A third person who won office in 2017, Vrej Agajanian, also promoted more affordable housing and stricter rent controls. He received a comparable number of votes (9,551) as compared to those received by Sinanyan and Najarian. See City of Glendale, "Election Results 2017," https://www.glendalevotes.org/election-archives/election-results-2017 (accessed March 15, 2019.

17. See City of Glendale, "General Municipal Election Results—2013," https://www.glendalevotes.org/home/showpublisheddocument/13169/635379269400630000 (accessed February 10, 2022).

18. See City of Glendale, "Election Results 2015," https://www.glendalevotes.org/past-elections/election-results-2015 (accessed February 10, 2022).

19. When we spoke, Fuentes was also working with the Filipino American Business Association of Glendale to build the Filipino American Friendship Monument in the city. Among other things, the monument would commemorate Filipinos' over thirty-year presence in and contributions to Glendale.

20. For Abrajano and Hajnal (2015), "white backlash" refers to the defection of Democratic white voters to the Republican Party owing to immigration; I am referring merely to the political consolidation of white Glendale voters in response to the emergence of ethnopolitical entrepreneurs (whose votes depend on immigrants as well as other co-ethnic populations).

6. THE ARMENIAN AMERICAN MUSEUM

1. The Armenian Cultural Foundation, a nonprofit organization, advances and preserves Armenian heritage through educational and cultural initiatives.

2. Sahakian has also served as the chair of the City of Glendale Arts and Culture Commission, chair of the Glendale Youth Alliance, and president of the Glendale Parks and Open Space Foundation. In addition, before his museum appointment, Sahakian had previously been a member of the Armenian Genocide Centennial Committee.

3. See "More than $2.2 Million Raised at 2nd Annual Armenian American Museum Gala," *Asbarez*, December 12, 2019, https://asbarez.com/more-than-2-2-million-raised-at-2nd-annual-armenian-american-museum-gala/.

4. Arsine Torosyan, "Senator Anthony J. Portantino Visits Armenian American Museum Construction Site," Armenian American Museum and Cultural Center of California, February 4, 2022, https://www.armenianamericanmuseum.org/senator-anthony-j-portantino-visits-armenian-american-museum-construction-site/.

5. See "Congressman Schiff Tours Armenian American Museum and Cultural Center," *Glendale News-Press*, March 1, 2022, https://glendalenewspress.outlooknewspapers
.com/blog/2022/03/01/congressman-schiff-tours-armenian-american-museum-and
-cultural-center/.

6. Some examples featured in the daily news cycle included ascertainment (and the General Services Administration), certification procedures, safe harbor day, and the Twenty-Fifth Amendment.

7. Geoffrey Skelley, Elena Mejía, Amelia Thomson-DeVeaux, and Laura Bronner, "Why the Suburbs Have Shifted Blue," FiveThirtyEight, December 16, 2020, https://
fivethirtyeight.com/features/why-the-suburbs-have-shifted-blue/.

8. It should be noted that four of these seats featured candidates who ran unopposed (the non-Armenian candidate also ran unopposed).

9. Quoted in "Landslide Victory for ANCA Endorsed Candidates in California," *Armenian Weekly*, April 6, 2017, http://armenianweekly.com/2017/04/06/landslide-victory
-for-anca-endorsed-candidates-in-california/.

10. Larry Zarian, the first Armenian American voted into office in 1983, accomplished this task with very low voter turnout among Armenian Americans (see chapter 1).

11. See Alene Tchekmedyian, "Jewel City Shines in FBI Report," *Glendale News-Press*, November 13, 2014, https://www.latimes.com/socal/glendale-news-press/news/tn-gnp
-jewel-city-shines-in-fbi-report-20141113-story.html; see also Katie McEntire, "California's 50 Safest Cities," SafeWise, June 22, 2021, https://www.safewise.com/blog/safest
-cities-california/.

EPILOGUE

1. Quoted in Elise Kalfayan, "'Re-imagined' Glendale Central Library to Open May 1," *Asbarez*, April 27, 2017, http://asbarez.com/162683/re-imagined-glendale-central-library
-to-open-may-1/. The TUMO Center for Creative Technologies is an education and technology center. It opened in Armenia in 2011 and now has centers in France, Lebanon, Russia, and elsewhere. The centers provide free, hands-on training for Armenian teenagers in various disciplines that integrate digital technology and engineering.

2. Quoted in Aline Smithson, "Ara Oshagan and Collaborators: Landscape of Memory: Witnesses & Remnants of the Armenian Genocide," *Lenscratch*, May 28, 2017, http://
lenscratch.com/2017/05/the-states-project-maine-5/.

References

Abrahamian, Levon. 2006. *Armenian Identity in a Changing World*. Armenian Studies Series, no. 8. Costa Mesa, CA: Mazda Publishers.

Abrajano, Marisa. 2010. *Campaigning to the New American Electorate: Advertising to Latino Voters*. Stanford, CA: Stanford University Press.

Abrajano, Marisa, and Zoltan Hajnal. 2015. *White Backlash: Immigration, Race, and American Politics*. Princeton, NJ: Princeton University Press.

Abrams, Dominic, and Michael A. Hogg. 2006. *Social Identifications: A Social Psychology of Intergroup Relations and Group Processes*. London: Routledge.

Abramson, Scott. 2013. "Lebanese Armenians: A Distinctive Community in the Armenian Diaspora and in Lebanese Society." *Levantine Review* 2 (2): 188–216.

Acemoglu, Daron, and James A. Robinson. 2020. *The Narrow Corridor: States, Societies, and the Fate of Liberty*. New York: Penguin.

Adriaans, Rik. 2017. "Dances with Oligarchs: Performing the Nation in Armenian Civic Activism." *Caucasus Survey* 5 (2): 142–159.

——. 2018. "Of Oligarchs, Orientalists, and Cosmopolitans: How 'Armenian' Is *Rabiz* Music?" *Nationalities Papers* 46 (4): 704–716.

Airgood-Obrycki, Whitney, Bernadette Hanlon, and Shannon Rieger. 2021. "Delineate the U.S. Suburb: An Examination of How Different Definitions of the Suburbs Matter." *Journal of Urban Affairs* 43 (9): 1263–1284.

Alba, Richard, Glenn Deane, Nancy Denton, Ilir Disha, Brian McKenzie, and Jeffrey Napierala. 2014. "The Role of Immigrant Enclaves for Latino Residential Inequalities." *Journal of Ethnic and Migration Studies* 40 (1): 1–20.

Alba, Richard, and Victor Nee. 1997. "Rethinking Assimilation Theory for a New Era of Immigration." *International Migration Review* 31 (4): 826-874.

——. 2003. *Remaking the American Mainstream: Assimilation and Contemporary Immigration*. Cambridge, MA: Harvard University Press.

Albarracín, Julia. 2016. *At the Core and in the Margins: Incorporation of Mexican Immigrants in Two Rural Midwestern Communities*. East Lansing: Michigan State University Press.

Alexander, Benjamin F. 2005. "Armenian and American: The Changing Face of Ethnic Identity and Diasporic Nationalism, 1915–1955." PhD diss., City University of New York.

Anacker, Katrin B., ed. 2016. *The New American Suburb: Poverty, Race and the Economic Crisis*. New York: Routledge.

Antaramian, Richard. 2022. "Confessionalism, Centralism, Armenians, and Ottoman Imperial Governance in the 18th and 19th Centuries." *International Journal of Middle East Studies* 54 (2): 319–337.

Appadurai, Arjun. 1996. "Global Ethnoscapes: Notes and Queries for a Transnational Anthropology." In *Modernity at Large: Cultural Dimensions of Globalization*, 48–65. Minneapolis: University of Minnesota Press.

Arroyo, Juliet. 2006. *Glendale, 1940–2000: Images of America*. Charleston, SC: Arcadia Publishing.

Aslanian, Sebouh. 2014. *From the Indian Ocean to the Mediterranean: The Global Trade Networks of Armenian Merchants from New Julfa.* Berkeley: University of California Press.

Bakalian, Anny. 1993. *Armenian-Americans: From Being to Feeling Armenian.* New Brunswick, NJ: Transaction Publishers.

Bakalian, Anny, and Mehdi Bozorgmehr. 2009. *Backlash 9/11: Middle Eastern and Muslim Americans Respond.* Berkeley: University of California Press.

Barreto, Matt, and Sergio Garcia. 2011. *An Analysis of Voting Patterns in Glendale, CA.* Glendale, CA: Redistricting Partners. Accessed April 26, 2017. http://www.glendale.edu/home/showdocument?id=14288.

Barrett, James R. 1992. "Americanization from the Bottom Up: Immigration and the Remaking of the Working Class in the United States, 1880–1930." *Journal of American History* 79 (3): 996–1020.

Barry, James. 2019. *Armenian Christians in Iran: Ethnicity, Religion, and Identity in the Islamic Republic.* Cambridge: Cambridge University Press.

Barsoumian, Hagop Levon. 1980. "The Armenian Amira Class of Istanbul." PhD diss., Columbia University.

Baumann, Markus, Marc Debus, and Jochen Müller. 2015. "Personal Characteristics of MPs and Legislative Behavior in Moral Policymaking." *Legislative Studies Quarterly* 40 (2): 179–210.

Bevelander, Pieter, and Ravi Pendakur. 2009. "Social Capital and Voting Participation of Immigrants and Minorities in Canada." *Ethnic and Racial Studies* 32 (8): 1406–1430.

Biavaschi, Costanza, Corrado Giulietti, and Zahra Siddique. 2017. "The Economic Payoff of Name Americanization." *Journal of Labor Economics* 35 (4): 1089–1116.

Bleich, Erik, Irene Bloemraad, and Els de Graauw. 2015. "Migrants, Minorities and the Media: Information, Representations and Participation in the Public Sphere." *Journal of Ethnic and Migration Studies* 41 (6): 857–873.

Bloemraad, Irene. 2006. *Becoming a Citizen: Incorporating Immigrants and Refugees in the United States and Canada.* Berkeley: University of California Press.

Bonacich, Edna. 1973. "A Theory of Middleman Minorities." *American Sociological Review* 38 (5): 583–594.

Bonilla-Silva, Eduardo. 2004. "From Bi-racial to Tri-racial: Towards a New System of Racial Stratification in the USA." *Ethnic and Racial Studies* 27 (6): 931–950.

Bourdieu, Pierre. 1991. *Language and Symbolic Power.* Cambridge, MA: Harvard University Press.

Bournoutian, George A. 1994. *A History of the Armenian People: 1500 AD to the Present.* Vol. 2. Costa Mesa, CA: Mazda Publishers.

Boyles, Andrea S. 2015. *Race, Place, and Suburban Policing: Too Close for Comfort.* Berkeley: University of California Press.

Bozorgmehr, Mehdi. 1997. "Internal Ethnicity: Iranians in Los Angeles." *Sociological Perspectives* 40 (3): 387–408.

Bozorgmehr, Mehdi, and Georges Sabagh. 1988. "High Status Immigrants: A Statistical Profile of Iranians in the United States." *Iranian Studies* 21 (3/4): 5–36.

Branton, Regina. 2007. "Latino Attitudes toward Various Areas of Public Policy: The Importance of Acculturation." *Political Research Quarterly* 60 (2): 293–303.

Briggs, Xavier de Souza. 2013. "Conclusion: Rethinking Immigrant Political Incorporation: What Have We Learned, and What Next?" In Hochschild et al. 2013, 321–342.

Browning, Rufus, Dale Marshall, and David Tabb. 1984. *Protest Is Not Enough: The Struggle of Blacks and Hispanics for Equality in Urban Politics.* Berkley: University of California Press.

——. 1990. *Racial Politics in American Cities*. Harlow, England: Longman Publishing Group.

Brubaker, Rogers. 2004. *Ethnicity without Groups*. Cambridge, MA: Harvard University Press.

——. 2005. "The 'Diaspora' Diaspora." *Ethnic and Racial Studies* 28 (1): 1–19.

——. 2015. *Grounds for Difference*. Cambridge, MA: Harvard University Press.

——. 2017. "Revisiting 'The "Diaspora" Diaspora.'" *Ethnic and Racial Studies* 40 (9): 1556–1561.

Bueker, Catherine Simpson. 2005. "Political Incorporation among Immigrants from Ten Areas of Origin: The Persistence of Source Country Effects." *International Migration Review* 39 (1): 103–140.

Bulbulian, Berge. 2000. *The Fresno Armenians: History of a Diaspora Community*. Fresno: Press at California State University, Fresno.

Burden, Barry C. 2007. *Personal Roots of Representation*. Princeton, NJ: Princeton University Press.

Burns, Peter F. 2006. *Electoral Politics Is Not Enough: Racial and Ethnic Minorities and Urban Politics*. Albany: State University of New York Press.

Calvo, Rocío, Joanna M. Jablonska-Bayro, and Mary C. Waters. 2017. "Obamacare in Action: How Access to the Health Care System Contributes to Immigrants' Sense of Belonging." *Journal of Ethnic and Migration Studies* 43 (12): 2020–2036.

Carpio, Genevieve, Clara Irazábal, and Laura Pulido. 2011. "Right to the Suburb? Rethinking Lefebvre and Immigrant Activism." *Journal of Urban Affairs* 33 (2): 185–208.

Cattacin, Sandro. 2009. "Differences in the City: Parallel Worlds, Migration, and Inclusion of Differences in the Urban Space." In Hochschild and Mollenkopf 2009, 250–259.

Chahin, Mark. 2001. *The Kingdom of Armenia*. London: Routledge.

Chahinian, Talar, and Anny Bakalian. 2016. "Language in Armenian American Communities: Western Armenian and Efforts for Preservation." *International Journal of the Sociology of Language*, no. 237: 37–57.

Chakravorty, Sanjoy, Devesh Kapur, and Nirvikar Singh. 2016. *The Other One Percent: Indians in America*. New York: Oxford University Press.

Chandra, Kanchan, ed. 2012. *Constructivist Theories of Ethnic Politics*. New York: Oxford University Press.

Chandra, Kanchan, and Cilanne Boulet. 2012. "A Baseline Model of Change in an Activated Ethnic Demography." In Chandra 2012, 229–276.

Chang, Yoonmee. 2010. *Writing the Ghetto: Class, Authorship, and the Asian American Ethnic Enclave*. New Brunswick, NJ: Rutgers University Press.

Chao, Melody Manchi, Chi-yue Chiu, Wayne Chan, Rodolfo Mendoza-Denton, and Carolyn Kwok. 2013. "The Model Minority as a Shared Reality and Its Implication for Interracial Perceptions." *Asian American Journal of Psychology* 4 (2): 84–92.

Ching, Francis D. K., Mark M. Jarzombek, and Vikramaditya Prakash. 2017. *A Global History of Architecture*. Hoboken, NJ: John Wiley & Sons.

City of Glendale. 2018. *Workforce Demographics, 2003 through 2016*. Glendale, CA: City of Glendale. https://www.glendaleca.gov/home/showdocument?id=43136.

City of Glendale, South Glendale Historic Context, Historic Resources Group. 2014. *City of Glendale, South Glendale Historic Context Statement, September 30, 2014*. Glendale, CA: City of Glendale, South Glendale Historic Context, Historic Resources Group. https://www.glendaleca.gov/home/showpublisheddocument/42068/63651 2648973800000.

Clerge, Orly. 2019. *The New Noir: Race, Identity, and Diaspora in Black Suburbia*. Berkeley: University of California Press.

Cohen, Robin. 2008. *Global Diasporas: An Introduction*. London: Routledge.

Cohen, Robin, and Carolin Fischer, eds. 2019. *Routledge Handbook of Diaspora Studies*. London: Routledge.

Collet, Christian. 2005. "Bloc Voting, Polarization, and the Panethnic Hypothesis: The Case of Little Saigon." *Journal of Politics* 67 (3): 907–933.

Cook, Maria Lorena. 2013. "Is Incorporation of Unauthorized Immigrants Possible? Inclusion and Contingency for Nonstatus Migrants and Legal Immigrants." In Hochschild et al. 2013, 43–64.

Coon, David R. 2014. *Look Closer: Suburban Narratives and American Values in Film and Television*. New Brunswick, NJ: Rutgers University Press.

Coser, Lewis. 1956. *The Functions of Social Conflict*. Glencoe, IL: Free Press.

Craver, Earlene. 2009. "On the Boundary of White: The Cartozian Naturalization Case and the Armenians, 1923–1925." *Journal of American Ethnic History* 28 (2): 30–56.

Dadrian, Vahakn N. 2003. *The History of the Armenian Genocide: Ethnic Conflict from the Balkans to Anatolia to the Caucasus*. New York: Berghahn Books.

Dahl, Robert. 1961. *Who Governs? Democracy and Power in an American City*. New Haven, CT: Yale University Press.

De Brey, Cristobal, Thomas D. Snyder, Anlan Zhang, and Sally A. Dillow. 2021. *Digest of Education Statistics 2019*. NCES 2021-009. Washington, DC: National Center for Education Statistics.

de la Garza, Rodolfo O., Angelo Falcon, and F. Chris Garcia. 1996. "Will the Real Americans Please Stand Up: Anglo and Mexican-American Support for Core American Political Values." *American Journal of Political Science* 40 (2): 335–351.

Diamond, John B., and Linn Posey-Maddox. 2020. "The Changing Terrain of the Suburbs: Examining Race, Class, and Place in Suburban Schools and Communities." *Equity and Excellence in Education* 53 (1–2): 7–13.

Dufoix, Stéphane. 2008. *Diasporas*. Berkeley: University of California Press.

——. 2017. *The Dispersion: A History of the Word Diaspora*. Leiden: Brill.

Eckstein, Susan. 2006. "Transnational Family Based Social Capital: Remittances and the Transformation of Cuba." *International Journal of Sociology of the Family* 32 (2): 141–171.

——. 2009. *The Immigrant Divide: How Cuban Americans Changed the US and Their Homeland*. New York: Routledge.

Eckstein, Susan, and Mette Berg. 2009. "Cubans in the United States and Spain: The Diaspora Generational Divide." *Diaspora: A Journal of Transnational Studies* 18 (1/2): 159–183.

Entzinger, Han, and Renske Biezeveld. 2003. *Benchmarking in Immigrant Integration*. Rotterdam: Erasmus University.

Faist, Thomas. 2010. "Diaspora and Transnationalism: What Kind of Dance Partners?" In *Diaspora and Transnationalism: Concepts, Theories and Methods*, edited by Rainer Bauböck and Thomas Faist, 9–34. Amsterdam: Amsterdam University Press.

Fearon, James D. 1999. "Why Ethnic Politics and 'Pork' Tend to Go Together." Paper presented at the SSRC-MacArthur sponsored conference "Ethnic Politics and Democratic Stability," University of Chicago, May 1999.

Fee, Molly. 2021. "Lives Stalled: The Costs of Waiting for Refugee Resettlement." *Journal of Ethnic and Migration Studies*. Published online, February 18, 2021. https://doi.org/10.1080/1369183X.2021.1876554.

Fehlings, Susanne. 2016. "The Ignoble Savage in Urban Yerevan." *Central Asian Survey* 35 (2): 195–217.

Feiock, Richard C., Moon-Gi Jeong, and Jaehoon Kim. 2003. "Credible Commitment and Council-Manager Government: Implications for Policy Instrument Choices." *Public Administration Review* 63 (5): 616–625.

Fishman, Robert L. 1987. "American Suburbs / English Suburbs: A Transatlantic Comparison." *Journal of Urban History* 13 (3): 237–251.

——. 2008. *Bourgeois Utopias: The Rise and Fall of Suburbia.* New York: Basic Books.

Fittante, Daniel. 2017. "But Why Glendale? A History of Armenian Immigration to Southern California." *California History* 94 (3): 2–19.

——. 2018. "The Armenians of Glendale: An Ethnoburb in Los Angeles's San Fernando Valley." *City & Community* 17 (4): 1231–1247.

——. 2019. "Constructivist Theories of Political Incorporation." *Ethnicities* 19 (5): 809–829.

——. 2020. "Glendale's Ethnopolitical Entrepreneurs: Suburban Immigrant Political Incorporation." *Ethnopolitics.* Published online, February 13, 2020. https://doi.org/10.1080/17449057.2020.1725284.

——. 2020. "Perceptual Disconnect: An Ethnographic Account of Immigrant Political Incorporation." *International Migration* 58 (2): 3–14.

Fittante, Daniel, and Bryan Wilcox-Archuleta. 2020. "The Armenians of Los Angeles: Rethinking "Americanization." *Nationalism and Ethnic Politics* 26 (3): 221–239.

Foner, Nancy. 1997. "What's New about Transnationalism? New York Immigrants Today and at the Turn of the Century." *Diaspora: A Journal of Transnational Studies* 6 (3): 355–375.

——. 2001. *New Immigrants in New York.* New York: Columbia University Press.

Fong, Timothy P. 1994. *The First Suburban Chinatown: The Remaking of Monterey Park, California.* Philadelphia: Temple University Press.

Force, Peter, ed. 1886. *Tracts and Other Papers, relating Principally to the Origins of the Colonies in North America.* Vol. 3. Washington.

Forsyth, Ann. 2012. "Defining Suburbs." *Journal of Planning Literature* 27 (3): 270–281.

Fox, Cybelle. 2012. *Three Worlds of Relief: Race, Immigration, and the American Welfare State from the Progressive Era to the New Deal.* Princeton, NJ: Princeton University Press.

Frasure, Lorrie A., and Michael Jones-Correa. 2010. "The Logic of Institutional Interdependency: The Case of Day Laborer Policy in Suburbia." *Urban Affairs Review* 45 (4): 451–482.

Frasure-Yokley, Lorrie. 2015. *Racial and Ethnic Politics in American Suburbs.* New York: Cambridge University Press.

Frey, William H. 2011. *Melting Pot Cities and Suburbs: Racial and Ethnic Change in Metro American in the 2000s.* Washington, DC: Brookings Institution. https://www.brookings.edu/research/melting-pot-cities-and-suburbs-racial-and-ethnic-change-in-metro-america-in-the-2000s/.

Gans, Herbert J. 1979. "Symbolic Ethnicity: The Future of Ethnic Groups and Cultures in America." *Ethnic and Racial Studies* 2 (1): 1–20.

——. 1997. "Toward a Reconciliation of 'Assimilation' and 'Pluralism': The Interplay of Acculturation and Ethnic Retention." *International Migration Review* 31 (4): 875–892.

——. 1999. "The Possibility of a New Racial Hierarchy in the Twenty-First-Century United States." In *The Cultural Territories of Race: Black and White Boundaries,* edited by Michèle Lamont, 371–390. Chicago: University of Chicago Press.

Gerstle, Gary. 2001. *American Crucible: Race and Nation in the Twentieth Century.* Princeton, NJ: Princeton University Press.

——. 2013. "Acquiescence or Transformation? Divergent Paths of Political Incorporation in America." In Hochschild et al. 2013, 306–320.

Gerstle, Gary, and John Mollenkopf. 2001. *E Pluribus Unum? Contemporary and Historical Perspectives on Immigrant Political Incorporation*. New York: Russell Sage Foundation.

Geertz, Clifford. 1973. *The Interpretation of Cultures : Selected Essays*. New York: Basic Books.

Ghazarian, Jacob G. 2018. *The Armenian Kingdom in Cilicia during the Crusades: The Integration of Cilician Armenians with the Latins, 1080–1393*. London: RoutledgeCurzon.

Ghougassian, Vazken Sarkis. 1998. *The Emergence of the Armenian Diocese of New Julfa in the Seventeenth Century*. Atlanta, GA: Scholars Press.

Glazer, Nathan, and Daniel Patrick Moynihan. 1970. *Beyond the Melting Pot: The Negroes, Puerto Ricans, Jews, Italians, and Irish of New York City*. Cambridge, MA: MIT Press.

Golding, Shaun A., and Richelle L. Winkler. 2020. "Tracking Urbanization and Exurbs: Migration across the Rural–Urban Continuum, 1990–2016." *Population Research and Policy Review* 39: 835–859.

Gomez, Edmund Terence, and Hsin-Huang Michael Hsiao, eds. 2004. *Chinese Enterprise, Transnationalism, and Identity*. New York: Routledge.

Gordon, Colin. 2019. *Citizen Brown: Race, Democracy, and Inequality in the St. Louis Suburbs*. Chicago: University of Chicago Press.

Gregg, Heather S. 2002. "Divided They Conquer: The Success of Armenian Ethnic Lobbies in the United States." Rosemary Rogers Working Paper Series, no. 13. Massachusetts Institute of Technology, Cambridge, MA.

Grossman, Jonathan. 2019. "Toward a Definition of Diaspora." *Ethnic and Racial Studies* 42 (8): 1263–1282.

Hajnal, Zoltan, and Taeku Lee. 2011. *Why Americans Don't Join the Party: Race, Immigration and the Failure of Political Parties to Engage the Electorate*. Princeton, NJ: Princeton University Press.

Hajnal, Zoltan, and Jessica Trounstine. 2014. "What Underlies Urban Politics? Race, Class, Ideology, Partisanship, and the Urban Vote." *Urban Affairs Review* 50 (1): 63–99.

Hamel, Pierre, and Roger Keil, eds. 2015. *Suburban Governance: A Global View*. Toronto: University of Toronto Press.

Hanlon, Bernadette. 2009. *Once the American Dream: Inner-Ring Suburbs of the Metropolitan United States*. Philadelphia: Temple University Press.

Hardwick, Susan Wiley. 1993. *Russian Refuge: Religion, Migration, and Settlement on the North American Pacific Rim*. Chicago: University of Chicago Press.

Harris, Richard, and Robert Lewis. 2001. "The Geography of North American Cities and Suburbs, 1900–1950: A New Synthesis." *Journal of Urban History* 27 (3): 262–292.

Haynes, Bruce D. 2001. *Red Lines, Black Spaces: The Politics of Race and Space in a Black Middle-Class Suburb*. New Haven, CT: Yale University Press.

Haynes, Chris, and S. Karthick Ramakrishnan. 2015. "How Much Do They Help? Ethnic Media and Political Knowledge in the United States." In *Just Ordinary Citizens? Towards a Comparative Portrait of the Political Immigrant*, edited by Antoine Bilodeau, 113–129. Toronto: University of Toronto Press.

Heitman, Sidney. 1987. *The Third Soviet Emigration: Jewish, German, and Armenian Emigration from the USSR since World War II*. Cologne: Bundesinstitut für ostwissenschaftliche und internationale Studien.

Herzig, Edmund M. 1996. "The Rise of the Julfa Merchants in the Late Sixteenth Century." *Pembroke Papers* 4 (1): 305–322.

Hett, Benjamin Carter. 2018. *The Death of Democracy: Hitler's Rise to Power and the Downfall of the Weimar Republic*. New York: Henry Holt.

Hewsen, Robert H. 2001. *Armenia: A Historical Atlas*. Chicago: University of Chicago Press.

Hill, Howard C. 1919. "The Americanization Movement." *American Journal of Sociology* 24 (6): 609–642.

Hochschild, Jennifer, Jacqueline Chattopadhyay, Claudine Gay, and Michael Jones-Correa, eds. 2013. *Outsiders No More? Models of Immigrant Political Incorporation*. New York: Oxford University Press.

Hochschild, Jennifer, and John Mollenkopf, eds. 2009a. *Bringing Outsiders In: Transatlantic Perspectives on Immigrant Political Incorporation*. Ithaca, NY: Cornell University Press.

——. 2009b. "Modeling Immigrant Political Incorporation." In Hochschild and Mollenkopf 2009a, 15–30.

Horton, John. 1995. *The Politics of Diversity: Immigration, Resistance, and Change in Monterey Park, California*. Philadelphia: Temple University Press.

Hovannisian, Richard, ed. 1998. *Remembrance and Denial: The Case of the Armenian Genocide*. Detroit: Wayne State University Press.

——, ed. 2009. *The Armenian Genocide in Perspective*. New Brunswick, NJ: Transaction Publishers.

Itzigsohn, José. 2009. *Encountering American Faultlines: Race, Class, and the Dominican Experience in Providence*. New York: Russell Sage Foundation.

Jackson, Kenneth T. 1987. *Crabgrass Frontier: The Suburbanization of the United States*. New York: Oxford University Press.

Jiménez, Tomás. 2010. *Replenished Ethnicity: Mexican Americans, Immigration, and Identity*. Berkeley: University of California Press.

Jones, Philip E. 2009. "Politicians Are People Too." In *The Future of Political Science: 100 Perspectives*, ed. Gary King, Kay L. Schlozman, and Norman H. Nie, 16–18. New York: Routledge.

Jones-Correa, Michael. 2005. "Bringing Outsiders In: Questions of Immigrant Incorporation." In *The Politics of Democratic Inclusion*, edited by Christina Wolbrecht and Rodney Hero, 75–101. Philadelphia: Temple University Press.

——. 2008. "Race to the Top? The Politics of Immigrant Education in Suburbia." In *New Faces in New Places: The Changing Geography of American Immigration*, edited by Douglas Massey, 308–340. New York: Russell Sage Foundation.

——. 2013. "Thru-Ways, By-Ways, and Cul-de-Sacs of Immigrant Political Incorporation." In Hochschild et al. 2013, 176–191.

Joppke, Christian. 2013. "Tracks of Immigrant Political Incorporation." In Hochschild et al. 2013, 65–81.

Joyce, James. 1986. *Ulysses*. Ed. Hans Walter Gabler. New York: Vintage Books.

Kapur, Devesh. 2010. *Diaspora, Development, and Democracy: The Domestic Impact of International Migration from India*. Princeton, NJ: Princeton University Press.

Kasinitz, Philip. 1992. *Caribbean New York: Black Immigrants and the Politics of Race*. Ithaca, NY: Cornell University Press.

Kasinitz, Philip, John Mollenkopf, and Mary C. Waters, eds. 2004. *Becoming New Yorkers: Ethnographies of the New Second Generation*. New York: Russell Sage Foundation.

Katouzian, Homa. 1981. *The Political Economy of Modern Iran*. New York: New York University Press.

Kévorkian, Raymond. 2011. *The Armenian Genocide: A Complete History*. London: Bloomsbury Publishing.

Kitchen, Peter, Allison M. Williams, and Melissa Gallina. 2015. "Sense of Belonging to Local Community in Small-to-Medium Sized Canadian Urban Areas: A Comparison of Immigrant and Canadian-Born Residents." *BMC Psychology* 3: 1–17.

Koopmans, Ruud, Paul Statham, Marco Giugni, and Florence Passy. 2005. *Contested Citizenship: Immigration and Cultural Diversity in Europe*. Minneapolis: University of Minnesota Press.

Kymlicka, Will. 1995. *Multicultural Citizenship: A Liberal Theory of Minority Rights*. Oxford: Oxford University Press.

Laitin, David D. 1998. *Identity in Formation: The Russian-Speaking Populations in the Near Abroad*. Ithaca, NY: Cornell University Press.

Laitin, David D., and A. Maurits van der Veen. 2012. "Ethnicity and Pork: A Virtual Test of Causal Mechanisms." In Chandra 2012, 341–358.

Lal, Barbara Ballis. 1997. "Ethnic Identity Entrepreneurs: Their Role in Transracial and Intercountry Adoptions." *Asian and Pacific Migration Journal* 6 (3–4): 385–413.

LaPiere, Richard T. 1930. "The Armenian Colony in Fresno County, Calif.: A Study in Social Psychology." PhD diss., Stanford University.

Lassiter, Matthew D. 2006. *The Silent Majority: Suburban Politics in the Sunbelt South*. Princeton, NJ: Princeton University Press.

Lee, Sugie, and Nancey Greene Leigh. 2007. "Intrametropolitan Spatial Differentiation and Decline of Inner-Ring Suburbs: A Comparison of Four U.S. Metropolitan Areas." *Journal of Planning Education and Research* 27 (2): 146–164.

Levitt, Peggy. 1998. "Social Remittances: Migration Driven Local-level Forms of Cultural Diffusion." *International Migration Review* 32 (4): 926–948.

——. 2009. "Roots and Routes: Understanding the Lives of the Second Generation Transnationally." *Journal of Ethnic and Migration Studies* 35 (7): 1225–1242.

Levitt, Peggy, and B. Nadya Jaworsky. 2007. "Transnational Migration Studies: Past Developments and Future Trends." *Annual Review of Sociology* 33: 129–156.

Levitt, Peggy, and Deepak Lamba-Nieves. 2011. "Social Remittances Revisited." *Journal of Ethnic and Migration studies* 37 (1): 1–22.

Lewis, Paul G., and S. Karthick Ramakrishnan. 2007. "Police Practices in Immigrant-Destination Cities: Political Control or Bureaucratic Professionalism?" *Urban Affairs Review* 42 (6): 874–900.

Li, Wei. 1998. "Anatomy of a New Ethnic Settlement: The Chinese Ethnoburb in Los Angeles." *Urban Studies* 35 (3): 479–501.

——. 2009. *Ethnoburb: The New Ethnic Community in Urban America*. Honolulu: University of Hawaii Press.

Li, Wei, Emily Skop, and Wan Yu. 2016. "Enclaves, Ethnoburbs, and New Patterns of Settlement among Asian Immigrants." In *Contemporary Asian America: A Multidisciplinary Reader*, edited by Min Zhou and Anthony C. Ocampo, 193–214. 3rd ed. New York: New York University Press.

Lichter, Daniel T., Domenico Parisi, and Michael C. Taquino. 2015."Toward a New Macro-Segregation? Decomposing Segregation within and between Metropolitan Cities and Suburbs." *American Sociological Review* 80 (4): 843–873.

——. 2017. "Together but Apart: Do US Whites Live in Racially Diverse Cities and Neighborhoods?" *Population and Development Review* 43 (2): 229–255.

Lin, Jan, and Paul Robinson. 2005. "Spatial Disparities in the Expansion of the Chinese Ethnoburb of Los Angeles." *GeoJournal* 64 (1): 51–61.

Lin, Wan-Ying, and Hayeon Song. 2006. "Geo-ethnic Storytelling: An Examination of Ethnic Media Content in Contemporary Immigrant Communities." *Journalism* 7 (3): 362–388.

Luce, Caroline. 2013. "Reexamining Los Angeles' 'Lower East Side': Jewish Bakers Union Local 453 and Yiddish Food Culture in 1920s Boyle Heights." In *Jews in the Los Angeles Mosaic*, edited by Karen S. Wilson, 25–42. Los Angeles: Autry National Center of the American West, in association with University of California Press.

Lung-Amam, Willow. 2017. *Trespassers? Asian Americans and the Battle for Suburbia*. Berkeley: University of California Press.

——. 2020. "Out of the Urban Shadows: Uneven Development and Spatial Politics in Immigrant Suburbs." *City & Community* 19 (2): 303–309.

Maghbouleh, Neda. 2017. *The Limits of Whiteness: Iranian Americans and the Everyday Politics of Race*. Stanford, CA: Stanford University Press.

Malcolm, M. Vartan. 1910. *The Armenians in America*. Boston: Pilgrim Press.

Mandel, Maud. 2003. *In the Aftermath of Genocide: Armenians and Jews in Twentieth-Century France*. Durham, NC: Duke University Press.

Marrow, Helen B. 2009. "Immigrant Bureaucratic Incorporation: The Dual Roles of Professional Missions and Government Policies." *American Sociological Review* 74 (5): 756–776.

Martin, Barbara. 2021. "The Sakharov-Medvedev Debate on Détente and Human Rights: From the Jackson-Vanik Amendment to the Helsinki Accords." *Journal of Cold War Studies* 23 (3): 138–174.

Massey, Douglas, ed. 2008. *New Faces in New Places: The Changing Geography of American Immigration*. New York: Russell Sage Foundation.

McCabe, Ina Baghdiantz. 1999. *The Shah's Silk for Europe's Silver: The Eurasian Trade of the Julfa Armenians in Safavid Iran and India (1530–1750)*. University of Pennsylvania Armenian Texts and Studies, no. 15. Atlanta, GA: Scholars Press.

McGirr, Lisa. 2001. *Suburban Warriors: The Origins of the New American Right*. Princeton, NJ: Princeton University Press.

McKay, James. 1982. "An Exploratory Synthesis of Primordial and Mobilizationist Approaches to Ethnic Phenomena." *Ethnic and Racial Studies* 5 (4): 395–420.

McManus, Ruth, and Philip J. Ethington. 2007. "Suburbs in Transition: New Approaches to Suburban History." *Urban History* 34 (2): 317–337.

Meier, Kenneth J., and Laurence J. O'Toole Jr. 2006. *Bureaucracy in a Democratic State: A Governance Perspective*. Baltimore: Johns Hopkins University Press.

Mekdjian, Sarah. 2009. "De l'enclave au kaléidoscope urbain: Los Angeles au prisme de l'immigration arménienne." PhD diss., Université Paris Nanterre.

Mikelbank, Brian A. 2004. "A Typology of U.S. Suburban Places." *Housing Policy Debate* 15 (4): 935–964.

Minnite, Lorraine. 2009. "Lost in Translation? A Critical Reappraisal of the Concept of Immigrant Political Incorporation." In Hochschild and Mollenkopf 2009, 48–60.

Mirak, Robert. 1983. *Torn between Two Lands: Armenians in America, 1890 to World War I*. Cambridge, MA: Harvard University Press.

Mollenkopf, John. 1983. *The Contested City*. Princeton, NJ: Princeton University Press.

——. 2013. "Dimensions of Immigrant Political Incorporation." In Hochschild et al. 2013, 107–118.

Morawska, Ewa. 2001. "Immigrants, Transnationalism, and Ethnicization: A Comparison of This Great Wave and the Last." In *E Pluribus Unum? Contemporary and Historical Perspectives on Immigrant Political Incorporation*, edited by Gary Gerstle and John Mollenkopf, 175–212. New York: Russell Sage Foundation.

——. 2013. "Structuring Immigrants' Civic-Political Incorporation into the Host Society." In Hochschild et al. 2013, 137–161.

Nalbantian, Tsolin. 2013. "Going beyond Overlooked Populations in Lebanese Historiography: The Armenian Case." *History Compass* 11 (10): 821–832.

Narayan, Kirin. 1993. "How Native Is a 'Native' Anthropologist?" *American Anthropologist* 95 (3): 671–686.

Ng, Franklin. 1998. *The Taiwanese Americans*. Westport, CT: Greenwood Press.

Nichanian, Marc. 1999. "Enlightenment and Historical Thought." In *Enlightenment and Diaspora: The Armenian and Jewish Cases*, edited by Richard Hovannisian and David N. Meyers, 87–123. Atlanta, GA: Scholars Press.

Nicolaides, Becky M. 2002. *My Blue Heaven: Life and Politics in the Working-Class Suburbs of Los Angeles, 1920–1965*. Chicago: University of Chicago Press.

Nicolaides, Becky M., and Andrew Wiese, eds. 2006. *The Suburb Reader*. New York: Routledge.

Oh, Sookhee, and Angie Chung. 2014. "A Study on the Sociospatial Context of Ethnic Politics and Entrepreneurial Growth in Koreatown and Monterey Park." *GeoJournal* 79 (1): 59–71.

Olzak, Susan. 2006. *The Global Dynamics of Racial and Ethnic Mobilization*. Stanford, CA: Stanford University Press.

Orfield, Myron, and Thomas F. Luce. 2013. "America's Racially Diverse Suburbs: Opportunities and Challenges." *Housing Policy Debate* 23 (2): 395–430.

Orleck, Annelise. 2001. "Soviet Jews: The City's Newest Immigrants Transform New York Jewish Life." In *New Immigrants in New York*, edited by Nancy Foner, 111–140. New York: Columbia University Press.

Panossian, Razmik. 2006. *The Armenians: From Kings and Priests to Merchants and Commissars*. New York: Columbia University Press.

Park, Robert Ezra. 1950. *Race and Culture*. Glencoe, IL: Free Press.

Park, Robert Ezra, and Ernest W. Burgess. 2019. *The City*. Chicago: University of Chicago Press.

Pattie, Susan. 1997. *Faith in History: Armenians Rebuilding Community*. 1997.Washington, DC: Smithsonian Institution Press.

——. 2004. "From the Centers to the Periphery: 'Repatriation' to an Armenian Homeland in the Twentieth Century." In *Homecomings: Unsettling Paths of Return*, edited by Fran Markowitz and Anders H. Stefansson, 109–124. Lanham, MD: Lexington Books.

Phillips, Bruce A. 2016. "Not Quite White: The Emergence of Jewish 'Ethnoburbs' in Los Angeles, 1920–2010." *American Jewish History* 100 (1): 73–104.

Pincetl, Stephanie. 1994. "Challenges to Citizenship: Latino Immigrants and Political Organizing in the Los Angeles Area." *Environment and Planning A: Economy and Space* 26 (6): 895–914.

Portes, Alejandro, Cristina Escobar, and Renelinda Arana. 2008. "Bridging the Gap: Transnational and Ethnic Organizations in the Political Incorporation of Immigrants in the United States." *Ethnic and Racial Studies* 31 (6): 1056–1090.

Portes, Alejandro, and Rubén G. Rumbaut. 2001. *Legacies: The Story of the Immigrant Second Generation*. Berkeley: University of California Press.

——. 2006. *Immigrant America: A Portrait*. Berkeley: University of California Press.

Portes, Alejandro, and Min Zhou. 1993. "The New Second Generation: Segmented Assimilation and Its Variants." *Annals of the American Academy of Political and Social Science* 530: 74–96.

Posner, Daniel N. 2017. "When and Why Do Some Social Cleavages Become Politically Salient Rather than Others?" *Ethnic and Racial Studies* 40 (12): 2001–2019.

Putnam, Robert. 2000. "Bowling Alone: America's Declining Social Capital." In *Culture and Politics: A Reader*, edited by Lane Crothers and Charles Lockhart, 223–234. New York: Palgrave Macmillan.

Quigley, John M., and Steven Raphael. 2005. "Regulation and the High Cost of Housing in California." *American Economic Review* 95 (2): 323–328.

Rafter, Nicole, and Sandra Walklate. 2012. "Genocide and the Dynamics of Victimization: Some Observations on Armenia." *European Journal of Criminology* 9 (5): 514–526.

Ramakrishnan, S. Karthick. 2013. "Incorporation versus Assimilation: The Need for Conceptual Differentiation." In Hochschild et al. 2013, 27–42.

Ramírez, Ricardo, and Luis Fraga. 2008. "Continuity and Change: Latino Political Incorporation in California since 1990." In *Racial and Ethnic Politics in California*, vol. 3, *Continuity and Change*, edited by Sandra Bass and Bruce E. Cain, 61–93. Berkeley: IGS Press, Institute of Governmental Studies, University of California, Berkeley.

Riker, William H. 1986. *The Art of Political Manipulation*. New Haven, CT: Yale University Press.

Robertson, Shanthi, Alexandra Wong, Christina Ho, Ien Ang, and Phillip Mar. 2022. "Sydney as 'Sinoburbia': Patterns of Diversification across Emerging Chinese Ethnoburbs." *Urban Studies*, 59 (16): 3422–3441.

Rogers, Reuel. 2006. *Afro-Caribbean Immigrants and the Politics of Incorporation: Ethnicity, Exception, or Exit*. New York: Cambridge University Press.

——. 2009. "Political Institutions and Rainbow Coalitions: Immigrant-Minority Relations in New York and Hartford." In Hochschild and Mollenkopf 2009, 93–110.

Rothstein, Richard. 2017. *The Color of Law: A Forgotten History of How Our Government Segregated America*. New York: Liveright Publishing Corporation.

Rumbaut, Rubén G. 2008a. "The Coming of the Second Generation: Immigration and Ethnic Mobility in Southern California." *Annals of the American Academy of Political and Social Science* 620: 196–236.

——. 2008b. "Reaping What You Sow: Immigration, Youth, and Reactive Ethnicity." *Applied Development Science* 12 (2): 108–111.

Sabagh, Georges, Mehdi Bozorgmehr, and Claudia Der-Martirosian. 1990. "Subethnicity: Armenians in Los Angeles." ISSR Working Paper. Institute for Social Science Research, University of California, Los Angeles.

Safran, William. 1991. "Diasporas in Modern Societies: Myths of Homeland and Return." *Diaspora: A Journal of Transnational Studies* 1 (1): 83–99.

Saito, Leland T. 1998. *Race and Politics: Asian Americans, Latinos, and Whites in a Los Angeles Suburb*. Urbana: University of Illinois Press.

Schiller, Nina Glick, Linda Basch, and Cristina Szanton Blanc. 1995. "From Immigrant to Transmigrant: Theorizing Transnational Migration." *Anthropological Quarterly* 68 (1): 48–63.

Schleunes, Karl A. 1970. *The Twisted Road to Auschwitz: Nazi Policy toward German Jews, 1933–1939*. Urbana: University of Illinois Press.

Schneider, Jason. 2014. "From Urban Enclave to Ethnoburb: Discourse, Space, and Community in Polish Chicago." *Iowa Journal of Cultural Studies* 15 (1): 80–102.

Schneider, Mark, and Paul Teske. 1992. "Toward a Theory of the Political Entrepreneur: Evidence from Local Government." *American Political Science Review* 86 (3): 737–747.

Segura, Gary M. 2013. "Behavioral and Attitudinal Components of Immigrant Political Incorporation." In Hochschild et al. 2013, 254–269.

Shefter, Martin. 1986. "Political Incorporation and the Extrusion of the Left: Party Politics and Social Forces in New York City." *Studies in American Political Development* 1: 50–90.

Simmel, Georg. 1955. *"Conflict" and "The Web of Group-Affiliations."* Translated by Kurt H. Wolff and Reinhard Bendix. Glencoe, IL: Free Press.

Simon, Bernd, and Bert Klandermans. 2001. "Politicized Collective Identity: A Social Psychological Analysis." *American Psychologist* 56 (4): 319–331.

Smith, Timothy L. 1978. "Religion and Ethnicity in America." *American Historical Review* 83 (5): 1155–1185.

Soehl, Thomas. 2013. "The Ambiguities of Political Opportunity: Political Claims-Making of Russian-Jewish Immigrants in New York City." *Ethnic and Racial Studies* 36 (12): 1977–1996.

Soysal, Yasemin. 1994. *Limits of Citizenship: Migrants and Postnational Membership in Europe.* Chicago: University of Chicago Press.

Statesman's Year-Book. 1921. "Russia: Principal Towns: Caucasia." London: Macmillan and Company.

Statham, Paul. 1999. "Political Mobilisation by Minorities in Britain: Negative Feedback of 'Race Relations'?" *Journal of Ethnic and Migration Studies* 25 (4): 597–626.

Steinberg, Stephen. 1981. *The Ethnic Myth: Race, Ethnicity, and Class in America.* New York: Atheneum.

Sugrue, Thomas J. 2014. *The Origins of the Urban Crisis.* Princeton, NJ: Princeton University Press.

Suny, Ronald Grigor. 1993. *Looking toward Ararat: Armenia in Modern History.* Bloomington: Indiana: University Press.

——. 1999. "Provisional Stabilities: The Politics of Identities in Post-Soviet Eurasia." *International Security* 24 (3): 139–178.

——. 2019. *The Baku Commune, 1917-1918: Class and Nationality in the Russian Revolution.* Princeton, NJ: Princeton University Press.

——. 2021. "Armenian Genocide." In *Encyclopedia Britannica* (chrome-extension://efai dnbmnnnibpcajpcglclefindmkaj/https://encyclopedia.1914-1918-online.net/pdf /1914-1918-Online-armenian_genocide-2015-05-26.pdf).

Suro, Roberto, Jill H. Wilson, and Audrey Singer. 2011. "Immigration and Poverty in America's Suburbs." Metropolitan Opportunity Series. Washington, DC: Brookings Institution.

Tajfel, Henri, John C. Turner, William G. Austin, and Stephen Worchel. 1979. "An Integrative Theory of Intergroup Conflict." *Organizational Identity: A Reader,* 56: 65.

Takooshian, Harold. 1986. "Armenian Immigration to the United States from the Middle East." *Journal of Armenian Studies* 3 (1–2): 133–155.

Tarrow, Sidney. 1994. *Power in Movement: Social Movements, Collective Action and Mass Politics in the Modern State.* Cambridge: Cambridge University Press.

Taylor, Laura. 2011. "No Boundaries: Exurbia and the Study of Contemporary Urban Dispersion." *GeoJournal* 76 (4): 323–339.

Teaford, Jon C. 2011. "Suburbia and Post-Suburbia: A Brief History." *International Perspectives on Suburbanization: A Post-Suburban World?,* edited by Nicholas A. Phelps and Fulong Wu, 15–34. Basingstoke: Palgrave Macmillan.

——. 2020. *The American Suburb: The Basics.* New York: Routledge.

Tehranian, John. 2000. "Performing Whiteness: Naturalization Litigation and the Construction of Racial Identity in America." *Yale Law Journal* 109 (4): 817–48.

Tichenor, Daniel. 2002. *Dividing Lines: The Politics of Immigration Control in America.* Princeton, NJ: Princeton University Press.

Tilly, Charles, and Sidney G. Tarrow. 2015. *Contentious Politics.* New York: Oxford University Press.

Tolnay, Stewart E. 2003. "The African American 'Great Migration' and Beyond." *Annual Review of Sociology* 29: 209–232.

Tölölyan, Khachig. 1991. "The Nation-State and Its Others: In Lieu of a Preface." *Diaspora: A Journal of Transnational Studies* 1 (1): 3–7.

——. 1996. "Rethinking Diaspora(s): Stateless Power in the Transnational Moment." *Diaspora: A Journal of Transnational Studies* 5 (1): 3–36.

——. 2000. "Elites and Institutions in the Armenian Transnation." *Diaspora: A Journal of Transnational Studies* 9 (1) 107–136.

——. 2005. "Armenian Diaspora." In *Encyclopedia of Diasporas: Immigrant and Refugee Cultures around the World*, edited by Melvin Ember, Carol R. Ember, and Ian Skoggard, 2:35–46. Boston: Springer.

Tuan, Mia. 1999. *Forever Foreigners or Honorary Whites? The Asian Ethnic Experience Today*. New Brunswick, NJ: Rutgers University Press.

Tygiel, Jules. 2001. "Introduction: Metropolis in the Making: Los Angeles in the 1920s." In *Metropolis in the Making: Los Angeles in the 1920s*, edited by Thomas Sitton and William Deverell, 1–10. Berkeley: University of California Press.

Vallianatos, Mark. 2017. "To Serve and to Protect: Food Trucks and Food Safety in a Transforming Los Angeles." In *Food Trucks, Cultural Identity, and Social Justice: From Loncheras to Lobsta Love*, edited by Julian Agyeman, Caitlin Matthews, and Hannah Sobel, 67–83. Cambridge, MA: MIT Press.

van der Veen, A. Maurits, and David D. Laitin. 2012. "Modeling the Evolution of Ethnic Identity." In Chandra 2012, 277–311.

Van Nuys, Frank. 2002. *Americanizing the West: Race, Immigrants, and Citizenship, 1890–1930*. Lawrence: University Press of Kansas.

Vassilian, Hamo B., ed. 1995. *Armenian American Almanac: An Encyclopedic Guide to Armenian Organizations, Churches, Print and Non-print Media, Libraries, Armenian Studies, Bookstores, Armenian Schools, Etc*. Glendale, CA: Armenian Reference Books Company.

Voicu, Bogdan, and Mircea Comşa. 2014. "Immigrants' Participation in Voting: Exposure, Resilience, and Transferability." *Journal of Ethnic and Migration Studies* 40 (10): 1572–1592.

Voskanian, N. A., K. A. Korkotian, and A. M. Savalian. 1988. *Hay girk'ĕ 1512–1800 t'vakannerin: Hay hnatip grk'i matenagitut'yun*. Erevan: Haykakan SSH Kulturayi Ministrut'yun, Al. Myasnikyani Anvan Zhoghovurdneri Barekamut'yan Shk'anshanakir HSSH Petakan Gradaran.

Voss, Kim, and Irene Bloemraad. 2011. *Rallying for Immigrant Rights: The Fight for Inclusion in 21st Century America*. Berkeley: University of California Press.

Waldinger, Roger. 2007. "Transforming Foreigners into Americans." In *The New Americans: A Guide to Immigration since 1965*, edited by Mary C. Waters and Reed Ueda, 137–148. Cambridge, MA: Harvard University Press.

——. 2012. "Beyond Transnationalism: An Alternative Perspective on Immigrants' Homeland Connections." In *The Oxford Handbook of the Politics of International Migration*, edited by Marc Rosenbaum and Daniel Tichenor, 74–102. New York: Oxford University Press.

——. 2015. *The Cross-Border Connection: Immigrants, Emigrants, and Their Homelands*. Cambridge, MA: Harvard University Press.

——. 2016. "A Cross-Border Perspective on Migration: Beyond the Assimilation/Transnationalism Debate." *Journal of Ethnic and Migration Studies* 43 (1): 3–17.

Waldinger, Roger, and Mehdi Bozorgmehr, eds. 1996. *Ethnic Los Angeles*. New York: Russell Sage Foundation.

Waldinger, Roger, and David Fitzgerald. 2004. "Transnationalism in Question." *American Journal of Sociology* 109 (5): 1177–1195.

Waldinger, Roger, and Yen-Fen Tseng. 1992. "Divergent Diasporas: The Chinese Communities of New York and Los Angeles Compared." *Revue européenne des migrations internationales* 8 (3): 91–115.

Walker, Kyle. 2018. "Immigrants in U.S. Suburbs." In *The Routledge Companion to the Suburbs*, edited by Bernadette Hanlon and Thomas J. Vicino, 193–207. London: Routledge.

Walzer, Michael. 1981. *Spheres of Justice: A Defense of Pluralism and Equality.* New York: Basic Books.

Wen, Ming, Diane S. Lauderdale, and Namratha R. Kandula. 2009. "Ethnic Neighborhoods in Multi-ethnic America, 1990–2000: Resurgent Ethnicity in the Ethnoburbs?" *Social Forces* 88 (1): 425–460.

Wiese, Andrew. 2004. *Places of Their Own: African American Suburbanization in the Twentieth Century.* Chicago: University of Chicago Press.

Wilson, Karen S., ed. 2013. *Jews in the Los Angeles Mosaic.* Berkeley: University of California Press.

Wolfinger, Raymond. 1965. "The Development and Persistence of Ethnic Voting." *American Political Science Review* 59 (4): 896–908.

Wong, Janelle, S. Karthick Ramakrishnan, Taeku Lee, and Jane Junn. 2011. *Asian American Political Participation: Emerging Constituents and Their Political Identities.* New York: Russell Sage Foundation.

Yang, Alan, and Rodolfo O. de la Garza. 2016. "Americanizing Latinos, Latinoizing America: The Political Consequences of Latino Incorporation." *Social Science Quarterly* 98 (2): 690–727.

Yeretzian, Aram Serkis. 1923. "A History of Armenian Immigration to America with Special Reference to Conditions in Los Angeles." Master's thesis, University of Southern California.

Young, Donald. 1932. *American Minority Peoples: A Study in Racial and Cultural Conflicts in the United States.* New York: Harper & Brothers.

Zarsadiaz, James. 2022. *Resisting Change in Suburbia: Asian Immigrants and Frontier Nostalgia in L.A.* Berkeley: University of California Press.

Zepeda-Millán, Chris. 2017. *Latino Mass Mobilization: Immigration, Racialization, and Activism.* New York: Cambridge University Press.

Zhou, Min. 1997. "Segmented Assimilation: Issues, Controversies, and Recent Research on the New Second Generation." *International Migration Review* 31 (4): 975–1008.

——. 2009. "Suburbanization and New Trends in Community Development: The Case of Chinese Ethnoburbs in the San Gabriel Valley, California." In *Contemporary Chinese America: Immigration, Ethnicity, and Community Transformation,* 77–96. Philadelphia: Temple University Press.

Zhou, Min, and Carl L. Bankston III. 2020. "The Model Minority Stereotype and the National Identity Question: The Challenges Facing Asian Immigrants and Their Children." *Ethnic and Racial Studies* 43 (1): 233–253.

Zhou, Min, Yen-Fen Tseng, and Rebecca Y. Kim. 2008. "Rethinking Residential Assimilation: The Case of a Chinese Ethnoburb in the San Gabriel Valley, California." *Amerasia Journal* 34 (3): 53–83.

Zhou, Min, and Yang Sao Xiong. 2005. "The Multifaceted American Experiences of the Children of Asian Immigrants: Lessons for Segmented Assimilation." *Ethnic and Racial Studies* 28 (6): 1119–1152.

Zolberg, Aristide. 2006. *A Nation by Design: Immigration Policy in the Fashioning of America.* New York: Russell Sage Foundation; Cambridge, MA: Harvard University Press.

Index

Figures, notes, and tables are indicated by f, n, and t following the page number.

www.ingramcontent.com/pod-product-compliance
Lightning Source LLC
Chambersburg PA
CBHW030835270326
41928CB00007B/1070